# SUNRISE OVER
# AYODHYA

# ADVANCE PRAISE FOR THE BOOK

'A former Oxford don and now a practising lawyer and politician, Salman Khurshid casts his analytical and engaged eye on the Ayodhya–Ram Janmabhoomi controversy and the Supreme Court's verdict on it. The result is an incisive and evocative book that is imbued with rare and remarkable optimism'—Rudrangshu Mukherjee, chancellor and professor of history, Ashoka University

'While there exist many accounts of the politics which led to and followed upon the destruction of the Babri Masjid, this remarkable analysis focuses on its juridical history and consequences. More than a lament about communal violence, it looks at the new risks as well as possibilities created by legal interventions in the dispute. Written by an eminent lawyer and former law minister, the book offers a new understanding of the ways in which the judicial settlement of contending religious claims has altered India's constitutional history'—Faisal Devji, professor of Indian history, University of Oxford

'Intuition, instinct, intellect have been wonderfully combined by the author to dispassionately analyse the Ayodhya saga . . . A great contribution to the understanding of contemporary history and legal process'—Malvika 'Mala' Singh, publisher, *Seminar* magazine

'An admirably thoughtful and measured assessment of intensely divisive issues, the Ayodhya case and the Supreme Court's judgment, in a context of growing religious polarization. At a time of declining trust in the judiciary, Salman Khurshid reaffirms faith in the institution and the secular Indian Constitution of which it is guardian, in ways that are both persuasive and poignant. Anchored in extensive legal knowledge and political experience, this valuable work is vital reading for students of law, politics, history, religion and many other disciplines'—Rochana Bajpai, reader in politics and senior fellow, HEA, Department of Politics and International Studies, SOAS University of London

SUNRISE OVER

# AYODHYA

## NATIONHOOD IN OUR TIMES

SALMAN
KHURSHID

VINTAGE
An imprint of Penguin Random House

VINTAGE

USA | Canada | UK | Ireland | Australia
New Zealand | India | South Africa | China

Vintage is part of the Penguin Random House group of companies
whose addresses can be found at global.penguinrandomhouse.com

Published by Penguin Random House India Pvt. Ltd
4th Floor, Capital Tower 1, MG Road,
Gurugram 122 002, Haryana, India

First published in Vintage by Penguin Random House India 2021

10 9 8 7 6 5 4

ISBN 9780670096145

Typeset in Adobe Caslon Pro and Calibri by Manipal Technologies Limited, Manipal
Printed in India

www.penguin.co.in

*For Dr Rajeev Dhavan,*
*erudite, pugnacious advocate, eagle-eyed commentator,*
*who argued the brief for Babri Masjid*
*with commitment to secular values,*
*and whom I have had reasons to admire since*
*our days as law teachers in the UK*

# Contents

# Introduction

Many books have been written over the years on the protracted Ayodhya saga,* but we are yet to see more recent works that take into account developments in the Supreme Court except for short articles with responses of persons who had the ringside seats. Much of the public discourse in the run-up to the hearing before the Supreme Court was sadly a priori, based on implicit or explicit assumptions or elements of subconscious expectations of faith or even cynical political strategies. Since the pronouncement of the judgment there has been conspicuous restraint by both sides of the dispute, although discreet but closer scrutiny reveals that some people have raised questions about the legal soundness of the judgment on the issue of better possessory title of Hindus over the inner courtyard of the mosque (the structure with the three domes). With the gavel having descended upon the contestations, the ground reality is abundantly clear, irrespective of how people

_____

* The dispute over the Ayodhya or Ram Janmabhoomi site has been the focus of a dispute throughout the history of independent India, with several, often contentious, political, cultural and legal dimensions. The dispute, seemingly, has come to an end with the pronouncement of the judgment of the hon'ble Supreme Court of India in 2019.

on different sides reconcile themselves with that reality. Despite
the court's effort to present the dispute as a purely legal contest,
one cannot see it in a standalone manner, removed from the
prevailing political situation in the country. But the continuing
confusion needs to be addressed in the national interest, and
therefore this book. The history of the dispute and the uneven
path that culminated in the judgment must lay at rest alternative
versions once the Supreme Court has spoken.

There might be a question as to why the book is titled *Sunrise
over Ayodhya* when many features of the story suggest that *Sunset
over Ayodhya* might have been more appropriate. Unless one has a
fatalistic view of national life, irrespective of one's opinion about
the developments, it is important to look at the brighter side. Of
course, the proponents of Hindutva will see it as an appropriate
recognition of their moment in history. Life comes with many
imperfections, including in terms of justice, but we need to adjust
and accommodate for life to go on. It is quite another matter that
a point comes in history when this is no longer possible. But as
Thomas More of *A Man for all Seasons* would say, you do not seek
martyrdom over every disagreement but when the point comes,
no price is too high. This book is an attempt to see hope in what
might be a judicious decision, even if some people think it was not
entirely fair. When people begin to disagree about what is fair,
there are cracks that need attention beyond all sentiments natural
to human beings.

Given that public memory is short, people will very soon forget
the facts of the saga of Ayodhya and merely focus attention on the
outcome of the judgment. An impressive Ram Mandir will surely
mark the skyline of Ayodhya and, understandably, there will be
many claimants to the honour of having contributed to that. Who
will recall the historical beginnings or the sequence of the dispute,
how at each stage the courts dealt with them and how the decisions
of successive governments gradually but inevitably led to the final
outcome? Could mistakes have been avoided, and might that have

made a difference? What indeed did the Supreme Court say in the several hundred pages that it devoted to the judgment? Is there a national imperative that we continue to claim adherence to high principles of secularism, social inclusion and the rule of law but submit to reality and pragmatism to preserve the delicate bonds of national unity? Instead of people having to search fragments of information from the huge expanse of relevant records, it would be useful to bring all the information together in one place for convenient access and, of course, to facilitate living knowledge of critical events in the modern history of our land. Besides, intertwined with every society's history are personal histories as well. Recording them has a palliative impact when history has been harsh or difficult to understand. It may also help friends and well-wishers understand the author's public-life motivations and attitudes better. Ultimately, what people feel intensely is best not kept confined and under cover and thus be allowed to fester.

The decades-long span of simmering disquiet and subdued anxiety finally ended with the Ayodhya verdict of the Constitutional Bench of the Supreme Court.* In a sense, it is fortunate that the court delivered a unanimous judgment of five judges. All sides and political parties, which had either exploited public sentiment or indeed suffered politically, had categorically committed to accept the adjudicated outcome. Initial reactions suggest that the decision was received widely with a sense of relief that the fire of passion, real or contrived, had finally been doused, even if some people feel a bit disappointed and legally trained professionals will continue to dissect the findings for their impact as precedents for future decisions.

Despite the predictable 1045 pages (a modest size compared to the recent trend of lengthy judgments on pivotal constitutional

---

* 'M. Siddiq (Dead) through Legal Representatives v Mahant Suresh Das and Others' (Ram Janmabhoomi Temple Case), 2020, 1 SCC 1; 2019 SCC OnLine SC 1440.

issues), the judgment makes for easy reading, and should not be difficult to absorb and understand for legal experts as well as ordinary people. What, of course, stands out conspicuously is that the disputed plot of 2.75 acres, along with the surrounding land acquired by the Central government post the demolition, was handed over to a trust established by the government, and the Waqf Board accepted 5 acres a few kilometers from the temple site. This was not by an act of obeisance towards Ram Lalla (the deity), or, in other words, by submission to the faith of Hindus, but by an interesting balancing of principles of establishing title. The court held that the right to the inner courtyard of the mosque, claimed by Muslims, was not uninterruptedly free of opposing claims and periodic attempts by Hindus to assert their rights. On the other hand, Muslims had themselves admitted that Shri Ram Chanderji was born in Ayodhya and that the *chabutra* or platform in the outer courtyard had been undisputedly in the possession of Hindus for decades and puja was conducted uninterrupted. Although a close analysis of the interface of competing claims might throw up questions, the fact remains that the present decision, undoubtedly made very thoughtfully by the court, was made possible by the conduct of the Muslim side over the decades. Be that as it may, ultimately the court made a delicate balancing effort of subscribing to legal principles and healing a festering civilizational wound. Muslims, who had all along committed themselves to accepting the court verdict, now have a chance to show grace and generosity, and to reach out to claim a place as contributors to true national integration and unity.

The Supreme Court might have found the Hindu cause marginally more persuasive than the Muslim cause, but it has done a great deal more to facilitate and inspire Muslims to see this as a moment of reconciliation rather than defeat. There could not have been clearer condemnation by the highest court of the land of the acts of intrusion in 1949, when the idol of Ram Lalla was placed under the middle dome of the mosque, as indeed of the act of vandalism when the mosque was demolished in 1992. The court was also clear that the Archaeological Survey of India report showing evidence of previous civilizations did not prove that a temple, least of all a Ram temple, was demolished to construct the Babri Masjid under the instructions of Emperor Babar. Reaffirmation of India's secular character in the judgment should not be obscured by the baseline outcome. This is the truth that preceded reconciliation. Furthermore, the direction that 5 acres of other land be given to the Sunni Waqf Board was a gesture that underscored that the court and the nation treat all citizens as equals. The court recognized that all citizens have their respective faiths and manners of worship, and that while faith has a place in our national life, it does not trump legal rights in an unqualified sweep.

The greatest opportunity that the judgment offers is for a reaffirmation of India as a secular society. It is a decision that refutes the idea of Hindu Rashtra and amplifies the practical handling of sensitive religious concerns in a secular system. Upholding the purpose and effect of the Places of Worship Act, among other matters, is a clear indication that the secular edifice of India and the commitment of its highest court to the Constitutional principles we cherish have not only remained undisturbed but have indeed been fortified. If we have all placed our trust in the court, it is imperative that we recognize our trust has been redeemed. But there is silence on one issue: the failure of periodic attempts to find a solution outside the courtroom does not seem to have found a place under the sun. Perhaps there is a lesson in it for us: if this is what was to happen, could we all not have done it ourselves? Has the court gently nudged us to rethink our approach to our national life? As we look back, we will be able to see how much we have lost over Ayodhya through the years of conflict. If the loss of a mosque is preservation of faith, if the establishment of a temple is emancipation of faith, we can all join together in celebrating faith in the Constitution. Sometimes a step back to accommodate is several steps forward towards our common destiny.

Since the judgment is of considerable length (though thankfully it was a unanimous judgment), it would take considerable effort for a lay reader, indeed even a professional, to capture its essence. It is therefore thought appropriate to include the text from the judgment in this book extensively, for the purpose of quick cross-reference. Other associated judgments in the run-up to the final pronouncement have been included as well, so as to ensure an unbroken narrative.

The Supreme Court has put its stamp on history and in a sense turned the last page. It has, in the process, written itself into the history of Ayodhya. If that has laid the foundation of a grand reconciliation or perpetuated the stress of majoritarian might versus right, or a mixture of the two, only time will tell. The last word, as always, will be that of time.

# One

# The Long Demolition

The legal dispute over Ayodhya dates back to 1858 (although there is some evidence of an earlier tussle). An FIR was filed on 30 November 1858 by one Mohd Salim against a group of Nihang Sikhs who had reportedly installed a Nishan Saheb and written 'Ram' inside the Babri Masjid. They also performed *havan* and puja. Sheetal Dubey, the thanedar (station-house officer) of Avadh, in his report of 1 December 1858 verified the complaint, but it seems no further action was taken, and the possession of the mosque was restored to the Muslims at some stage.

The formal dispute over Ayodhya began in 1885, when Mahant Raghubar Das filed a suit (no. 61/280) against the Secretary of State for India in Council in the civil court of Faizabad. Das claimed that he was a mahant, and that he was located at the chabutra in the outer courtyard and sought permission to construct a temple there. The suit was dismissed. In 1886, a civil appeal (no. 27) was filed against the 1885 judgment. The district judge of Faizabad, F.E.R. Chamier, decided to visit the spot for inspection before passing the order and ultimately dismissed the appeal.

A second civil appeal (no. 122) was filed against this dismissal, which was also dismissed by the court of judicial commissioner.

1

For the next sixty-three years, there was no further progress in the matter. In 1934, things came to head when a riot took place in Ayodhya and Hindus demolished a portion of the structure at the disputed site. The damaged portion was repaired under the directions of the British.

Matters rested there till the night of 22–23 December 1949, when some persons entered the mosque and placed the idol of Ram Lalla or infant Ram. What followed was a huge congregation of devotees gathering for *darshan*. The top echelons of government in Uttar Pradesh and Delhi got into flurried activity even as the district magistrate, K.K. Nayer, dragged his feet. Thereafter, the entire structure was sealed under orders of the magistrate (with a side door left open for the priest to go in for the puja) and remained so till the locks were opened under court orders in 1986, following the application of a local advocate seeking to enforce his right to worship. People believe that this was done to counterbalance the Hindu sentiment stirred by the 1985 Shah Bano* judgment and its rejection by Parliament.

Having seen an opportunity to build on the Hindu sentiment, the Vishva Hindu Parishad and other Hindu organizations conducted a Ram shila pujan, a religious ceremony to consecrate the bricks to be used for the temple. Bricks, for eventual use, were carried across long distances to Ayodhya and stored on the adjacent land acquired by the UP government for tourism purposes.

After the 1989 general election, the Janata Dal, under V.P. Singh, came to power, with outside support of the BJP. In September 1990, L.K. Advani, then the president of his party and Hindu hardliner, launched the Ram Rath Yatra—a procession in a *rath* (chariot)—from the restored Somnath temple in Gujarat, which would cover some 10,000 kilometres

---

* 'Mohd. Ahmed Khan vs Shah Bano Begum and Ors', 1985, AIR 945, 1985 SCR (3) 844.

across western and northern India, to culminate in Ayodhya. As the Rath Yatra wound its way through the Hindi heartland, it sparked serious communal tensions and sporadic violence. The events took a dramatic turn when Advani was arrested by the Janata Dal administration of Lalu Prasad Yadav in Bihar in late October, and the BJP used this as a pretext for withdrawing support to V.P. Singh's government, which finally exited in November that year.

On 30 October, a small group of *karsevaks* attempted to storm the heavily guarded Babri Masjid, and managed to place a saffron flag on top of the middle dome, causing some damage to it. Retaliatory action by the police resulted in the deaths of more than fifty people in police firings. Thousands of karsevaks were arrested, and trains were suspended to defuse the situation and prevent the Rath Yatra from igniting further communal trouble. This direct confrontation with the state government, headed by someone the BJP called a 'pro-Muslim pseudo secularist' (Mulayam Singh), created a heroic legend of the martyrdom of karsevaks in Ayodhya, and an opportunity for the BJP to carry the ashes of the martyrs across the country. On the other hand, Muslims began to see Mulayam Singh as a secular saviour, giving him political capital that he exploited for several years. But as recent elections have shown, he was unable or unwilling to consolidate his OBC–Muslim alliance into anything more than an election arrangement. Politics, though, was never to be what it had been before these events in Ayodhya.

In a logical conclusion to the steadily growing saffron mood in the country, the BJP was elected to office in 2014 and, once again, in 2019, and took firm decisions on several contested issues that had been under a cloud of ambiguity for decades, such Article 370,*

---

* In August 2019, the government took the final decision to abrogate Article 370 of the Constitution of India, which recognized the special status of Jammu and Kashmir.

Triple Talaq,\* NRC in Assam.† Buoyed by the passive response on those decisions, the government of the day disturbed the equilibrium on citizenship by passing amendments to the Citizenship Act 1956‡ that led to widespread public outcry and even horrible, avoidable violence. The self-certification by the BJP, of having made riots a thing of the past, was rudely refuted by the riots in north-east Delhi, not to mention the innumerable incidents of lynching of innocent people by self-appointed conscience-keepers of society.

There are moments in history that shape how people look at their future. All major conflicts—such as the American Civil War; power-play partitions of land and society, as in Korea and Vietnam, the Balfour Declaration and the birth of Israel and Palestine; outcomes of military operations, such as the division of post-World War II Berlin; break-up of political entities, as in the Indian Partition of 1947 and the birth of Bangladesh in 1973—ultimately end in some form of conciliation and reconciliation. Which of the last two processes will operate in Indian national life beyond Ayodhya is still unclear. We must consciously and concertedly steer ourselves to the preferred path, instead of leaving it all to chance. The national project is too valuable and critical for succeeding generations of Indians for us to sit back and allow events to take shape unguided and unplanned. This book is a modest attempt to participate in an endeavour to help the nation understand where we are today, how and why we got here, and how we should proceed from here. It is in that sense an objective look at contemporary history. It is also an attempt to work on the fabric of our national

---

\* In July 2019, the government promulgated the Muslim Women (Protection of Rights on Marriage) Act, 2019, criminalizing the act of Triple Talaq.
† In 2013–14, the government implemented the National Register of Citizens (NRC) in the state of Assam, ostensibly to tackle the issue of illegal immigration from Bangladesh.
‡ The Citizenship (Amendment) Act, 2019 was passed by the Parliament of India on 11 December 2019. It amended the Citizenship Act, 1955 by providing a pathway to Indian citizenship for persecuted religious minorities from other countries.

life, to fortify it against the toxic political winds blowing across the globe. Even if we can steer the conversation to conciliation and reconciliation, we would have added to national integration.

My own political career spans the years during which Ayodhya became a burning topic and, bit by bit, consumed the Congress Party. Before 1989, the first election I contested from Farrukhabad, graffiti about the Ram Mandir ('*mandir wahin banayege*') would periodically appear, somewhat innocuously, all over the town. Kanshi Ram's DS4 (the Dalit Shoshit Samaj Sangharsh Samiti) similarly took to decorating their message through slogans painted across walls but did little more than deface the walls. That was the time when Meira Kumar could trounce Behen Mayawati from Bijnor. But of course, before 1989, attempts to storm the Babri Masjid had been foiled by Mulayam Singh. The 1989 campaign had been steady and somewhat uneventful till I reached a large Muslim village, Dundwa Buzurg, for door-to-door campaigning. I went from one house to another where the residents were busy rolling *beedis* sitting on the floor. I reached out to one young man to shake his hand, but he refused to respond and simply said, 'I hate you.' My colleagues rushed me away, much to my distress. 'What is this about?' I asked. 'Don't you know about the *shilanyas* [foundation stone-laying ceremony]? BBC reported it,' I was told.* There were no mobile phones and no Internet. Newspapers were few and only in vernacular languages.

We quickly gathered a crowd of the faithful and made a passionate speech. In a few hours that night, I discovered that my flags and posters were all gone and so was the vote. As I discovered later, the home minister, Sardar Buta Singh, had hoped that permitting the foundation ceremony away from the mosque building would lower temperatures during the ensuing election. However, the BBC report indicated that the proposed temple

---

* Mark Tully, BBC's India correspondent, who was present at the scene, famously reported the events and has recounted them many times since.

structure built from that point would lead to the *garb griha*, or sanctum sanctorum, where the idols were placed in the mosque. That was considered an admission by the government of the day of the claim by the Hindu side. It was a turning point for the election but entirely adverse to us in the Congress.

'Maulana' Mulayam had emerged as a messiah of Muslims and hero to secular Hindus, to sweep away years of bonding between the two communities. Politics was to be an uphill task on a slippery slope from thereon. Yet I won some months later in the next election, in 1991, and became a junior minister under Narasimha Rao, but in the shadow of our leader Rajiv Gandhi's assassination. That heartbreaking, terrible event happened two days before the late leader was to address a rally in Farrukhabad, from where I was contesting.

In that tenure of 1991–96 came the demolition of 1992. At a social gathering at Tariq Anwar's house, a boy asked me why I had not resigned in light of the demolition. I said, 'I could and go on to win all future elections. But would that be fair to the nation?' Some years later, Farrukhabad elected me again, but the toxic cocktail of the BJP's Hindutva and the BSP–SP combine showed me the door in subsequent elections. We lost crucial years as voters continued to nurture the hope that their salvation lay in strengthening the two parties to the detriment of the Congress. Yet when the curtains came down on the Ayodhya litigation, there was no sign of the two parties.

It seems ironic that during those difficult years, when we were looked upon with hostility and accusing eyes, our questions as to who else would find a solution acceptable to Muslims were never answered. Even as every step taken by us to address the feelings of the community, that they were being let down, was resolutely dismissed, the regional parties that had grabbed our political space were not even prodded for an alternative. There was a promising anti-Congress industry that served its masters at the cost and expense of the Congress.

Before the fateful day of 6 December 1992, I spoke several times to my ministerial colleague Ranga Kumaramangalam, who was working closely with Prime Minister Narasimha Rao and the PMO team, which included Naresh Chandra, cabinet secretary, and A.N. Verma, principal secretary. We pored over pencil drawings of possible solutions, including leaving the actual spot untouched, with land on the two sides given to the temple and the mosque. There were certainly some people who believed that the angst was directed at the structure of a standing mosque and that its removal from sight would quell the storm. Of course, they did not dare to suggest that, but the eventual demolition indicates that it might have defeated other options not entirely unacceptable to the cynics. When it did happen, it left us perplexed and numbed. It took a while for the implications to sink in. Over the years, I came to understand a deep dichotomy in our public attitudes: we castigated and complained about certain situations, like the demolition, but continued to hope that we had to do nothing with it. The Supreme Court judgment has probably put the 6 December ritual into cold storage. Even the ritual of remorse has ended. But periodic whiffs of smoke rise meaninglessly from the embers, as when the Ayodhya judgment is mentioned by the critics of Chief Justice Ranjan Gogoi.

The immediate aftermath was a stunned silence, till the storm burst in Mumbai a week later and blew people off their feet over the next two months. It was a riot the likes of which had not been seen since Partition. The state, through its police force and with rare exceptions, seemed to be actively complicit in the genocide-like killing and looting. Months later, the underworld, dominated by Muslims and described as D-Company, etc., retaliated with a series of bomb blasts at important commercial centres of the city, causing untold misery and agony to innocent people.

Justice B.N. Srikrishna, then a relatively junior judge of the Bombay High Court, accepted the task of investigating the causes of the riots. For five years until 1998, he examined victims, witnesses and alleged perpetrators. Detractors came initially from left quarters; they were wary of a judge who was a devout and practising Hindu. The commission was disbanded by the Shiv Sena-led government in January 1996. On public opposition to the move, it was later reconstituted on 28 May 1996, though its terms of reference were extended to include the Bombay bomb blasts of March 1993. The report of the commission stated that the tolerant and secular foundations of the city were in place, even if they were a little shaky. Justice Srikrishna indicted those he alleged as largely responsible for the second phase of the bloodshed and to some extent the first, the Shiv Sena.

According to the Srikrishna Commission, the riots had started as a result of communal tension prevailing in the city after the Babri Masjid demolition on 6 December 1992. The commission identified two phases of the riots. The first was mainly a Muslim instigation, as a result of the demolition, in the week following 6 December. The second phase was a Hindu backlash, occurring as a result of the killings of Hindu *mathadi kamgar* (workers) by Muslim fanatics in Dongri (an area of South Bombay), stabbing of Hindus in Muslim-majority areas and burning of six Hindus, including a disabled girl, in Radhabai Chawl. This phase occurred in January 1993, with most incidents reported between 6–20 January.

The report found that the communal passions among Hindus were aroused to fever pitch by provocative writings in the print media, particularly *Saamana* and *Navakal*, which gave exaggerated accounts of the mathadi murders and the Radhabai Chawl incident. An estimated 575 Muslims and 275 Hindus were killed at the end of the riot. The communal violence and rioting triggered off by the burnings at Dongri and Radhabhai Chawl, and the following retaliatory violence by the Shiv Sena, were hijacked by local criminal elements and the land mafia, who saw an opportunity to make quick gains. By the time the right-wing Hindu organization Shiv Sena realized that enough had been done by way of 'retaliation', the matter had gone out of their hands.

The Srikrishna Commission report was, not surprisingly, criticized as 'politically motivated' by those directly held culpable. For a while its contents were a closely guarded secret, and no copies were available to the public. The BJP–Shiv Sena government rejected its recommendations. Since under the Commissions of Inquiry Act an inquiry is not a court of law (even if it conducts proceedings like a court of law) and the report of an inquiry is not binding on governments, the Srikrishna Commission's recommendations were not automatically enforced; they were neither accepted nor acted upon by the Maharashtra government. Many indicted policemen were subsequently promoted by the government, and indicted politicians continue to hold high political office even today. And now, of course, the Shiv Sena leads an alliance government, with the Congress and Nationalist Congress as partners. For those unfamiliar with the politics of Maharashtra, it would come as a surprise that this could not have happened without wholehearted support of the leading Muslims of the state.

Successive Congress governments, at the centre and in the state, have also been targeted for going slow on the report or not implementing it. Although never actually articulated in public, the considered view in the Congress has been that some wounds should be allowed to heal with the passage of time, and that any attempt to implement the commission's recommendations will only make the wounds fester and bring greater problems for Muslims. Ironically, that did not just prove right but perhaps laid the foundation for the Shiv Sena–Congress alliance in Maharashtra to form a government that keeps the BJP out of power. The initial doubts about such an enterprise were put to rest by Muslim public figures. The jury is out on whether this experiment would inevitably fail as a form of power-seeking hypocrisy, or mature into an evolution of ideologies past their sell-by dates.

One might contrast this with Nelson Mandela's 'Truth and Reconciliation"* process to get beyond seemingly irreconcilable histories of oppressors and their victims. Perhaps we have attempted an ad-hoc version of Mandela's articulated and structured scheme feasible for situations of complete change in order, whereas in India we have to deal with a varying mix of the past and the present.

Although the wounds of the 1993 riots were consciously covered, it was quite another matter for accountability to be imposed on the perpetrators of the Bombay blasts. The investigation was a humongous one and led to the accused across continents. The trial court had, in September 2006, convicted 100 and acquitted twenty-three accused. Of them, ninety-nine were handed out sentences ranging from three years to life sentence, while one was released under the Probation of Offenders Act (POA). The Supreme Court converted all but one to life sentence. The first execution in the case was carried out in July 2015, when Yakub Memon was hanged in Nagpur Jail, hopefully ending a horrible chapter in the history of modern India.

Post the demolition, as passions continued to swell and ebb across north India, my irrepressible friend Rajesh Pilot, with whom I often travelled to political destinations, took me to Faizabad by a special aircraft. From there we took a short car journey, by the Sarayu River, to Ayodhya. That was my, and Rajesh's, first visit to Ramkot, the hillock where the masjid stood. The place was heavily barricaded, although not many visitors could be seen. We first went to the terrace of a nearby building, from where the police had kept a watch on the fateful day. Rajesh asked his usual questions about how tough it was to be vigilant and how things got out of hand. We then proceeded to the temporary temple, made of bamboo

---

* Mandela founded the Truth and Reconciliation Commission (TRC) as a quasi-judicial body in South Africa after the apartheid; the TRC's focus was on restorative justice.

and tarpaulin. Rajesh went straight to where Ram Lalla was placed while I deliberately walked around to look at the neighbourhood. Given the sensitivities of political emotion, I was uncertain how my going near the temple would be received or interpreted in light of the raging dispute. Rajesh did not seem to notice the hesitation. The young priest perceptively stepped out and placed prasad in my palms. We departed without any further problem.

Those were the days when Muslims looked at us with anger and once, some young people even reacted to my description of the Babri Masjid 'structure (*dhancha*)', as though it amounted to conceding the opposition claim. I went back to Ayodhya several times for social-harmony events and even went up to the temple mound, which now had an elaborate marquee and ASI excavation trenches. There was a strange sense of inevitability about the developments; an implied, self-imposed restraint was exercised by all in even expressing the hope that the mosque would be reconstructed. Indeed, for a while the attitude of Muslims seemed to have veered towards the view that it might be impossible to reconstruct the mosque but, at least, let nothing be built on the land where the mosque once stood.

In the days before the demolition, instead of helplessly watching, we decided to register our presence in Ayodhya and took a special plane to Lucknow, where we would pick up Narayan Dutt Tiwari before proceeding to Faizabad. At the Lucknow airport, Tiwariji and Jitendra Prasada got into a convoluted conversation, in which the affable Raja Anand Singh, former MP from Gonda, untiringly cautioned against underestimating the mood in Ayodhya. This despite the fact that the previous day Nirmal Khatri had organized an impressive march through the streets. Tiwariji could not get over the fact that karsevaks had put up saffron flags on his gate. This was a colossus of UP politics, who had spent his golden years at the helm of UP, showing nervousness about the public mood.

The discussions at the airport took so long that finally the pilots indicated that the short hop to Faizabad was no longer possible because of fading sunlight. We got into the aircraft and departed for Delhi. En route, we were informed that Arjun Singh, considered to be the right-hand/second to the PM, had been in Lucknow to intercede on behalf of Zafar Ali Naqvi, a Congress leader close to him, along with the chief minister, Kalyan Singh. We assumed things were in control if our top leaders were in conversation with the state's leadership. Yet a few hours later, all hell broke loose.

As the target date of 6 December 1992 approached and the proposed kar seva plans unfolded, the matter went up to the Supreme Court repeatedly. Between 20 November and 1 December several orders were passed,* taking on board the assurances of the state government that only symbolic kar seva would be conducted and no alterations or construction would be permitted. At that point, all counsel and the court were focused on plans for construction through kar seva and the materials that had been gathered for the purpose. Actual demolition, although part of the slogans, was not envisaged or directly in issue. The court asked the High Court to spare a district judge to monitor and send a report on the developments.

Among the inevitable steps after the demolition on 6 December was the initial reaction of the court, demanding that the demolished structure be restored, but it seems that the attorney general was able to persuade it not to take that preemptory step in the hope that a settlement would be found. But of course, contempt proceedings were inevitable. Ultimately, in 1994 the final orders on contempt were passed.† In view of the importance of the matter and the fact that the court was passing judgment in contempt on a chief minister of a state, it is important to reproduce the entire reasoning. However, it is also important to point out that, as in many other cases, we will encounter in the

---

* 20, 25, 28 November and 1 December.
† 'Mohd. Aslam vs Union of India', 1994, 4 SCC 442.

Ayodhya saga a sense of 'much ado about nothing'. In that matter the court held:

1. **These petitions raise certain important issues as to the amenability of the State and of its Ministers to be proceeded against in contempt for failure of obedience to the judicial pronouncements. These proceedings have the echo of the disastrous event that ended in the demolition on the 6-12-1992 of the disputed structure of 'Ram Janma Bhoomi-Babri Masjid' in Ayodhya. Thousands of innocent lives of citizens were lost, extensive damage to property caused and more than all a damage to the image of this great land as one fostering great traditions of tolerance, faith, brotherhood amongst the various communities inhabiting the land was impaired in the international scene.** Though the proceedings for suo motu contempt against the then Chief Minister of the State of Uttar Pradesh and its officers in relation to the happening of 6-12-1992 were initiated those are pending and shall be dealt with independently.

2. The subject-matter of the present contempt proceedings, however, arises out of certain antecedent events that occurred during the month of July 1992 in relation to an extent of 2.77 acres of land in Ayodhya which was acquired by the State Government pursuant to a notification dated 7-10-1991, under Section 4 of the Land Acquisition Act, 1894. The acquisition was ostensibly for the purpose of developing the acquired land as an amenity for pilgrims at Ayodhya. The acquisition proceedings were challenged both before the High Court and this Court. In those proceedings, three interlocutory orders came to be made—two by the High Court and one by this Court. **In order to put the complaint of wilful disobedience of these orders by the State of Uttar Pradesh and its Chief Minister, Shri Kalyan Singh, it is necessary to advert to two of these orders.**

3.  On 15-11-1991 in WP No. 1000 of 1991 [Naveed Yar Khan v. State
    of U.P., 1992 Supp (2) SCC 221] this Court made the following order
    (SCC p. 222, para 1): The petitioners have approached this Court
    by way of these petitions under Article 32 of the Constitution as
    public interest litigation challenging the acquisition covered by two
    notifications dated 7-10-1991 and 10-10-1991 made under Section
    4(1) of the Land Acquisition Act, 1894 under which certain property
    in Faizabad close to Ram Janma Bhoomi–Babri Masjid complex has
    been notified for acquisition for the purpose of development of
    pilgrimage and providing amenities to them at Ayodhya.

    This Court further said (SCC pp. 223–24, paras 7–8): In
    the meantime, as we have been told at the Bar, there was a
    meeting at the national level of the Integration Council and the
    Chief Minister of the State as it appears from the affidavit of
    the Home Secretary of the respondent-State dated 13-11-1991
    made certain statements to the Council. These have been
    extracted in paragraph 3 of the affidavit and read thus: 'The
    Chief Minister has made several statements at the National
    Integration Council meeting on 2-11-1991. On the basis of the
    statements, the resolution of National Integration Council was
    passed on 2-11-1991. The Resolution itself states:

    **'The Council noted the following assurances given by the Chief
    Minister of Uttar Pradesh:**

    **(i)  All efforts will be made to find an amicable resolution of
    the issue;**

    **(ii) Pending a final solution, the Government of Uttar Pradesh
    will hold itself fully responsible for the protection of the
    Ram Janma Bhumi-Babri Masjid structures;**

    **(iii) Orders of the Court in regard to the land acquisition
    proceedings will be fully implemented; and**

    **(iv) Judgment of the Allahabad High Court in the cases pending
    before it will not be violated.'**

We shall take it, and Mr Jaitley has no objection to our doing so, that the State of Uttar Pradesh remains bound by what has been stated in this paragraph and this shall be the obligation of the State of Uttar Pradesh to stand by our order of today which is made after taking into account the stand of the State of Uttar Pradesh as disclosed by the Chief Minister and reiterated in the affidavit of the Home Secretary. It shall, therefore, be taken as a representation to the Court on which we have made this Order.

4.  On 15-7-1992 the High Court of Allahabad in CMA No. 83(O) of 1992 made an order to the following effect:

'Learned Advocate General has prayed for and is allowed three days' time to file counter-affidavit. Three days' time is allowed for filing rejoinder to the petitioner (.) List immediately thereafter (.) In the meantime the opposite parties are restrained from raising any construction on the land (.) If there is any necessity for doing something on the land for its use, prior permission from the Court would be obtained (.)'

5.  The grievance in these contempt proceedings is that these orders have been deliberately and wilfully flouted and disobeyed by the State of Uttar Pradesh, though the petitions for contempt which were lodged in the months of February and March 1992 respectively, merely alleged there were demolitions of certain structures in violation of the interdiction in that behalf contained in the order of this Court dated 15-11-1991. However, later on as events developed, certain subsequent events were brought to the notice of the Court by affidavits which came to be filed pointing out that large-scale construction work of a permanent nature was carried out on the land in utter disregard of the orders of this Court. By order dated 5-8-1992 this Court while recording the finding that the alleged demolitions did not strictly fall within the interdiction of the order of this Court dated

15-11-1991, however, found that there were certain constructional activities undertaken on the land which prima facie violated the orders of this Court.

[. . .]

Thereafter, counter-affidavits were filed by the officers of the U.P. Government. Shri Kalyan Singh, however, did not choose to file an affidavit of his own.

8.  The gravamen of the charge in these contempt petitions is that Shri Kalyan Singh, the then Chief Minister of the State, in view of his ideological and political affinity with the Bharatiya Janata Party and the Vishwa Hindu Parishad and their commitment to the building of Sri Ram temple, deliberately encouraged and permitted the grossest violation of the Courts' orders.

9.  The defence in substance, is that the constructions were initially of the nature of 'levelling operations' done by the State Government for enabling the Parikrama facilities for the pilgrims. However, later, the large congregation of Sadhus who had assembled on the land took upon themselves to make the constructions and that even those constructions which were in the nature of a platform did not amount to permanent structure such as were prohibited by the order of the Court.

10. The questions that therefore arise for consideration are:

    (i)  Whether the undertaking given by the Chief Minister before the National Integration Council which was in terms recapitulated and incorporated in the order dated 15-11-1991 of this Court could be said to be an undertaking given by the Chief Minister personally or was merely an undertaking on behalf of the U.P. Government;

    (ii) Whether there was any construction of a permanent nature carried on the land in wilful disobedience of the orders of the Court;

(iii) Whether these constructional activities were carried on by or at the instance of the State Government or its authorities or were done in connivance with and assistance and encouragement of the State Government; or were they carried out in spite of all reasonable steps taken in that regard by the State Government and the Chief Minister to prevent the same; and

(iv) Whether the State Government and the Chief Minister were not liable for contempt for any alleged wilful disobedience of the orders of this Court.

11. The purport of the defence—as gatherable from the various affidavits and counter-affidavits filed from time to time—does not seem to dispute that constructions of a substantial nature were carried out on the land in the month of July 1992. Implicit in these admissions is that had these works and activities been carried out by the State Government and its authorities, there would be no doubt whatsoever that they constitute a flagrant violation of the orders of the Court. What was, however, sought to be pleaded was that the area in question, by a long religious tradition in Ayodhya, attracts a large number of pilgrims and particularly in the month of July which coincides with the period of 'Chaturmas' where a large number of Sadhus congregate to celebrate 'Sarvadev Anusthan'. It was urged that these pilgrim-Sadhus embarked upon the construction of the cement concrete platform and that their number was so large that any coercive preventive action would have triggered off an adverse reaction which might have endangered the safety of the disputed 'Ram Janma Bhoomi–Babri Masjid structure' which was situated in the immediate vicinity and for whose protection the Government stood committed. In view of these conflicting considerations and of the risks involved in the operations, the Government felt compelled to abstain from any coercive steps to prevent the constructions by the pilgrims. We shall later advert to the merits

and bona fides of this version. Suffice it to say here that at no point of time did the Chief Minister seek before Court to be absolved of his undertaking in view of these alleged conditions. They are now put forward as a defence in the contempt action.

12. But it is necessary to say that in a Government of laws and not of men the executive branch of Government bears a grave responsibility for upholding and obeying judicial orders. It is perhaps worthwhile recalling what the Supreme Court of United States observed in William G. Cooper, Members of the Board of Directors of the Little Rock v. John Aaron [358 US 1 : 3 L Ed 2d 5 : 78 S Ct 1401 (1958)] where, in his concurring opinion Justice Frankfurter said:

'The use of force to further obedience to law is in any event a last resort and one not congenial to the spirit of our Nation . . . Violent resistance to law cannot be made a legal reason for its suspension without loosening the fabric of our society. What could this mean but to acknowledge that disorder under the aegis of a State has moral superiority over the law of the Constitution?

The historic phrase 'a Government of laws and not of men' epitomizes the distinguishing character of our political society. When John Adams put that phrase into the Massachusetts Declaration of Rights he was not indulging in a rhetorical flourish. He was expressing the aim of those who, with him, framed the Declaration of Independence and founded the Republic.

Compliance with decisions of this Court, as the constitutional organ of the supreme law of the land, has often, throughout our history, depended on active support by State and local authorities. It presupposes such support. To withhold it, and indeed to use political power to try to paralyse the supreme law, precludes the maintenance of our federal system as we have known and cherished it for one hundred and seventy years.

Lincoln's appeal to 'the better angels of our nature' failed to avert a fratricidal war. But the compassionate wisdom of Lincoln's First and Second Inaugurals bequeathed to the Union, cemented with blood, a moral heritage which, when drawn upon in times of stress and strife, is sure to find specific ways and means to surmount difficulties that may appear to be insurmountable.'

[. . .]

14. In these formative years of our nation building, it is more important than ever to recognise that in a pluralist society law is the greatest and the only integrating factor. Respect for law and its institutions is the only assurance that can hold a pluralist nation together. Any attempt to achieve solutions to controversies, however, ideologically and emotionally surcharged, not on the basis of law and through judicial institutions, but on the strength of numbers will subvert the fundamental values of our chosen political organisation. It will demolish public faith in the accepted constitutional institutions and weaken people's resolve to solve issues by peaceful means. It will destroy respect for the Rule of Law and the authority of courts and seek to place individual authority and strength of numbers above the wisdom of law. This is courting disaster, fratricidal wars, civil commotion, disruption of everything that we hold sacred. The highest cherished value of our nationhood which is tolerance will be distorted by such misguided enthusiasm.

15. On the issue whether there was construction—massive construction—in violation of the Courts' orders, no other material than the very admissions of the State authorities are sufficient to justify a finding that there were such violation of the Courts' orders.

16. In the Chief Engineer's Report appended to the counter-affidavit of Shri Prabhat Kumar, Principal Secretary to the Government, Home Department, the following description of the nature of the work occurs:

'Foundation concrete has been laid in three layers as described in the enclosed site map in the plan. It was seen on digging from the outer side, that the lowest layer had an average thickness of 62 cm, the middle layer had an average thickness of 60 cm and the upper layer had an average thickness of 60 cm. Middle and upper layers have not been laid on the whole of the area in which foundation concrete has been laid on the lowest layer.

Brick wall has been constructed in some part, the height of which is 1.56 metres, on the lowest layer of the foundation concrete, the location of which has been shown in the enclosed site map in the plan. The brickwork of the wall has been done with cement and sand mortar. A brick wall touching the cut in the earth on mount close to the pipe barricading, has been constructed, the average height of which is 2.25 metres and cement and sand mortar has been used in it. Its location has been shown in the enclosed site map in the plan.'

17. Commenting on the possible purpose of this structure, Shri Prabhat Kumar himself says, '[H]owever, according to the statements of those involved in the construction work it was intended to be the first step towards putting up of the "Singh Dwar" of the proposed "Ram Mandir" as and when the same would be constructed'.

18. In the report dated 18-7-1992 by the District Magistrate and Senior Superintendent of Police to the Chief Secretary, as to the nature and extent of construction, while admitting the progress of construction, the District Magistrate says:

'On 18-7-1992 at 8.45 to 9.30 a.m. we met Shri Ashok Singhal and Shri Onkar Bhave and requested them to have the work stopped in compliance with order dated 15-7-1992 of the High Court, responsibility for which had been entrusted to us. They informed that at 5 p.m. on 17-7-1992 decision was taken in the meeting of about 50 saints at the Digamber Akhara that construction will not be stopped. In view of this decision construction could not be stopped and they suggested that talks may be held with members of Temple Renovation Committee.'

19. This Court constituted a committee consisting of Shri S. Rai, Registrar General, Supreme Court; Professor K.K. Nayar, IIT Delhi; and Professor Arvind Krishan, School of Planning and Architecture, New Delhi. In the report of the Committee, the nature and the extent of construction is described thus:

'The area built-up can be visualised as 5 north-south strips arranged from the east to the west (for the purpose of computation and reference as shown in Appendix A2-1). Areas and dimensions of the first four strips increase step by step from one another. The fifth strip is cut back both in area and dimension. There are 3 layers of concrete in the structure (Annexure A1-2). The first layer is about 0.62 m thick and it covers the full area of 1060 sq. m except for a circular opening of 7.1 m diameter in the centre of the fourth strip. On the northern side, the top level of this layer of concrete merges with the ground. On all other sides this layer is only 10 cm below the ground level. The second layer is 0.6 m thick and has an area of 560 sq. m, including the circular opening. It is laid on the first layer over the strips 2 to 5 and with setbacks. Both these layers are fairly symmetrical about the east-west axis, except for small irregularities in the dimensions. The third layer is also 0.6 m thick but covers only a small area of 130 sq. m. Bulk of concrete is laid on the south-west region of the structure. In general, the second and third layers have poor surface finish. The concrete casting work is unfinished.

However, if one desires, a modified form of a classical temple can be related to this configuration.

As already stated in Paragraphs 2(a).04.1 to 2(a).04.4, the magnitude of the work is such that it could not have been carried out without the use of construction equipments such as water-tankers, cement concrete mixers, concrete vibrators, earth-moving equipment etc.'

20. There is, therefore, no manner of doubt that substantial work, indeed very substantial work, involving tonnes of cement and concrete deployed with the help of constructional machinery was carried on at the site. The photographs produced by the complainant—which are not disputed—indicate the gathering of workers. A mere perusal of the photographs justifies an inference that the large workforce at the site does not consist of mere Sadhus but justifies the inference that professional workmen had been deployed at the site.

21. [. . .] **We have no hesitation in finding that there was massive work undertaken and executed on the land in violation of the Courts' orders.**

22. The next question is whether these activities were carried on by a congregation of Sadhus at the site and not by the State Government and despite Government's efforts. Apart from a glib suggestion that any attempt to prevent the work would have created a violent situation endangering the safety of the 'Ram Janma Bhoomi–Babri Masjid structure' itself, nothing is indicated as to what was sought to be done at all to prevent constructional material coming in. There is no mention in any of the affidavits of any of the officers as to what reasonable measures the Government took to prevent the inflow of constructional material such as large quantities of cement, mortar, sand, constructional equipment, water-tankers etc. that were necessary for the work. The report of the Expert Committee has indicated that constructional machinery was indispensable having regard to the nature and magnitude of the work carried out. While it is understandable that the prevention of the gathering of Sadhus might have created some resentment, it is ununderstandable why large quantities of building materials were allowed to be brought on the land unless it be—and that must be the reasonable

presumption—that the Government itself was not too anxious to prevent it. It is not merely positive acts of violation but also surreptitious and indirect aids to circumvention and violation of the orders that are equally impermissible. If reasonable steps are not taken to prevent the violation of the orders of the Court, Government cannot be heard to say that violation of the orders were at the instance of others. The presumption is that the Government intended not to take such preventive steps. In the facts and circumstances of the case, we are unable to persuade ourselves to the view that the Government was helpless and the situation that had developed was in spite of all reasonable steps taken by the Government. Indeed there is no indication that the Government bestirred itself to take any steps, reasonable or otherwise, to prevent large-scale building material getting into the site. The Chief Minister having given a solemn assurance to the National Integration Council and permitted the terms of that assurance to be incorporated as his own undertaking to this Court and allowed an order to be passed in those terms cannot absolve himself of the responsibility unless he placed before the Court sufficient material which would justify that he had taken all reasonable steps and precautions to prevent the occurrence. Indeed, if such reasonable steps had been taken he could not be faulted merely because he did not do the best by the standards of others. In this case, we find no explanation at all apart from the fact that the Sadhus had congregated in that place in large number, as to what steps the Government took to prevent the constructional equipment from getting into site. If any reasonable effort had been made and evidence of that placed before Court, it might have been possible for the Court to assess the situation in the light of that explanation to find out whether such steps had been taken. **In the absence, we are constrained to hold that the Government failed to take steps to prevent the grossest violation of the order of this Court. We record a finding accordingly.**

23. The last question is whether the undertaking furnished by the Chief Minister was a personal undertaking or was on behalf of the State of U.P. It was both.

24. **There is no immunity for any authority of Government, if a personal element is shown in the act of disobedience of the order of the Court, from the consequence of an order of the Court. Even in England where the maxim 'Crown can do no wrong' has had its influence, a distinction is made between the Crown as such and the Executive.**

25. In a recent pronouncement of far-reaching impact, the House of Lords in M. v. Home Office [(1994) 1 AC 377 : (1993) 3 All ER 537] observed (as per Lord Templeman):

'My Lords, Parliament makes the law, the executive carry the law into effect and judiciary enforce the law. The expression 'the Crown' has two meanings; namely the monarch and the executive. In the seventeenth century Parliament established its supremacy over the Crown as monarch, over the executive and over the judiciary. Parliamentary supremacy over the Crown as monarch stems from the fact that the monarch must accept the advice of a Prime Minister who is supported by a majority of Parliament. Parliamentary supremacy over the Crown as executive stems from the fact that Parliament maintains in office the Prime Minister who appoints the ministers in charge of the executive. Parliamentary supremacy over the judiciary is only exercisable by statute. The judiciary enforce the law against individuals, against institutions and against the executive. The judges cannot enforce the law against the Crown as monarch because the Crown as monarch can do no wrong but judges enforce the law against the Crown as executive and against the individuals who from time to time represent the Crown. A litigant complaining of a breach of the law by the executive can sue the Crown as executive bringing his action against the minister who is responsible for the department of

State involved, in the present case the Secretary of State for Home Affairs. To enforce the law the courts have power to grant remedies including injunctions against a minister in his official capacity. If the minister has personally broken the law, the litigant can sue the minister, in this case Mr Kenneth Baker, in his personal capacity. For the purpose of enforcing the law against all persons and institutions, including ministers in their official capacity and in their personal capacity, the courts are armed with coercive powers exercisable in proceedings for contempt of court.

* * *

My Lords, the argument that there is no power to enforce the law by injunction or contempt proceedings against a minister in his official capacity would, if upheld, establish the proposition that the executive obey the law as a matter of grace and not as a matter of necessity, a proposition which would reverse the result of the Civil War. For the reasons given by my noble and learned friend Lord Woolf and on principle, I am satisfied that injunctions and contempt proceedings may be brought against the minister in his official capacity and that in the present case the Home Office for which the Secretary of State was responsible was in contempt.'

26. However, in that case it was found as a matter of fact that there was no personal element involved in the violation at the instance of the Home Secretary, Mr Baker. Therefore, Lord Templeman observed:

'I am also satisfied that Mr Baker was throughout acting in his official capacity, on advice which he was entitled to accept and under a mistaken view as to the law. In these circumstances I do not consider that Mr Baker personally was guilty of contempt.'

In the leading speech Lord Woolf said:

> 'This was the first time that a minister of the Crown had been found to be in contempt by a court. The finding of contempt was made for not complying with an injunction granted by Garland, J. ordering M., who had made a claim for asylum, which was rejected by the Home Office, to be returned to this country.

\* \* \*

Nolan, L.J. considered that the fact that proceedings for contempt are 'essentially personal and punitive' meant that it was not open to a court, as a matter of law, to make a finding of contempt against the Home Office or the Home Secretary. [See M. v. Home Office, (1992) 4 All ER 97, 144 : (1992) 1 QB 270, 311] While contempt proceedings usually have these characteristics and contempt proceedings against a government department or a minister in an official capacity would not be either personal or punitive (it would clearly not be appropriate to fine or request the assets of the Crown or a government department or an officer of the Crown acting in his official capacity), this does not mean that a finding of contempt against a government department or minister would be pointless. The very fact of making such a finding would vindicate the requirements of justice. In addition an order for costs could be made to underline the significance of contempt. A purpose of the courts' powers to make findings of contempt is to ensure that the orders of the court are obeyed. This jurisdiction is required to be coextensive with the courts' jurisdiction to make the orders which need the protection which the jurisdiction to make findings of contempt provides.

\* \* \*

Normally it will be more appropriate to make the order against the office which a minister holds where the order which has been breached has been made against that office since members of the department concerned will almost certainly be involved and investigation as to the part played by individuals is likely to be at least extremely difficult, if not impossible, unless privilege is waived (as commendably happened in this case). In addition the object of the exercise is not so much to punish an individual as to vindicate the rule of law by a finding of contempt. This can be achieved equally by declaratory finding of the court as to the contempt against the minister as representing the department. By making the finding against the minister in his official capacity the court will be indicating that it is the department for which the minister is responsible which has been guilty of contempt. The minister himself may or may not have been personally guilty of contempt. The position so far as he is personally concerned would be the equivalent of that which needs to exist for the court to give relief against the minister in proceedings for judicial review.

* * *

To draw a distinction between his two personalities would be unduly technical. While he was Home Secretary the order was one binding upon him personally and one for the compliance with which he as the head of the department was personally responsible.'

[. . .]

28. The State Government is, therefore, liable in contempt.
    A Minister or Officer of Government is also either in his official capacity or if there is a personal element contributing to contempt, in his personal capacity, liable in contempt.

29. We find that the undertaking given by Shri Kalyan Singh was both in his personal capacity and on behalf of his Government.

There has been a flagrant breach of that undertaking. There has been willful disobedience of the order.

30. **It is unhappy that a leader of a political party and Chief Minister has to be convicted of an offence of contempt of court. But it has to be done to uphold the majesty of law. We convict him of the offence of contempt of court. Since the contempt raises larger issues which affect the very foundation of the secular fabric of our nation, we also sentence him to a token imprisonment of one day. We also sentence him to pay a fine of Rs 2000. The fine shall be paid within a period of two months. For the sentence of imprisonment a warrant will issue.**

31. The contempt petitions are partly disposed of accordingly.

\* \* \*

The demolition led to several BJP state governments, which had supported their party's programme regarding Ayodhya, being dismissed. The dismissals were challenged in the high courts and finally came to be decided by a nine-judge bench of the Supreme Court in the case of 'S.R. Bommai v Union of India'.* The court upheld the dismissal but in the process declared secularism to be part of the basic structure of the Constitution, a finding specifically referred to in the Ayodhya judgment. As for the then chief minister, Kalyan Singh, he served the sentence till the rising of court and went on to become governor of Rajasthan, with constitutional immunity from prosecution during his tenure; but he was forced to face prosecution upon laying down office. Curiously, he did not figure as a prominent invitee to the bhoomi pujan on 5 August 2020 along with some other front-line activists of the Ram Mandir movement. L.K. Advani, who also faced prosecution at the time, had to be satisfied with a suo-motu statement about his dream having come true. In the end, he, as indeed many others, were acquitted and freed of any blame.

---

* 'S.R. Bommai v Union of India', 1994, 3 SCC 1.

# Two

# A Sunset in the East

The Babri Masjid–Ram Janmabhoomi controversy revolves around issues of faith, power and politics. It might not be wrong to say that the first, both deeply felt and lightly assumed, would have the least share in the issue while the other two make up the most of it. For the BJP government, while Triple Talaq and Article 370 might have been contrived for impact, the Ram Mandir judgment was a godsend, so to speak. The subject matter of the issue deals with the past—the past of temple and mosque demolitions, depending on where you stand, as well as the past of faiths and belief systems.

Y. Sudershan Rao, former chairperson, Indian Council for Historical Research (ICHR), says, '. . . colonial and Marxist historians have dominated history writing in India for long . . . People do not care whether Ram is historical or not. He is truth for them. India's need is a special study of its past and the truth of its past cannot be denied. We need to Indianise our history writing."* This is not useful criticism since it does not explain what the process of Indianization—the term in itself is abstract

---

* R. Chopra, 'Ramayan, Mahabharat Historical Sources, West Dubs Them Myth: Y Sudershan Rao', *Economic Times*, 17 November 2014, https://economictimes.

and ambiguous—entails. What is the idea of India? Surely there
cannot be only one. But since all historical work is based on an
argument about the present, it is argued here that it will be useful
to understand the Ramayana's symbology for Indians in 2020 to
address the current political and judicial crisis. I argue that the
Babri Masjid–Ram Janmabhoomi controversy tells a story of the
long-drawn process of the communalization of Indian society, and
it all begins because of the question of faith.

As A.G. Noorani argued, 'Vishwa Hindu Parishad's case is
based on false history, a perverted course of justice in the courts
and politics based on naked force and intimidation.'* The historical
evidence presented here does support that line of thought, though
it is not per say a historical account of the Babri Masjid–Ram
Janmabhoomi issue, because even though the origins of this
dispute lie in the past, it is no longer a matter of only historical
records.

Reactions to the Ayodhya judgment range across a broad
spectrum of perceptions. Some people think it was sensible and
inevitable; others think of it as the final closure that was desirable
and justified. Some think there is an intrinsic contradiction in
the court holding that the mosque was never abandoned, despite
several unlawful attempts to interfere with it, and Muslims being
denied title in what was admittedly a title suit; yet others believe
that as the verdict of the final court we have to accept it but
Muslims, being denied justice, should abjure the offer of 5 acres to
build a mosque elsewhere.

As we will see here, mistakes were made by the lawyers of the
Muslim side. My suggestion, that it might be a good gesture to
accept the offer with grace, was met with foul derision by some

indiatimes.com/opinion/interviews/ramayan-mahabharat-historical-sources-
west-dubs-them-myth-y-sudershan-rao/articleshow/45171587.cms?from=mdr
* A.G. Noorani, 'The Babri Masjid-Ram Janmabhoomi Question', *Economic and
Political Weekly*, vol. 24, no. 44/45, 4–11 November 1989, pp. 2461–2466.

people and, of course, some colleagues have already rejected the land as unwanted charity. Perhaps the Waqf Board has chosen wisely to accept the offer, but it is surprising that instead of the acquired land, or somewhere else within the municipal limits of Ayodhya, they accepted a site several kilometres away. Be that as it may, the fact remains that it is imperative that we find closure and carry on with our national life. It is therefore important to put the Ayodhya saga into perspective beyond the narrative of the 'other'. We had, after all, announced that we would all accept and honour the judgment of the Supreme Court, but that surely must be in letter and spirit. Yet we heard muted disappointment and open encouragement to reject the 5 acres of land for a mosque.

There is a tragedy here that has implications for future reconciliation efforts. Some people have arrogated to themselves the right to make critical decisions about the future of their community. In the past, the same people took to campaigning against Congress leaders in parliamentary elections, including in my constituency. When the Waqf Amendments were passed, the same people screamed that it was done to defeat their claim on Babri Masjid. Now that the judgment has been pronounced, do they not feel remorse at having questioned others on intentions and ability? Instead, they insist on taking further decisions without consultation or deference. It had to be left to young people to take to the streets without waiting for instructions from the likes of the All India Muslim Personal Law Board.

Ayodhya will almost certainly be a turning point in the political history of India. It is another matter whether the road ahead leads to greater reconciliation and bonding, or to collective sullenness of one community and triumphant assertion by the other. Even to help succeeding generations choose wisely and somehow preserve the beauty of India's unity, we need to establish the truth about how and why the dispute arose; how indeed unsuccessful attempts were made to find an amicable solution outside courts; how the Supreme Court charted the course not to be swept by claims of faith and steered the country to a workable resolution of a seemingly intractable conflict. This book attempts to do just that, in the hope that ostensible formal acceptance of the Ayodhya verdict will leave no subcutaneous scars on the soul of India.

India is not alone in having to deal with interreligious conflicts that manifest themselves around places of worship. However, many of those conflicts, even the past ones in India, emerged and were mostly resolved before a fully democratic government was established. In that sense the present case is different. But either way, there are lessons from the past that might be helpful in understanding the present predicament and to set at rest apprehensions felt in certain quarters about the Ayodhya judgment becoming a precedent for future adventurism by political forces seen to have gained advantage.

Although it is now clear that 67 acres, acquired in the vicinity of the 2.77 acres contested by way of the suits decided by the Allahabad High Court, will go as intended to the successful party, and that an uninterrupted area of Hindu dominance will emerge in Ayodhya, the fact remains that the holy city has over 500 mosques and many more temples. Yet the accommodation exhibited by other communities in Haridwar and Amritsar will undoubtedly be continued to be shown in Ayodhya. How comfortably, and indeed wholesomely, the proposed masjid will adorn the Ayodhya landscape and skyline remains to be seen. But the shaping of that reality will depend a great deal on how various actors in the Ayodhya saga write the script for the future.

In one way or the other, this moment in history will be marked as the crossroads of pluralist democracy. While mandir and masjid are important to Indians, Hindus and Muslims alike, in a civilizational sense, our constitutional imperative of equal regard and respect for all citizens is of paramount importance. It is here that a distinction needs to be made between honest acceptance and being forced to accept and comply. Must justice operate in entirety or inevitably in aggregate? While it is understandable that people expect that each and every moment must be addressed in terms of justice, it makes sense to state that justice may not be a mathematical exercise. Be that as it may, once a judgment is examined closely, it would be useful to take the final call on how just that judgment is. Meanwhile, as the sun sets on a social conflict and legal dispute, it remains to be seen whether it will rise on the beginning of a fresh period of hope and fulfilment.

It is necessary to remain aware of the fact that the dramatis personae involved in this issue are innumerable, all claiming to speak on behalf of entire communities. The curse of the Sole Spokesman that tore India apart in the run-up to Independence and pushed us to Partition, which continues to hurt several decades later, remains a distortion of our democratic impulses. If, hopefully, the Ayodhya contention has one way or the other come to an end, it is equally important that its parting memory be wholesome.

Curiously, many of the non-BJP parties that made their fortune out of the Ayodhya dispute had precious little to say about the decision. Caste affiliations have certainly dominated politics in north India, but these parties have used bulk voting by Muslims for effective impact in terms of votes. Now, their alibi is gone, and the BJP has eaten into their vote banks. Would it now appeal to them to shed traditional formulae and engage in the real politics of growth and development? Meanwhile, the BJP has no intention to bow out of the Ram Mandir story and put it away as a gesture of obeisance. The fanfare with which Prime Minister Narendra Modi and Uttar Pradesh's chief minister, Yogi Adityanath, arrived in Ayodhya for the shila pujan in August 2020, despite COVID-19, indicated their intention to squeeze political advantage to the last. Thus far, there are no signs that they are at peace in terms of their religious quest and that they would reach out to Muslims with a hand of comfort and reconciliation anytime soon.

# Three

# Lord Ram's Ayodhya: Triumph and Tragedy

In order to grasp the full significance of the Ayodhya judgment and subsequent developments, it is necessary to keep the story of Lord Ram before us, as despite the repeated caution of the Supreme Court that the decision was on legal principles of title, the backdrop of obeisance to the deity and the concept was never obscured, and the subsequent conduct of persons in government more than demonstrates that.

In dealing with the significance of the birthplace of Lord Ram, it is important to take a closer look at the average Indian's (particularly Hindu) perception and the place of Ram in their ethical world view. The story or legend of Lord Ram has innumerable dimensions interwoven with faith, mythology, culture and history. Scholars have delved into original sources, including Jain and Buddhist texts, to construct a consistent narrative to the extent possible, yet different streams continue to influence our understanding and perception. The epic has multiple layers and nuances often defying attempts to reconcile and harmonize. Ultimately, deep faith controls willing suspension of disbelief. Since the legend was not frozen in time and space, temporal influences of the age in which something was added lend a wonderful elasticity to the narrative, but in keeping with the prevailing thought of the times. There is a great deal that is difficult to explain to a modern, rational mind, except to insist that we see the narrative as allegorical rather than factual.

There is generally no real disagreement on the fact that Lord Ram was born in Ayodhya, even if some people continue to debate where Ayodhya actually was situated and if there was but one Ayodhya. It is a collective memory, a faith, a legacy drawn from Tulsidas's *Ramcharitmanas* and Valmiki's Ramayana, while for some it is a romanticized fragment of history. Periodically, one hears voices pronouncing that Lord Ram is mere imagination, but such assertions are dismissed with contempt. It is another matter that no one really can point to the exact spot of Lord Ram's birth, other than by assuming that it is under where the central dome of the Babri Masjid used to be. But a Vaidik once told me that according to Vaishnava tradition, the umbilical cord is buried where a child is born, making the place impure for building a temple. Of course, this fact was not argued before the courts. Much after the judgment, some people raised the objection about a mandir being proposed on land where Muslims lie buried. Be that as it may, one wonders if the precise point could have been identified in the pre-GPS days.

Whether Lord Ram, also described as Maryada Purushottam,* was God in the sense of many other religions or indeed unique as a human avatar of Lord Vishnu remains a matter of study and debate. The mind boggles at the thought of a God among many, including at different levels of interaction in the legend, as opposed to one single God familiar to Islam and the unified Trinity of Christianity. Curiously, the Brahma–Vishnu–Maheshwara trinity,

---

* Sanskrit phrase in which 'Maryada' translates to 'honour and righteousness', and 'Purushottam' translates to 'the supreme man'.

too, is part of a single entity. For instance, the gods in heaven (all themselves part of Param Brahma), perturbed by Ravana straying from dharma, persuaded Brahma to send the avatar of Lord Vishnu (himself part of Brahma) to kill the *rakshasa*. But then Ravana had a certain boon granted by Brahma, making him difficult to kill except in conditions that only Lord Ram could satisfy. Ravana was secured from gods, but in his conceit he had not bothered to seek protection against a human adversary.

In order to cross the sea to get to Lanka, Ram had to pray to the sea god for several days. During the combat with Ravana's son, Indrajit, the latter became invisible, and both Ram and Lakshman were helpless against the former's arrows (serpent darts) charged with sorcery. But the poisonous darts disappeared when Garuda came upon the scene. Ram did not know then that he was Vishnu and that Garuda was his own bird, which he rode. But what might surprise many people is to know that Ram said to Vibhishana, the latter lamenting his brother Ravana's gruesome death in battle: 'Ravana fought like a true warrior and fell fighting like a hero. Death has washed his sins. It calls for no mourning. Ravana has entered Heaven.' All of Ravana's demon kin having fallen in battle against the forces of Lord Ram, it would fall upon Vibhishana to perform the last rites of his brother.

Be that as it may, Lord Ram remains for Hindus a close link between humans and gods, with the latter descending to human existence to the extent of suffering all forms of human striving and pain, and yet alleviating humankind's gravest dangers. By any measure, the triumph accomplished by Lord Ram in slaying Ravana also had its tragic side, with Sita ultimately withdrawing to the womb of her mother, the Earth Goddess (Bhumi) and Lord Ram finally submitting himself to Jalabhishek, or *samadhi*, in the Sarayu River at Ayodhya, in the company of his two surviving bothers and devoted followers. But even in that regard it is argued that Ram once again merged with Vishnu and therefore, in truth, did not take samadhi.

In the Ramayana it is stated in the Bala Kanda (the first book of the Valmiki Ramayana) that Lord Ram was born to King Dasharatha (ruler of the Kingdom of Kosala) and his Queen Kaushalya in the city of Ayodhya. The kingdom of Kosala is mentioned in Buddhist and Jain texts as one of the sixteen *mahajanapadas* of ancient India, and as an important centre of pilgrimage. It is therefore difficult for experts to conclude upon the excavation records. However, there is some scholarly dispute whether the modern Ayodhya (present-day Uttar Pradesh) is indeed the same as the site/city mentioned in ancient texts.

The Valmiki Ramayana is a Sanskrit text, while the *Ramcharitmanas* retells the Ramayana in the Awadhi dialect of the Hindi language, commonly understood in northern India, and thus forms the basis of the script for the immensely popular annual Ramlilas. The *Ramcharitmanas* was composed in the sixteenth century by the poet Tulsidas. The popular text is notable for synthesizing the epic story in a Bhakti-movement framework, wherein the original legends and ideas morph into an expression of spiritual *bhakti* (devotional love) for a personal God.

Tulsidas's account was one of many later versions of the Ramayana which were inspired by the allegorical interpretation of the Adhyatma Ramayana. In this Sanskrit text, which spans the thirteenth to fifteenth centuries, Ram and other characters of the Valmiki Ramayana along with their attributes (*saguna* narrative), were transposed into spiritual terms and an abstract rendering of an atma (soul) without attributes (*nirguna* reality)*. In the *Ramcharitmanas*, Ram's story combines mythology, philosophy and religious beliefs with a life narrative, a code of ethics and a treatise on universal human values. The text debates human

---

* John Nicol Farquhar, *An Outline of the Religious Literature of India*, Oxford University Press, 1920, pp. 324–325.

dilemmas, the ideal standards of behaviour, duties towards loved ones and mutual responsibilities.*

Being the eldest son and heir apparent, Lord Ram was a thorn in the eyes of his foster mother, Kaikeyi, who on the eve of his coronation persuaded the king to send him to exile for fourteen years. As a noble and obedient son, Lord Ram left the palace with his wife Sita; they were accompanied by Lakshman, who refused to let his elder brother go unattended. Upon the demise of Dasharatha, Bharat was offered the throne, owing to Ram's absence. Bharat turned down the offer and travelled to the place of exile to usher Ram to return, but despite his entreaties Ram refused to defy his father's wishes. So Bharat chose to place Ram's *kharaon* (sandals) on the throne in Nandigram, awaiting the return of Ram from exile.

What might have been an uneventful completion of exile and the reunion of the family was upset by the unpleasant intervention by Ravana, who, slyly using Maricha disguised as a golden deer to draw away Ram and Lakshman, abducted Sita to avenge the treatment meted out to his own sister, Surpanakha. Surpanakha had been harshly reprimanded and disfigured by Lakshman for trying to stalk him and for threatening Sita. What followed was the decision on the part of the brothers to set out in hot pursuit of the abductor and seek the release of Sita from captivity. The assistance of the *vaanar* king Sugriva and his minister Hanuman came as a timely boon after some interesting side adventures. Hanuman made a heroic journey to search for Sita, who was kept in captivity in the kindom of Lanka. Ram's troops then built the Ram Setu across the sea, remnants of which are said to exist in the Palk Strait. War ensued, with Ravana's brother Vibhishan transferring his allegiance to Ram, which led to the killing of Ravana and his other brother Kumbhkaran, besides many other rakshasas, and of

---

* A. Kapoor, Gilbert Pollet (ed.), *Indian Epic Values: Ramayana and Its Impact*, Peeters Publishers, 1995, pp. 181–186.

course the eventual, triumphant return of Lord Ram and Sita to Ayodhya. Every event and step in the saga is replete with side tales and passing encounters that cast light on the character of Ram, and are a continuing source of immense debate and scholarship.

The saga of Ram and the victory of the forces of good over evil is celebrated with gaiety and gusto each year on the occasion of Dussehra (the killing of the ten-headed one) or Vijayadashami, when effigies of the demons Ravana, Kumbhkaran and Meghnath are ignited. In India it is not really regarded as an exclusively religious event and attracts people of all communities; it's celebrated as a social statement of unity of good against all evil, a part of the cultural identity of India. If such critical moments in the life and times of Lord Ram are seen as matters of cultural importance to Hindus, Muslims, Christians, Sikhs, Buddhists and Parsis et al., then it seems strange that the event and place of his birth remain an issue of contest and conflict between two communities. It was the great poet Allama Iqbal who called Ram Imam-e-Hind:

*Hai raam ke vajūd pe hindostāñ ko naaz*
*Ahl-e-nazar samajhte haiñ is ko Imām-e-Hind*

(India is proud of the existence of Rama
Spiritual people consider him prelate of India)

As stated before, Hindus speak of Lord Ram as God, although he is really an avatar of Lord Vishnu, the preserver or nurturer among the trinity of Brahma, Vishnu and Maheshwara. Scholars closely dissect different periods of Ram's life to posit that the specific period of his being an avatar ended with the killing of Ravana. But that seems to be an attempt to distinguish the expectations of his followers from an avatar–king as from just a beneficent ruler. The popular perception and cognizance of God is anthropomorphic, although the Supreme Court in the Ayodhya judgment specifically recognizes the Hindu God as

being formless,* not very different from Islam and other religions
described as 'faiths of the Book'. Referring to Lord Ram as
Maryada Purshottam is indicative of his human character, but
of a godly kind. Raising outstanding humans to near-godly or
saintly status, regarding them as mahatmas, is common in the
Indian ethos. Thus, the line between the human and the divine is
very thin, which indeed is the essence of Hindu thought.

The return of Ram and Sita to Ayodhya was the beginning of
Ram Rajya. But the tribulations of Lord Ram did not end with the
vanquishing of Ravana. As king of Ayodhya, Ram displayed all
attributes underscored in the Hindu concept of sovereign: a perfect
human, an obedient son, a devoted sibling, a faithful friend and
an affectionate husband. But he was conscious of his *rajadharma*.
Under the pressure of his subjects, he was persuaded to seek from
Sita, who had been held captive by a rakshasa before returning to
Ayodhya, a trial by fire for unblemished chastity. Even beyond
that, the issue somehow remained alive and the decision for a fresh
*agni pareeksha* was taken, ultimately forcing Sita to first return to
exile and then forsake the family of a husband she adored and her
two sons, to seek refuge in the bosom of Mother Earth.

It is said that during Ram's rule as king, one of his subjects,
while rebuking his wife for alleged infidelity, told her that he was
not as timid as the king, who would take his wife back after she
had lived with another man. Of course, Ram understood that the
aspersions cast upon Sita were entirely bereft of truth. Yet, in
his commitment to be a just ruler, he yielded to growing public
opinion, and Sita was forced into exile a second time, this time
while she was carrying Ram's progeny. The *rishi* (sage) Valmiki
provided Sita with shelter in his forest ashram on the banks of the
Tamsa River, where she is said to have given birth to twin sons
named Luv and Kush.

---

* The Ram Janmabhoomi Temple case, paras 128–134 ('The Hindu Idol and
  Divinity').

There is another interesting version of events according to which Sita gave birth only to one son whom she named Luv. One day, when Sita was going to take *snaan* (bath) in the river, she asked the Valmiki to watch over her son. Valmiki nodded, busy in his writings. As Sita walked away from the ashram she noticed that the *muni* (Sanskrit term meaning 'thinker') was immersed in thought, and so she took Luv with her. After some time, when Valmiki turned away from his work to look towards the child, he found him missing. Worried at how to face Sita, he created a boy-child from some nearby *kush* (a type of grass used for making mats and roofs of huts) and breathed life into this child. When mother and son returned, Valmiki was surprised, but he asked Sita to take care of the boy as her own. From the tender age of just five the brothers began formally training under the tutelage of Valmiki, who trained them in divine and celestial warfare. The boys proved to be skilled archers and it is said that they were able to shoot arrows at the speed of sound. While they became masters of archery, their identities were kept secret throughout.

Many years after Sita's exile, Ram carried out the Ashwamedha Yagya[*] to expand his kingdom. The horse he released wandered into the forest where Luv and Kush lived. Being but children, they captured the horse without knowing its significance. Ram sent Hanuman to rescue the horse. Hanuman promptly recognized Luv and Kush as the sons of his master, and let them capture him and tie him up. Worried for Hanuman's fate when he did not return, Ram sent his brothers to look for him and the horse. On spotting Hanuman, Ram's brother challenged the two young boys. However, the two young warriors emerged as the victors on the day, defeating their challengers and knocking them unconscious.

---

[*] A ritual where an emperor sent out a horse, along with an army, to other kingdoms, and the local king would either allow the horse to wander, indicating that his kingdom would submit, or tie up the horse to show resistance or challenge the sovereignty of the king.

The king heard of these acts and guessed that the two children at the hermitage could be no ordinary youngsters. Eventually, the king himself came to deal with the two boys, not knowing they were his own children. Witnessing their prowess as warriors, Ram invited them back to Ayodhya perform the *yagya* or *yajna* (a ritual done in front of a sacred fire).

Valmiki had composed the Ramayana (with 24,000 verses) and taught Luv and Kush to sing it. Luv and Kush recited the Ramayana to Ram at the Ashwamedha Yagya ceremony, in the presence of Ram's brothers Bharat and Lakshman, as well as many others present in court, including Valmiki. Ram was deeply moved by the ballad, particularly when it narrated the legend of Sita and her second exile. At that point, Valmiki produced Sita, from whom Ram learnt that Luv and Kush were his children. Having witnessed the acceptance of her children by Ram, Sita sought final refuge in the embrace of her mother, Bhumi, who opened her arms to receive her. As the ground opened, Sita disappeared into the depths of the earth mother.

Valmiki's Ramayana is divided in seven *kandas* or episodes: Bala Kanda, Ayodhya Kanda, Aranya Kanda, Kishkindha Kanda, Sundara Kanda, Yuddha Kanda and Uttara Kanda.

It is believed that the first and the last of the kandas were added much later than the rest of the epic and display distinct literary features. The word 'uttara' itself can have several meanings and is capable of being read as 'after' or 'epilogue' or 'answer'. And in a sense the text performs each of these functions in relaying the saga of Ram. Much is recorded in the Uttara Kanda to reinforce the idea of Ram as Vishnu. It is in the Uttara Kanda that Rama banishes his beloved Sita, persuaded by his sense of duty to his subjects, and bowing to popular pressure, despite her being with child. Later he is reunited with his sons, who are raised in exile by their mother and the rishi Valmiki, finding his legitimate heirs. He also watches over the death of his devoted brother Lakshman, whose submits himself to death to uphold Ram's promise to Yama, rather than bring a curse by the sage Durvasa over his beloved brother and the entire kingdom of Ayodhya.

The greatest contribution of this final section of Valmiki's saga is that it seeks to fill the gaps in the narrative, and answer questions—both existing and those that may yet come. The Uttara Kanda retells the stories of the sage, narrating them anew or reframing them from the viewpoint of another, reinforcing the stories and tucking away any loose threads that may have arisen through the epic. For example, in the Uttara Kanda Agastya tells Ram the story of Hanuman, and how as a youth he was cursed by sages to forget the extent of his powers, until he is reminded of them. This tale ties together the story of Hanuman's birth, told by Jambavan and recorded in the Kishkindha Kanda, when Hanuman comes to learn of the many boons bestowed on him at birth, and immediately puts those boons to use to leap to Lanka to aid in the rescue of Sita.

The efforts made by Valmiki to correct any inconsistencies or aberrations suggests that the work may have recognized itself, i.e., it understood its own limitations and sought to rectify them. It may also indicate that parts of the text, and perhaps contours of the story itself, were added later.

The first and final chapters of the saga (i.e. the Bala Kanda and Uttara Kanda, respectively) explicitly state that Vishnu, persuaded by the other gods to extinguish the demon Ravana, took on the human form of Ram; that Ram is thus a God, an avatar of Vishnu. Thus, the story of Ram became central to Vaishnavism. The Bala Kanda and Uttara Kanda are also the only two texts in which Valmiki himself appears to narrate the story, further reinforcing the suggestion that the author added these sections after the rest of the texts.

The tone and politics of the final part of Valmiki's Ramayana also seems to indicate a shift in paradigms, diverging from the impressions given by the middle texts. Ram's actions—exiling Sita, allowing Lakshman to sacrifice his life, taking the life of a lower-caste man—seem to serve a different purpose than those of the hero–warrior in the earlier part of the story. The drive seems to serve the purpose of justifying the rule of Ram as a just and fair ruler, even where he is pressed into situations where he has to make tough decisions to serve his people. Ram is shown as being a king and ruler who must treat all his subjects with an equal hand—even when those citizens are his wife or his brothers.

The Uttara Kanda also makes great efforts to show the ultimate fate of Ravana, and how it is determined by his rakshasa nature and his evil actions and predilections, reinforcing the concept of dharma. Ravana is plagued by several curses, ensuring that he meets his end at the hands of Ram. The book also emphasizes how his death is a result of the consequences of his actions in life and the deeds of his past. Again and again, the Uttara Kanda emphasizes his nature as a rakshasa or demon, in contrast to other books in the saga that even hinted at a sort of 'nobility' in his nature (more akin to the term *rakshak* or protector/warrior). There are yet other texts, other than the Ramayana, which speak of him as a worshipper of Shiva, rival of Vishnu.

It seems that the Uttara Kanda makes great efforts to serve its purpose—as any good epilogue would. It strives to bring full circle the stories narrated through the Ramayana, and emphasize the journey and growth of Ram—from a warrior–prince to a just and virtuous king—as well as the inevitable contrast between Ram as a human man and as an avatar of all-powerful God. Attempting to reconcile the differing roles and attitudes of the characters in the saga seems to be the focus of the final book. Valmiki strives to show the various facets of Ram and his story, including his own conflicts and tribulations—exiling Sita to show his dedication to his subjects, preserving the caste system by executing a lower-caste man with ambitions above his station, establishing the supremacy of his kingdom, restoring dharma to the world by vanquishing Ravana—making the entire saga richer and more complex, and lending new subtleties to the stories narrated in the rest of the books.

The final chapter of the saga seems to purposefully drive us to re-read the entire saga in a new light. And looking at the transformations within the text itself would give us a deeper insight into the transformation of Hinduism itself, as well as the changing times between the composition of the first and last chapters. The Ramayana has a deep and pervasive impact on the culture of India. For many Hindus Ram is the blueprint, the supreme man. Thus, understanding the transformational nature of Ram's saga, and the changing polity of the times, could provide a deeper understanding of the meaning of Hinduism in modern life.

The idea of Lord Ram's death upon earth or, more accurately speaking, his jal samadhi, remains the most obscure part of the legend. Although the renunciation of life and the taking of samadhi is common among sages and saints, particularly among Jain priests, the idea of a king taking samadhi is unusual. But Ram, born human, had to die. In an interesting contrast, the closest devotee of Ram, Hanuman, a celibate with a boon, was immortal and survived his lord and master. Although there is no indication of a 'second coming' in the Hindu text—as in Christianity and Islam in relation to Jesus Christ or Hazrat Mehdi, respectively—nor any mention of reincarnation, Lord Ram returns in every yuga with a purpose.

Many scholars believe that the popular Ramayana is incomplete, as indeed it tells us little beyond Sita's return to the bosom of Mother Earth. It narrates the legend in 1,00,000 verses—Hanuman narrates 60,000 of these and Valmiki narrates 24,000.

Over a period, European scholars in the colonial context interpreted the Ramayana in racial terms: Aryans vs Dravidians, Vaishnavas vs Shaivites, saints vs kings, etc. In recent works, the Ramayana has been subjected to interpretation in terms of gender and caste conflict, with the idea of devotion regarded only in feudal terms. One awaits a modern, reconstructed projection of the story that encapsulates eternal truths about human nature without the distraction caused by time and space constraints, which historical narratives are often subject to.

The annual Ramlila performed in the traditional style across the country is a much-awaited event that brightens the lives of common folk. The cast of performers, as well as the artisans who prepare the stage, come from various backgrounds, cutting across religious faiths. It is a natural reflection of our social reality, and our cultural assimilation and interdependence.

In 1987, the TV serial based on the Ramayana—written by Rahi Masoom Raza and produced by Ramanand Sagar—would bring the country to a standstill every Sunday morning, unlike anything before. But there was no sign of partisan response or religious divide. Ram and the Ramayana belonged to all. Yet, by 1992, the dispute over the birthplace of Ram led to a political crisis that ripped the secular heart of the nation. Curiously, on one level, the legend of Ram continues to inspire devotional passion, while on another, in the twenty-first century, the Ramayana continues to be criticized by feminists and deconstructed by academics. The epic basks in its grandeur, regularly refreshing the moral perceptions of millions.

* * *

Of the many versions of the Ramayana across history, the following are most prominent:

Before second century BCE: Oral telling by travelling bards
Second century BCE: Valmiki's Ramayana (Sanskrit)
First century CE: Vyasa's Ramopakhyan in his Mahabharata
Second century: Bhasa's play *Pratima Nataka* (Sanskrit)
Third century: Sanskrit Vishnu Purana
Fourth century: Vimalasuri's Prakrit Paumachariya (Jain)

Fifth century: Kalidasa's *Raghuvamsa* (Sanskrit)
Sixth century: Pali Dashratha Jataka (Buddhist)
Seventh century: Bhattikavya (Sanskrit)
Eighth century: Bhavabhuti's play *Mahaviracharita* (Sanskrit)
Ninth century: Bhagavata Purana (Sanskrit)
Tenth century: Murari's play *Anargharaghava* (Sanskrit)
Eleventh century: Bhoja's Champu Ramayana (Sanskrit)
Twelfth century: Kambvan's *Iramavataram* (Tamil)
Thirteenth century: Adhyatma Ramayana (Sanskrit)
Thirteenth century: Buddha Reddy's Ranganath Ramayana (Telugu)
Fourteenth century: Adbhut Ramayana (Sanskrit)
Fifteenth century: Krittivasa's Ramayana (Bengali)
Fifteenth century: Kandali's Ramayana (Assamese)
Fifteenth century: Balaram Dass's Dandi Ramayana (Odia)
Fifteenth century: Ananda Ramayana (Sanskrit)
Sixteenth century: Tulsidas's *Ramcharitmanas* (Avadhi)
Sixteenth century: Akbar's collection of Ramayana paintings
Sixteenth century: Eknath's *Bhavarth Ramayana* (Marathi)
Sixteenth century: Torave's Ramayana (Kannada)
Sixteenth century: Ezhuthachan's Ramayana (Malayalam)
Seventeenth century: Guru Gobind Singh's Braj Gobind
    Ramayana, as part of Dasam Granth
Eighteenth century: Giridhar's Ramayana (Gujarati)
Eighteenth century: Divakara Prakasa Bhatta's Ramayana (Kashmiri)
Nineteenth century: Bhanubhakta's Ramayana (Nepali)

In the twentieth and twenty-first centuries, modern versions were added to this list:

1921: *Sati Sulochana* (silent film)
1943: *Ram Rajya* (the only film reported to have been watched
    by Mahatma Gandhi)
1955: *Geet Ramayana* (radio, Marathi)
1970: Amar Chitra Katha's *Rama* (comic book)

1987: Ramanand Sagar's *Ramayan* (TV series, Hindi)
2003: Ashok Banker's *Ramayana* series (novel)

The Lakshman Rekha has acquired important literary and moral attributes in contemporary society, emanating from the saga of Ram's life in exile. However, Valmiki does not mention the existence of any Lakshman Rekha in the episode about Sita's abduction that is contained in the Aranya Kanda. Unable to bear Sita's harsh words for his not accompanying Ram, Lakshman goes out into the forest to catch the golden deer that fascinates her. Lakshman is reluctant to leave Sita alone but relents on her insistence. He is said to have just moved away from Sita, with folded hands. There is no verse mentioning the Lakshman Rekha. In *Ramcharitmanas*, Tulsidas introduced the proverbial account of the Lakshman Rekha, a perimeter drawn on the ground by Lakshman, crossing which any being or wild animal would be destroyed. It ensured Sita's absolute safety within it. This concept of the Lakshman Rekha has compelling appeal, and people use it as a metaphor to underscore situations where a line should never be crossed.

The first two kandas of the Valmiki version of the Ramayana depict Ram to be a human being of unparalleled virtues, a Maryada Purushottam. However, Ram is depicted as the incarnation of Lord Vishnu in the later kandas and in Tulsidas's *Ramcharitmanas*. Thus, in the Ramayana, Ram acquires all his skills with diligent practice and devotion, but according to *Ramcharitmanas*, Ram possesses unique powers and virtues as the incarnation of Lord Vishnu. Reading Valmiki's Ramayana without prior knowledge of Hindu mythology, one would indeed consider Ram to be a human being, but with unique skills and great virtues. In Valmiki's Ayodhya Kanda, there is a verse suggestive that Ram's future wives would be delighted. *Ramcharitmanas*, however, portrays Ram to be devoted to Sita alone throughout.

The characterization of Sita is also quite different in both the versions. Both follow the same high praise for Sita's character, of her being a deeply pious woman, devoted to her husband, one who puts dharma above everything. However, Valmiki portrayed Sita to be a strong and clear-headed woman, even assertive and equal to her husband. *Ramcharitmanas* shows her to be more submissive and somewhat reticent. This may have stemmed from the role of women in society in the sixteenth century. It is interesting that in contemporary practice, the greeting of 'Jai Shree Ram' has gained currency, particularly in a somewhat aggressive articulation by Hindutva followers. However, 'Ram Ram' is the version popular in places like Rajasthan. And gender-equality activists prefer 'Jai Sia Ram', a greeting that includes Sita.

There is relatively scarce material available about the 1000 years that Ram is said to have reigned over Ayodhya. We know that his life on earth came to an end with his taking Jalabhishek in the Saryu River, but there are no accounts of the circumstances under which it was performed. While *Ramcharitmanas* ends with the establishment of Ram Rajya in Ayodhya, Valmiki's Uttara Kanda goes further to the point of Jalabhishek.

After Sita's departure, Ram is said to have lost the zest for life, as the whole world appeared to him to be meaningless. He had a golden image made of Sita and performed various yagyas and sacrifices. There was contentment in the land, and all calamities were kept at bay. Then, Kaushalya passed away, and Kaikeyi followed her soon thereafter.

It is difficult to derive a sense of time from the chronology of events in Ayodhya. If, as we are told, Ram ruled for thousands of years, what of the other members of the royal court and family? Be that as it may, ultimately it was communicated to Ram that he was to return to heaven. But there was the complicating factor of Bharat's demise and the king's command that anyone who disturbed his conversation with the visiting sage would have to die. In the end, Ram chose to descend into the waters of the Sarayu to unite with Vishnu.

We are told that the sage Kala Deva came to see Ram, seeking seclusion. Bharat was instructed to keep all people at bay even at the pain of death. Then, sage Durvasa arrived and insisted on being allowed to enter and, when Bharat indicated his helplessness, even threatened to curse the entire Raghu clan and Ayodhya. Bharat chose to die to save Ayodhya. On hearing this, Ram figured his time had come to return to Vaikuntha. The problem was that Yama was concerned about Hanuman guarding the gates to Ayodhya. He therefore had to be distracted. In order to do that, Ram dropped his ring into a crack and asked Hanuman to retrieve it. Hanuman transformed into a beetle and entered the crack to find a cave, the Nag Lok, where he met Vasuki, the king of serpents. On sharing with latter that his purpose was to retrieve the ring, Hanuman was shown a whole mountain of rings and spotted Ram's ring on the top. Vasuki told him that all the rings belonged to Ram and represented the life cycle of the world called Kalpa. Each Kalpa had four yugas, and it was the second yuga, called Treta, that was concluding. According to that version, Ram comes upon the earth again and again, whenever humankind needs him.

At the preordained hour Ram descends into the Sarayu, along with his court retinue, and becomes Ananta Shesha again, to be united with Sita. As we experience the Kaliyuga, there would be hope of Lord Ram's return, quite like other religious movements await the coming of the prophet.

# Four

# The Great Religions of the World

It will be rewarding to examine how doctrines of other religions compare with Hinduism and the nature of God envisaged by each of them.

## Aristotle's God

Aristotle imagined God with attributes of absolute perfection. Thus, according to this view, God in a state of 'stasis' beyond the worldly experience of change. The 'unmoved mover',[*] as Aristotle described God, is unlike the God seen in most religions; it is likened to an entity placed to impact somewhat like a series of dominos, where pushing one of them causes a chain or domino effect. But the cause of the initial push, and why it happens when it does, remains unclear. Essentially, in the Aristotelian discourse about God, we are dealing with metaphysics.

---

[*] See Anthony J.P. Kenny, et al., 'Aristotle', Britannica.com, https://www. britannica.com/biography/Aristotle/The-unmoved-mover

## Abrahamic Tradition

The Abrahamic God has attributes that broadly remain common to all three Abrahamic religions/traditions—Judaism, Christianity, and Islam. In these traditions, God is conceived as the all-powerful, all-knowing and unending creator of the world/universe. God is also transcendent, outside space and outside time as we understand them, and therefore not subject to anything within creation. At the same time, however, He is considered anthropomorphic, interested in the world and the prayers of his creations, distinguishing between the good and evil actions of His creatures. Yet there remains the much-debated theological conundrum of predestination and free will in relation to cause and effect in the real world and God's judgment. God is variously sought, pursued, feared, loved, beseeched. God is merciful and forgiving. These are the various dimensions along which the human mind approaches the Almighty.

## Judaism*

Judaism is a monotheistic religion, characterized by belief in one transcendent God who revealed himself to the Hebrew Prophets, including Abraham and Moses, and by life lived in accordance with the Testament and rabbinic traditions. Followers of Judaism regard it as more than just a religion, but rather a way of life, encompassing its own theology, laws and traditions.

Interestingly, it seems there are no equivalent words for 'religion' in the Hebrew language, although there are words for similar concepts such as 'faith', 'law' and 'custom'. The Jewish tradition as a way of life includes the social, cultural and religious memory from times immemorial, of a widespread and diverse

---

* See David Novak, et al., 'Judaism', Britannica.com, https://www.britannica.com/topic/Judaism

community, which harbours intense and special feelings for the land of Israel.

Judaism has encompassed the intricate religious and cultural development of the Jewish people through more than thirty centuries of history, stretching from Biblical times to medieval Spain, the Enlightenment, and lastly the Holocaust, etched deep in the collective consciousness, and the founding of the modern state of Israel. That experience is reflected in the unique relationship between religious practice and nationhood, seen as peoplehood. Judaism like other religions has a theistic structure, but from a people's perspective, it is the group memory of the Jewish communities globally and their cultural bonds that are most conspicuous. It consists not only of the Torah (divine revelation) and mitzvoth (divine commandments) but also the aggregated culture of the Hebrew, Yiddish and Ladino languages. It includes not only the visible markers of religious observance, such as the *kippah* (slightly rounded brimless skull cap) and *tzitzit* (special knotted tassels found on the corners of the *tallit* or prayer shawl), but also the communal living structures of the *kehillah* (congregation/organization dealing with community and charitable affairs), the *mellah* (a Jewish quarter, particularly in the city of Morocco) and the *shtetl* (small village/town community).

Judaism is perhaps best understood in terms of a triad of three points of reference: God, the Torah and the people of Israel (the Jewish people).

## Christianity*

Christianity follows closely upon the Jewish tradition, being linked to it by the person of Jesus Christ. It perceives God as the creator of all life and the universe. Christians too believe God to be both

---

* See Matt Stefon, et al., 'Christianity', Britannica.com, https://www.britannica.com/topic/Christianity

transcendent, separate and above the world and yet immanent, an indivisible part of it. Christian scriptures underscore the belief that God is part of the universe through his only son, Jesus Christ, who died atoning for the sins of humankind. Christ himself is tied both to the mortal and the divine, being born of a woman, yet by immaculate conception, and being one part of the Holy Trinity.

Jesus and his earliest followers were Jews and thus inherited the monotheistic faith of the Jewish people. In time they came to be separated from those who believed in the one true God of Israel by their faith in the divinity of Christ and the belief that he was the son of God. Yet Jesus and his followers did not wish to challenge the scriptures of the Jewish tradition. In fact, the entire scripture was adopted by the earlier Christians as part of the same faith—the Old Testament—as at the time they were seen as the same faith, and only later came to be divided as separate religions. These were supplemented by the New Testament, comprising a collection of the several notes and books of the early followers of Christ, which came to be edited as the four Gospels. The New Testament made clear links to the inherited faith, with Christ called the 'King of the Jews'.

In the Christian conception, the Trinity is One God, existing concomitantly in three forms; three distinct 'persons' who are yet one 'substance, essence or nature'.* The New Testament speaks often of the 'Trinity' of the Father, the Son and the Holy Spirit, though the term 'trinity' does not explicitly appear in the Bible. But it is important to note that is not really a tritheism, i.e. acceptance of the idea of three gods. Trinitarians, who form the large majority of Christians, hold it as a core tenet of the faith. But nontrinitarian denominations define the Father, the Son and the Holy Spirit in somewhat different ways. This core belief has, in fact, developed over many years and is not without continued debate. It is widely

---

* Definition of the Fourth Lateran Council, quoted in the Catechism of the Catholic Church.

accepted that the conception was shored up in 325 AD (or CE) by the First Council of Nicaea, a council of Christian bishops, convened in the city of Nicaea (present-day Iznik in Turkey) by the Roman Emperor Constantine I. The aim of the council was to attain consensus among the church on debated issues, such as the divinity of Christ and the performing of many of his miracles. One of its main accomplishments was the settlement of the divine nature of Christ (God, the Son) and his relationship with God (God, the Father).

The Holy Bible comprises the two testaments, with Jesus Christ as the predicted messiah in the Old Testament and the fulfilment of that prediction in the New Testament. The Christian doctrine—Christ died, Christ has risen, Christ shall come again— is at variance with Islamic belief, which, not believing in the Trinity, holds that the Second Coming is due to Christ never having died on earth and would need to return to complete his natural life.

## Buddhism[*]

Estimated to be the world's fourth-largest religion, with over 520 million followers, Buddhism encompasses a variety of related traditions, beliefs and spiritual practices based on the original teachings of the Buddha ('the awakened one'). Buddhism originated in ancient India as a Sramana tradition, sometime between the sixth and fourth centuries BCE, spreading to Central and South-East Asia, China, Korea and Japan. Modern-day Buddhism exists across the globe. The three main types/sects of the faith that represent specific geographical areas are: Theravada Buddhism (Thailand, Sri Lanka, Cambodia, Laos, Myanmar); Mahayana Buddhism (China, Japan, Taiwan, Korea, Singapore,

---

[*] See Giuseppe Tucci, et al., 'Buddhism', https://www.britannica.com/topic/Buddhism

Vietnam); and Tibetan Buddhism (Tibet, Nepal, Mongolia, Bhutan, parts of Russia and India).

Siddhartha Gautama, who later came to be known as 'the Buddha', was born a wealthy prince. At the age of twenty-nine, moved by the suffering he saw in the world, he renounced his title and wealth, to lead the life of an ascetic. His failure to find fulfilment through the extremes of asceticism led him to prolonged meditation under a Bodhi tree, where in quiet contemplation he found enlightenment. He spent the rest of his life teaching others about the 'Middle Way' or 'Middle Path', a way to lead one's life away from the two extremes of extreme asceticism and sensual indulgence.

Most Buddhist traditions share the goal of overcoming suffering and the cycle of death and rebirth, by the attainment of nirvana. Buddhist schools vary in their interpretation of the path to liberation, the relative importance and canonicity assigned to the various Buddhist texts, and their specific teachings and practices. Widely observed practices include taking refuge in the Buddha, the Dharma and the Sangha, observance of moral precepts, monasticism, meditation and the cultivation of the Paramitas (perfections or virtues).

## Jainism[*]

Jainism does not support belief in a creator deity. This makes it somewhat abstract in contrast with other religions. According to Jain doctrine, the universe and its constituents—soul, matter, space, time and principles of motion—have always existed. These elements are eternal and indestructible.

Jain reality comprises two components, *jiva* ('soul' or 'living substance') and *ajiva* ('non-soul' or 'inanimate substance'). Jainism

---

[*] See Paul Dundas, et al., 'Jainism', Britannica.com, https://www.britannica.com/topic/Jainism

preaches a path to enlightenment through disciplined non-violence (*ahimsa*) towards all living creatures, the final goal being the complete purification of the soul (moksha or eternal liberation). In Jain philosophy, all things in the universe are linked through the universal chain of cause and effect and the concept of karmas. Unlike in Hinduism and Buddhism, for Jains karma is not simply a concept but rather a material particle, which clings to the soul as a result of interactions with the material world. The pursuit of true perfection and liberation of the soul thus involves freeing oneself of these karmic particles through cycles of death and rebirth.

In modern Jainism there are two sects, divided over disputes concerning monastic practice: the Shvetambara ('White-Clad') and the Digambara ('Sky-Clad'). While the origins of the schism that led to the separation of these sects seem unclear, they still exist in force today.

## Sikhism[*]

Sikhs, or Khalsa (the pure), follow Sikhism or the *panth* (the path), a monotheistic religion that originated in the fifteenth century in the Punjab region of the Indian subcontinent, based on the revelation of Guru Nanak. The term Sikh has its origin in the word *shishya* meaning 'disciple' or 'student'. According to Sikh tradition, Sikhism was founded by Guru Nanak, who was succeeded by nine other gurus, each of whom were inhabited by a single immutable spirit. After the death of Guru Gobind Singh, the final guru, the spirit transferred itself into the Guru Granth Sahib, the sacred scripture of Sikhism.

From the day of their initiation, once they have undergone the Khande Ki Pahul (baptism by Khanda), an initiation ceremony know as Amrit, Sikhs are known as Khalsa Amritdhari Sikhs, and

[*] See William Hewat McLeod, et al., 'Sikhism', Britannica.com, https://www.britannica.com/topic/Sikhism

are committed to the five Ks: *kesh* (uncut hair), *kara* (an iron or steel bracelet), *kirpan* (a dagger-like sword tucked into a *gatra* (strap) or *kamal kasar* (belt), *kachera* (a cotton undergarment) and *kanga* (a small wooden comb often tucked into the hair). Additionally, Sikhs must avoid four sins: cutting their hair, eating halal meat, adultery and consuming tobacco.

The Punjab region of the Indian subcontinent, having been ruled by the Sikhs for significant parts of the eighteenth and nineteenth centuries, became their natural historic homeland. The contemporary Punjab state has a majority Sikh population, while sizeable communities of Sikhs exist around the world, particularly the USA and Canada. It was essentially a farming community that, for historical reasons, became a marshal race.

Guru Nanak (1469–1539), the founder of Sikhism, was born in the village of Talwandi, present-day Nankana Sahib, near Lahore. Like many other founders of religions, he was a social reformer and reached out to the downtrodden, and was thus inevitably associated with the Bhakti saints. Nanak composed many hymns, which were collected in the Adi Granth by Guru Arjan, the fifth Sikh Guru, in 1604. After Guru Nanak, the most important of the gurus was Guru Gobind Singh, the founder of the Khalsa, through which all Sikhs would owe allegiance directly to the Guru.

Sikhism was born against the backdrop of Islam and in reaction to popular Hinduism. Sikhs use the term 'Waheguru' for God. Guru Nanak describes God as *nirankar* (from the Sanskrit *niraakaara*, meaning formless), *akal* (meaning eternal) and *alakh* (from the Sanskrit *alakshya*, meaning invisible or unobserved). The Guru Granth Sahib, the holy book of Sikhism, starts with the figure '1', signifying the unity of God—not very different from the Islamic idea of God that is the single, personal and transcendental creator of the universe. Sikhism advocates the belief in one god who is omnipresent (*sarav viapak*), with a nature represented (especially in the Guru Granth Sahib) by the term

*Ek Onkar.* Thus, God is omnipresent in all creation but visible to the spiritually awakened, seen with 'the inward eye'.

Sikhs insist that their tradition is unique and separate from Hinduism. Nevertheless, many scholars argue that Sikhism was a reform movement within the Hindu tradition, like the Bhakti movement associated with the great poet and mystic Kabir (1440–1518). The Sants, most of whom were poor, from dispossessed and illiterate families, composed hymns describing experience of the divine, which they sensed in all things. This tradition drew heavily on Vaishnavism (the devotional movement within the Hindu tradition centred on the worship of Lord Vishnu), though there are important differences between the two. Like the followers of Bhakti, the Sants believed that devotion to God is essential for liberation from the cycle of rebirth that all human beings endure. However, unlike the followers of Bhakti, the Sants believed that God is *nirgun* (without form) and not *sagun* (with form).

## Islam[*]

In Islam, Allah is the Absolute One, the all-powerful and all-knowing, and the creator of everything in existence, and Hazrat Muhammad is the chosen Prophet and Messenger of Allah. Islam constantly emphasizes that Allah is strictly singular (*tawheed*); unique (*waahid*); inherently one (*ahad*), and also all-merciful and omnipotent. Islam thus markedly repudiates the trinity of Christianity in favour of a classical monotheism.

According to Islam, God is neither a material nor a spiritual being. 'No vision can grasp him, but His grasp is over all vision: He is above all comprehension, yet is acquainted with all things.'

---

[*] See Muhsin S. Mahdi, 'Islam', Britannica.com, https://www.britannica.com/ topic/Islam; John L. Esposito (ed.), *The Oxford Encyclopedia of the Islamic World*, Oxford University Press, 2009.

An interesting poetic rendition speaks of '*jo manzar bhi hai nazir bhi* (the One who is the Vision as indeed the Beholder)'.*

Despite the central belief that there is only one God, there are ninety-nine names of that one God (*al-asmaa al-husnaa*, literal meaning: the best names), each of which evokes a distinct attribute of God. All these names refer to Allah, the supreme and all-comprehensive God. Among the ninety-nine names of God, the most familiar and frequent reiterated are the Compassionate (Ar-Rahmaan) and the Merciful (Ar-Rahim).

Allah is described in the Quran as: 'Say: He is God, the One; God, the Eternal, the Absolute; He begot no one, nor is He begotten; Nor is there to Him equivalent anyone.' There is thus a clear departure here from the theology of Christians, despite the reference to them and Jews as 'people of the Book'. Muslims thus deny the Christian doctrine of the Trinity. In Islam, God is beyond all comprehension or imagination, except to be the purest form of energy, light or *noor*. Both Allah and the Prophet are not represented in visual form, except for the latter as light.

The message of God is carried by prophets and messengers, many named in the Quran, starting with Adam and concluding with Prophet Muhammad. Muslims believe that creation of everything in the universe is brought into being by God's sheer command, 'Be', and that the purpose of existence is to please God, both by worship and by good deeds. However, in the backdrop is the insolence and arrogance of Iblis: in refusing to acknowledge the primacy of God's creation by prostrating before Adam and Eve, as did all other angels, he was disgraced and expelled from heaven. In retaliation, he, as *shaitan*, set upon to mislead humankind, beginning with the forbidden apple in the Garden of Eden and the serpent.

Islam is the world's second-largest religion, with over 1.8 billion followers, making up the majority of the populations in

---

* 'Hum Dekhenge', an Urdu poem by poet Faiz Ahmed Faiz.

forty-nine countries. The primary scriptures of Islam are the Quran, believed to be the verbatim word of God, as well as the teachings and normative examples (called the Sunnah, composed of accounts called the Hadith) of Prophet Muhammad, compiled by religious leaders. These two main sources are to be supplemented by *ijma* (consensus) and *ijtihad* (individual thought), though the latter two are means of interpretation of the first two.

Islamic life is anchored by the five 'Pillars of Islam': shahadah (the profession of faith), namaz (the five daily prayers), zakat (the giving of alms or charity), ramzaan (fasting during the month of Ramadan/Ramzaan), and hajj (pilgrimage to Mecca).

## Hinduism*

Hinduism, sometimes referred to as Sanatan dharma, has been called the oldest religion of the world, originating in Vedic times and comprising several sacred texts and scriptures, including the four Vedas, thirteen Upanishads and eighteen Puranas. It has been widely accepted among scholars that Hinduism is etymologically derived from the term Sindu (the ancient name for the Indus River), beyond which was the vast land occupied by people who came to be described as Hindus. While Hinduism is thought of as a religion, prescribed by its sacred texts, and comprising several and varied systems of philosophy, belief and ritual, it has also been thought to be a social and political identity, with Hindutva being its assertive dimension.

S. Radhakrishnan, in *The Hindu View of Life*,[†] says, 'At the outset, one is confronted by the difficulty of defining what Hinduism is. To many it seems to be a name without any content.

---

* See J.A.B. van Buitenan, 'Hinduism', Britannica.com, https://www.britannica.com/topic/Hinduism
† S. Radhakrishnan, *The Hindu View of Life*, HarperCollins, 1993.

Is it a museum of beliefs, a medley of rites, or a mere map, a geographical expression?'

It is widely assumed that Hinduism allows the worship of many gods and goddesses, but it is also important that we know that Brahman is believed to be the supreme God and pervasive force above all gods and the creator of the universe. The other prominent deities include Vishnu, who preserves and protects; and Shiva or Maheshwara, who destroys when the need arises. Besides the trinity of Brahman, Vishnu and Shiva, there is Devi, the goddess of dharma; Krishna, the god of compassion, tenderness and love; Lakshmi, the goddess of wealth; and Saraswati, the goddess of learning. One way to see it is that all gods and goddesses are an intrinsic part of Brahma and they help us to focus on specific dimensions of our existence and experience.

Thus, on the one hand, we have polytheism, which contemplates 330 million gods and imagines gods in trees, water and stones, and yet, on the other hand, the Bhagavad Gita (7:20) says that humans with materialistic desires 'surrender unto demigods'. The Chandogya Upanishad (6:2:1) speaks of *ekam evadvitiyam* or 'one without second'; the Svetasvatara (6:9) describes God as one who 'neither has parents nor lord'; the Svetasvatara (4:20) speaks of a God whose 'form is not to be seen, no one sees Him with the eye'. The Rig Veda, the oldest and holiest of scripture, explains, in hymn 164, verse 46, that 'sages call one God by many names'. These descriptions are not entirely at variance with other religions and might one day be the basis of a grand reconciliation among religious beliefs. Meanwhile, we may continue to wonder how much of Hinduism the average Hindu knows.

Like all other religions, Hinduism has a central philosophy or theology, whose application as faith and in prevailing rituals make up the popularly understood religion. However, popular religion may often be at variance with its theological precepts. Since the popular understanding of Hinduism includes a multitude of religious ideas woven together in normative conduct, it is referred to as a 'way of life', in contrast with the Abrahamic religions. Technically speaking, Hinduism is described as henotheistic, by virtue of the fact that Hindus worship an ultimate deity, known as Brahma, while at the same time recognizing other gods and goddesses, or multiple paths to reaching the ultimate. At the heart of philosophical Hinduism is the belief in the doctrines of *samsara* (the continuous cycle of life, death and reincarnation) and karma (the universal law of cause and effect), in parallel with dharma (the ethical code or path). Despite many variants and focus on particular gods, this stream of belief runs through most forms of Hinduism.

One of the key ideas of Hinduism is the *atman* or soul. All living creatures have a soul, and all souls are ultimately part of the supreme soul Brahman. The instinctive goal of each soul is to achieve moksha or salvation, which ends the cycle of reincarnation as the soul becomes one with Brahman. This simple idea is theoretically made complex by innumerable traditions and worldly conceptions.

In the Vedic period, the concept of monotheism manifested itself in the semi-abstract, semi-personified form of the creative soul dwelling in God. In the Vaishnava traditions, god is Vishnu, identified as Krishna. The Sanskrit term *ishvara*, comes from the root *ish*, which means someone with extraordinary power. The term is mentioned six times in the Atharva Veda and is central to several traditions.

Hinduism calls the metaphysical absolute concept Brahman, incorporating within it the transcendent and immanent realities. Different schools of thought interpret Brahman as either personal, impersonal or transpersonal. Ishwar Chandra Sharma describes it as 'Absolute Reality, beyond all dualities of existence and non-existence, light and darkness, and of time, space and cause'.[*]

---

[*] Ishwar Chandra Sharma, *Ethical Philosophies of India*, Harper & Row, 1970, p. 75.

It might thus be said that according to Hinduism, Brahman is the highest Universal Principle, the Ultimate Reality. In major schools of Hindu philosophy, it is the final cause of all that exists and is pervasive, genderless, infinite and eternal, unchanging, but is the cause of all change. Brahman as a metaphysical concept is the single binding unity behind the diversity that exists in the material universe.

Brahman is a Vedic Sanskrit word and is conceptualized in Hinduism, states the German Indologist Paul Deussen, as the 'creative principle which lies realized in the whole world'. Brahman is a key concept found in the Vedas, and it is extensively discussed in the early Upanishads. The Vedas conceptualize Brahman as the Cosmic Principle. In the Upanishads, it has been also described as Sat–Chit–Ananda (truth–consciousness–bliss).

As per the Advaita Vedanta school of Hindu philosophy, the notion of Brahman (the highest universal principle) is akin to that of god, except that unlike most other philosophies Advaita links Brahman and atman. Hindus following Advaita Vedanta consider atman within every living being to be part of Vishnu or Shiva or Devi, or ultimately identical to and connected to the eternal metaphysical Absolute called Brahman. Such a philosophical system of Advaita or non-dualism, as it developed in the Vedanta school of Hindu philosophy, and especially as set out in the Upanishads and popularized by Adi Shankara in the ninth century, has been influential on the contemporary philosophical understanding of Hinduism.

The term 'henotheism' (adherence to one particular god out of several) was used by scholars such as Max Müller to describe the theology of Vedic religion. He noted that the hymns of the Rig Veda made mention of several distinct gods and goddesses but praised them as the 'one ultimate, supreme God' or 'one supreme Goddess', asserting that these deities were all different iterations/manifestations of the same divine being. This idea, that there can be and are plural perspectives for the same divine or spiritual principle, repeats itself at several places in the Vedic texts. For example, hymn 5.3 of the Rig Veda states:

> You at your birth are Varuna, O Agni. When you are kindled, you are Mitra. In you, O son of strength, all gods are centered. You are Indra to the mortal who brings oblation. You are Aryaman, when you are regarded as having the mysterious names of maidens, O Self-sustainer.[*]

While Hinduism generally emphasizes the complete equivalence of Brahman and atman, it goes on to conceptualize Brahman as *saguna* Brahman (God with attributes) and *nirguna* Brahman (God without attributes). The latter is the Brahman in the ultimate, while the former Brahman is the path to realizing nirguna Brahman, in itself ultimately illusory. The saguna Brahman, such as in the form of avatars, is considered to be a useful symbol for the path of the spiritual journey.

The Bhakti movement (beginning in the eighth century in southern India and expanding across the north in the fifteenth century) too essentially built its theosophy around these two concepts of Brahman—nirguna (the concept of the Ultimate Reality as formless, without attributes or form and quality understood in human existence) and saguna (envisioned and developed as Brahman with form, attributes and quality). The two had parallels in the ancient pantheistic non-manifest and theistic manifest traditions, respectively, and are traceable to the Arjuna–Krishna dialogue in the Bhagavad Gita. It is the same Brahman but viewed from two perspectives: one from *nirguni* knowledge–focus and the other from *saguni* love–focus, which are united as Krishna in the Gita.

The Dvaita Vedanta tradition considers individual souls (*jivatmans*) and the eternal metaphysical Absolute (Brahman)

---

[*] Translated by Hermann Oldenberg.

as independent realities, distinct from each other. Such a philosophical system of Dvaita, or dualism, developed in the Vedanta school of Hindu philosophy, especially as set out in the Vedas and popularized by Madhvacharya, a Hindu philosopher and the chief proponent of the Dvaita school of Vedanta in the thirteenth century. Madhva said that in the beginning there was only one God, Narayana or Vishnu, and refused to accept any claims that other Hindu deities, such as Brahma or Shiva, might be equally elevated.

The Yogasutras written by Patanjali contain several uses of the term Ishvara, which have been widely and differently interpreted. Among the Yogasutras are verses which specify distinct characteristics of Ishvara—the special self unaffected by one's obstacles (*klesha*); one's circumstances created by one's actions (karma), one's life fruits (*vipaka*); and one's dispositions (*ashaya*). According to one commentary, the concept functions as a 'transformative catalyst or guide for aiding the yogin on the path to spiritual emancipation'.*

Among the various Bhakti-practising sects of Hinduism, which built upon the yoga school of Hinduism, Ishvara can also mean a specific deity, such as Krishna, Ram, Shiva, Lakshmi, Parvati and others.

Svayam Bhagavan, a Sanskrit theological term, is the concept of absolute representation of the monotheistic God, as Bhagavan himself within himself. It is most often used in Gaudiya Vaishnava Krishna-centered theology as referring to Krishna. The title Svayam Bhagavan is used exclusively to designate Krishna. Certain other traditions of Hinduism consider him to be the source of all avatars and the source of Vishnu himself, or to be the same as Narayana. He is therefore regarded as Svayam Bhagavan.

---

* Ian Whicher, *The Integrity of the Yoga Darsana: A Reconsideration of Classical Yoga*, State University of New York Press, 1999, p. 86.

The theological interpretation of Svayam Bhagavan differs with each tradition, and the literal translation of the term has been understood in several distinct ways. Translated from the Sanskrit, it means literally 'God Himself'. The Gaudiya Vaishnava tradition often translates it within its perspective as 'primeval Lord' or 'original Personality of Godhead', but also considers terms such as 'Supreme Personality of Godhead' and 'Supreme God' as equivalents to Svayam Bhagavan, and may also choose to apply these terms to Vishnu, Narayana and many of their associated avatars. Madhvacharya translated the term Svayam Bhagavan as 'he who has *bhagavatta*', meaning 'he who has the quality of possessing all good qualities'. Others have translated it simply as 'the Lord Himself'.

Thus, the concept of God in Hinduism obviously varies substantially across its diverse traditions. Hinduism, as we have seen above, has a remarkable ability to include a wide range of beliefs and practices, such as henotheism, monotheism, polytheism, panentheism, pantheism, pandeism, monism, atheism and non-theism.

Hinduism is often called a way of life rather than merely a religion because of its rich history. It is one of the oldest religions in the world that evolved simultaneously with its society. The diversity allowed within Hinduism is unlike any other religion in the world. This diversity has allowed different cultures to flourish in the subcontinent, making India so unique. The study of Hinduism involves the study of ancient India, where myth and history are intertwined in a manner that the task of a historian involves finding deeper meanings hidden below the surface of mythical texts. Such meanings were usually seen as involving natural phenomena or human values of the time period to which they belonged. As historian Romila Thapar says, '[M]yth is in a sense a prototype history since it is a selection of ideas composed in narrative form for the purpose of preserving and giving significance to an important aspect of the past. Although myths cannot be used as descriptive sources on the past, their analysis can reveal the more emphatic assumptions of a society. Myths record what a people like to think about their past and to that extent even some modern histories are not always free of an element of myth-making.* The interpretation of myths of the early canonical literature has resulted in varied explanations of Hinduism and of the past itself.

Thus it is impossible for any proposition to be generally applicable universally to Hinduism as a whole. The evolution of Hinduism is best understood in terms of the evolution of man and society in the Indian subcontinent. For the purposes of convenience and understanding, the concepts and development of Hinduism have been divided into chronological phases, with limited engagement with the philosophical debates surrounding relevant subtopics. However, it is imperative to swim across this pool of information to understand any modern interpretations of any of these texts, especially the Ramayana and the political significance it holds today.

In *A History of Ancient and Early Medieval India: From Stone Age to the 12th Century*, Upinder Singh writes:

> Hindu thinkers do not start with the certainty of God. They regard god only as a hypothesis that is not unworkable. The historical process of the phenomenal world is not dependent on god, on the contrary, gods themselves are believed to be subject to some universal laws like the law of karma. The concept of God may thus seem not to be central to Hinduism.[†]

---

* Romila Thapar, *Time as a Metaphor of History: Early India*, the Krishna Bharadwaj Memorial Lecture, Oxford Scholarship Online, 1996, https://oxford.universitypressscholarship.com/view/10.1093/acprof:oso/9780195637984.001.0001/acprof-9780195637984

† Upinder Singh, *A History of Ancient and Early Medieval India: From the Stone Age to the 12th Century*, Pearson, 2009.

Vedic literature is divided into *smritis* (remembered) and *shrutis* (that which has been heard). Shrutis include the Vedas that are further divided into Samhitas, Brahmanas, Aranyakas and Upanishads. The following table provides a broad division of Vedic literature, to place the epics in the context of the rest of the religious literature:

1.  Shruti

Samhitas
Rig Veda: 1028 hymns, ten *mandals* or books
Sam Veda: 1810 verses, borrowed from the Rig Veda, arranged according to the needs of musical notation
Yajur Veda: details of the performance of rituals
Atharva Veda: Spells and charms that reflect popular beliefs and practices
Brahmanas: Prose explanations of social and religious meanings of rituals, details of sacrificial ritual
Aranyaka: Forest Books; they interpret sacrificial ritual in symbolic and philosophical ways
Upanishads: They mark the first clear expression of certain key ideas that are associated with Hinduism and certain other Indian philosophical and religious traditions (the goal of the Upanishads is the realization of Brahman, ultimate reality)

2.  Smriti

Vedangana (limbs of the Vedas): Phonetics, metre, grammar, etymology, ritual and astronomy
Epics/*itihasa*: also known as traditional history
Ramayana: 5/4 BCE–3 BCE, written in the *kavya* form, occurs in the Treta Yuga
Mahabharata: Placed between 400 BCE and 400 CE, an encyclopedic work, occurs in the Dvapara Yuga

Puranas: They touch upon five concepts—creation (*sarga*), recreation (*prati sarga*), period of Manus (*manavantaras*), genealogy of gods and rishis (*vamsha*) and account of royal dynasties (Vamshanucharita—explore the concept of time and mention the emergence of religious cults based on devotion (Vishnu, Shiva and Shakti)

Dharmashastras: Links Dharmasutras, smritis, commentaries and Kalpasutra (Shrautasutras: Vedic sacrifices; Grihasutras: simpler domestic sacrifices)

The Rig Vedic gods are seen as being subservient to an all-pervading powerful force. 'Since they participate in this magic potence together with all other categories of existence, they cannot be said to be essentially distinct from the latter (the "potence" being more basic and more important than the "person" or "thing" in which it inheres); and that all these categories, including gods, are dependent on one another for their proper functioning." Gods are powerful, benevolent and anthropomorphic, and could be made to intervene in human affairs through sacrifices or recitation of a sacrificial formula.

According to R.N. Dandekar, 'Rig vedic Gods cannot be said to have assumed a finite and finished form at the moment. It would, therefore, be wrong to study Hindu mythology as a static phenomenon. A particular Vedic god is seen to have been dominant in a particular period, because the personality and character of that god reflected in the ethos of that period [. . .] The relationships among the various Rig vedic gods were governed culture-historical compulsions. The concepts of some of the principal dual divinities, for instance, have originated out of these compulsions.'†

---

* R.N. Dandekar, 'God in Hindu Thought', Annals of the Bhandarkar Oriental Research Institute, vol. 48/49, Golden Jubilee Volume 1917–1967 (1968), p. 433, available at https://www.jstor.org/stable/41694270
† Ibid.

Conspicuous changes in life and society took place during the later Vedic age—such as expansion of settlements from the Punjab and Sind regions towards the Ganga Doab basin. The presence of Panchalas could be seen in the regions around Bareilly, Badaun and Farrukhabad. Koshala emerged as an important city (associated with Ram, though not mentioned in the Vedic literature). There was widespread primitive agriculture. The Shatapatha Brahmana mentions ploughing rituals at length, for example, Balaram (Krishna's brother) is also called Haladhar (associating him with the *hala* or plough), thereby signifying the importance of ploughs in society. Another interesting dimension is reflected in the story of Sita's birth: with Janaka finding her while ploughing the earth. The main gods are Prajapati (the creator, who holds the supreme position), Rudra (the God of Animals, who was a minor god in the Rig Vedic age), and Vishnu (the preserver and protector of the people). Sacrifices replaced prayers during this period, and idolatry became the popular mode of prayer. Creation was perceived as a result of the primordial sacrifice mentioned in the Purusha Sukta; creation was is also seen as emanating from the sun, Hiranyagarbha.

There were trends to substitute the impersonal absolute of the Upanishads with a personal God. The six orthodox schools, the Shatdarshanas, emerged. These were Nyaya, Sankhya, Yoga, Vaisheshika, Purva Mimamsa and Uttara Mimamsa. Most of these schools of thought believed in the theory of karma and rebirth. Moksha (salvation) was believed to be the liberation from the cycle of birth and death and seen as the ultimate goal of human life.

The epics and the Puranas led to the development of the Samkhya doctrine. Nyaya, Vaisheshika, Samkhya, Yoga, Mimamsa and Vedanta were important schools of thought during this period. The Nyaya school followed a scientific and rational approach. Sage Gautama was the founder of this school. It banked upon various *pramanas* (mechanisms of attaining knowledge).

It believed that gaining knowledge through the five senses was the sole way of attaining liberation from the cycle of birth and death.

The Ramayana, considered in the previous chapter, is an ancient Indian epic composed sometime in the fifth century BCE. It is about the exile and then triumphant return of Lord Ram, the prince and heir apparent of Ayodhya. It was composed in Sanskrit by Maharishi Valmiki. It comprises around 24,000 verses in seven chapters, or kandas, and is also known as the Adi Kavya (original poem). Ram, the king of Ayodhya, was born in the Treta Yuga, thousands of years before the Kali Yuga, which is supposed to have started in the year 3102 BC. The epic contains the teachings of ancient Hindu sages Vishwamitra and Vashishtha. One of the most important and inspirational literary works of ancient India, it has greatly influenced art and culture in the Indian subcontinent and in South-East Asia, with versions of the story also appearing in the Buddhist canon from a very early date.

Ram was the eldest son of king Dasharatha, who ruled the kingdom of Kosala from the capital city of Ayodhya. He was a warrior king, placed on a par with Indra and other *devas*. Ayodhya literally means 'that which cannot be subdued by war'. Admittedly, the historicity of Ayodhya is contentious. Nonetheless, it is one of the seven holy places of Hindus because of its association with Ram. Its contemporary religious importance and political significance leads Hindu communalists to conclude: 'Ayodhya is the centre of our Hindu nationhood and Lord Rama our national leader.'

Interestingly, there is the idea of determinism looming behind every event that takes place in the epic. The very reason for Ram's birth is established in the initial part of the text—Vishnu's human avatar has to kill Ravana, the antagonist who has Brahma's boon that made him invincible against all except humans. Ravana, in his arrogance, did not care to ask for security against mankind, and therefore Vishnu had to be born as Ram, the perfect man, to defeat and kill Ravana. Ram won the hand of the beautiful princess

Sita but was exiled with her and his devoted brother Lakshman for fourteen years through the plotting of his stepmother, Kaikeyi. In the forest, Ravana abducts Sita. Ram gathers an army of monkeys and begins searching for her. The allies attack Lanka and kill Ravana. After Sita is rescued, she needs to prove her chastity by entering fire but is vindicated by the gods and restored to her husband. After the couple's triumphant return to Ayodhya, Ram's righteous rule, Ram Rajya, inaugurates a golden age for all mankind.

There are many ways of reading and understanding the Ramayana. There is a religious–iconic Ram, the poetic Ram, the linguistically and the culturally hybridized Ram. The mythical Ram as written by Valmiki, and even the Ram of Tulsidas has a difference in meanings and values attached. Finding the meaning of Ram and his place in the Indian society is a difficult task. There is no linear evolution of Ram, who emerges as the most-invoked deity of twenty-first-century India. The Ram we are looking for lies in the idea of India itself. The Ram that can explain the importance of the site of the Ram Janmabhoomi Sthal resides in a version of the imagination of India at the very point of India's birth. It goes back to the need for Ram's presence under whose shadow we as a nation, bound to fail, would survive.

The importance of the Ramayana in contemporary India is evident in the writings of a number of leaders and thinkers during the early years of Independence. C. Rajagopalachari's abridged version of the Ramayana, written in 1957, underscores the centrality of this text to our culture. He says:

> The Ramayana is not history or biography. It is a part of Hindu mythology. We cannot understand Greek life and Greek civilisation without knowing all about Zeus, Apollo, Hercules, Venus, Hector, Priam, Achilles, Ulysses and others. So also one cannot understand Hindu dharma unless one knows Rama and Seeta, Bharata, Lakshmana, Ravana, Kumbhakarna and

Hanuman. Mythology cannot be dispensed with. Philosophy alone or rituals alone or mythology alone cannot be sufficient. These are the three strands of all ancient religions. The attitude towards things spiritual which belongs to a particular people cannot be grasped or preserved or conveyed unless we have all these three . . . Let us keep ever in our minds the fact that it is the Ramayana and the Mahabharata that bind our vast numbers together as one people, despite caste, space and language that seemingly divide them.[*]

Looking at the plethora of religious literature in Hinduism, it is interesting to ask why the Ramayana fits perfectly in the political imagination of twenty-first-century India. Sheldon Pollock points out that in the Ramayana, 'on one hand, a divine political order can be conceptualised, narrated, and historically grounded, and, on the other, a fully demonised other can be categorised, counterposed, and condemned'.[†] The process of historical resonance for the India of 2020, then, can be seen in the supporters of Narendra Modi invoking metaphors of the rebirth of Vishnu in his Kalki avatar in contemporary India.

A pertinent question is: Why was the Mahabharata not able to achieve a similar significance? The Mahabharata revolves around the theme of a tragic dilemma that is repeated throughout the text. Man's position is questioned, he is represented as a slave to power, and the overarching problem is resolved through fratricidal struggle, leading to losses suffered not only by the defeated but also the victors. 'We are the living dead,' Yudhisthir reflects when, after the battle, the brothers return to Indraprastha. The Mahabharata underscores the common experience, not unfamiliar

---

[*] C. Rajagopalachari (tr.), *Ramayana* (33rd edition), Bharatiya Vidya Bhavan, 2013.

[†] Sheldon Pollock, 'Ramayana and Political Imagination in India', *Journal of Asian Studies*, vol. 52, no. 2, May 1993, pp. 261, https://www.jstor.org/stable/2059648

to contemporary India, that political divisions lead to chaos and destruction. It questions the complex meaning of victory in power struggles. Valmiki's solution to the paradox of political struggle and strife is the divinization of the king, making the sovereign a sage with unquestioned authority, capable of and destined to combating evil.

The symbology of otherness in the Ramayana makes it a precious tool in the hands of the ruling class. The deterministic approach in the text establishes the other, being Ravana, much before Ram's birth. Ravana's eventual demise at the hands of Ram is an essential message to human civilization: identify the political and moral other. Contemporary political leadership understands the importance of the Ramayana's storyline to continue the 'us-versus-them' syndrome for political outcomes. Far beyond the ideology of one political party post-Independence, modern India has intuitively sought identification with cultural icons for self-esteem and the shaping of a national personality.

* * *

Having thus examined Hindu mythology, philosophy and theology familiar to religious experts and practitioners alike, it would be rewarding to look at how jurisprudence approaches Hinduism.

Indian judicial understanding of Hinduism was expressed at considerable length by Chief Justice P.B. Gagendragadkar in 'Shastri Yagnapurushdasji':*

27. Who are Hindus and what are the broad features of Hindu religion, that must be the first part of our enquiry in dealing with the present controversy between the parties. **The historical and etymological genesis of the word 'Hindu' has given rise**

---

* Shastri Yagnapurushdasji and Others v Muldas Brudardas Vaishya and Another', 1966, 3 SCR 242; 1966 AIR 1119.

to a controversy amongst indologists; but the view generally
accepted by scholars appears to be that the word 'Hindu' is
derived from the river Sindhu otherwise known as Indus which
flows from the Punjab. 'That part of the great Aryan race,' says
Monier Williams, which immigrated from Central Asia, through
the mountain passes into India, settled first in the districts near
the river Sindhu (now called the Indus). The Persians pronounced
this word Hindu and named their Aryan brethren Hindus. The
Greeks, who probably gained their first ideas of India from the
Persians, dropped the hard aspirate, and called the Hindus
'Indoi'.

28. The Encyclopaedia of Religion and Ethics, Vol. VI, has described
'Hinduism' as the title applied to that form of religion which
prevails among the vast majority of the present population of
the Indian Empire . . . As Dr Radhakrishnan has observed: 'The
Hindu civilization is so called, since its original founders or earliest
followers occupied the territory drained by the Sindhu (the Indus)
river system corresponding to the North West Frontier Province
and the Punjab. This is recorded in the Rig Veda, the oldest of the
Vedas, the Hindu scriptures which give their name to this period
[of] Indian history. The people on the Indian side of the Sindhu
were called Hindu by the Persian and the later western invaders.'
That is the genesis of the word 'Hindu'.

29. When we think of the Hindu religion, we find it difficult, if not
impossible, to define Hindu religion or even adequately describe
it. **Unlike other religions in the world, the Hindu religion does
not claim any one prophet; it does not worship any one God;
it does not subscribe to any one dogma; it does not believe in
any one philosophic concept; it does not follow any one set of
religious rites or performances; in fact, it does not appear to
satisfy the narrow traditional features of any religion or creed.
It may broadly be described as a way of life and nothing more.**

30. Confronted by this difficulty, Dr Radhakrishnan realised that
'to many Hinduism seems to be a name without any content.

Is it a museum of beliefs, a medley of rites, or a mere map, a geographical expression?' Having posed these questions which disturbed foreigners when they think of Hinduism, Dr Radhakrishnan has explained how Hinduism has steadily absorbed the customs and ideas of peoples with whom it has come into contact and has thus been able to maintain its supremacy and its youth. The term 'Hindu', according to Dr Radhakrishnan, had originally a territorial and not a credal significance. It implied residence in a well-defined geographical area. Aboriginal tribes, savage and half-civilized people, the cultured Dravidians and the Vedic Aryans were all Hindus as they were the sons of the same mother. The Hindu thinkers reckoned with the striking fact that the men and women dwelling in India belonged to different communities, worshipped different gods, and practised different rites (Kurma Purana).

31. Monier Williams has observed that 'it must be borne in mind that Hinduism is far more than a mere form of theism resting on Brahmanism. It presents for our investigation a complex congeries of creeds and doctrines which in its gradual accumulation may be compared to the gathering together of the mighty volume of the Ganges, swollen by a continual influx of tributary rivers and rivulets, spreading itself over an ever-increasing area of country and finally resolving itself into an intricate Delta of tortuous steams and jungly marshes . . . The Hindu religion is a reflection of the composite character of the Hindus, who are not one people but many. It is based on the idea of universal receptivity. It has ever aimed at accommodating itself to circumstances, and has carried on the process of adaptation through more than three thousand years. It has first borne with and then, so to speak, swallowed, digested, and assimilated something from all creeds.'

32. **We have already indicated that the usual tests which can be applied in relation to any recognised religion or religious creed in the world turn out to be inadequate in dealing with the**

**problem of Hindu religion.** Normally, any recognised religion or religious creed subscribes to a body of set philosophic concepts and theological beliefs. Does this test apply to the Hindu religion? In answering this question, we would base ourselves mainly on the exposition of the problem by Dr Radhakrishnan in his work on Indian Philosophy. Unlike other countries, India can claim that philosophy in ancient India was not an auxiliary to any other science or art, but always held a prominent position of independence. The Mundaka Upanisad speaks of Brahmavidya or the science of the eternal as the basis of all sciences, 'sarva-vidyapratishtha'. According to Kautilya, 'Philosophy' is the lamp of all the sciences, the means of performing all the works, and the support of all the duties. 'In all the fleeting centuries of history,' says Dr Radhakrishnan, 'in all the vicissitudes through which India has passed, a certain marked identity is visible. It has held fast to certain psychological traits which constitute its special heritage, and they will be the characteristic marks of the Indian people so long as they are privileged to have a separate existence.' The history of Indian thought emphatically brings out the fact that the development of Hindu religion has always been inspired by an endless quest of the mind for truth based on the consciousness that truth has many facets. Truth is one, but wise men describe it differently. The Indian mind has, consistently through the ages, been exercised over the problem of the nature of godhead, the problem that faces the spirit at the end of life, and the interrelation between the individual and the universal soul. 'If we can abstract from the variety of opinion,' says Dr Radhakrishnan, 'and observe the general spirit of Indian thought, we shall find that it has a disposition to interpret life and nature in the way of monistic idealism, though this tendency is so plastic, living and manifold that it takes many forms and expresses itself in even mutually hostile teachings.'

33. The monistic idealism which can be said to be the general distinguishing feature of Hindu Philosophy has been expressed

in four different forms: (1) Non-dualism or Advitism; (2) Pure monism; (3) Modified monism; and (4) Implicit monism. It is remarkable that these different forms of monistic idealism purport to derive support from the same vedic and Upanishadic texts. Shankar, Ramanuja, Vallabha and Madhva all based their philosophic concepts on what they regarded to be the synthesis between the Upanishads, the Brahmasutras and the Bhagavad Gita. Though philosophic concepts and principles evolved by different Hindu thinkers and philosophers varied in many ways and even appeared to conflict with each other in some particulars, they all had reverence for the past and accepted the Vedas as the sole foundation of the Hindu philosophy. Naturally enough, it was realised by Hindu religion from the very beginning of its career that truth was many sided and different views contained different aspects of truth which no one could fully express. This knowledge inevitably bred a spirit of tolerance and willingness to understand and appreciate the opponents [sic] point of view. That is how the several views set forth in India in regard to the vital philosophic concepts are considered to be the branches of the self-same tree. The short cuts and blind alleys are somehow reconciled with the main road of advance to the truth. When we consider this broad sweep of the Hindu philosophic concepts, it would be realised that under Hindu philosophy, there is no scope for ex-communicating any notion or principle as heretical and rejecting it as such.

34. Max Muller, who was a great oriental scholar of his time, was impressed by this comprehensive and all-pervasive aspect of the sweep of Hindu philosophy. Referring to the six systems known to Hindu philosophy, Max Muller observed: 'The longer I have studied the various systems, the more have I become impressed with the truth of the view taken by Vijnanabhiksu and others that there is behind the variety of the six systems a common fund of what may be called national or popular philosophy, a large manasa (lake) of philosophical thought and language far

away in the distant North and in the distant past, from which each thinker was allowed to draw for his own purposes.'

35. **Beneath the diversity of philosophic thoughts, concepts and ideas expressed by Hindu philosophers who started different philosophic schools, lie certain broad concepts which can be treated as basic. The first amongst these basic concepts is the acceptance of the Veda as the highest authority in religious and philosophic matters. This concept necessarily implies that all the systems claim to have drawn their principles from a common reservoir of thought enshrined in the Veda.** The Hindu teachers were thus obliged to use the heritage they received from the past in order to make their views readily understood. The other basic concept which is common to the six systems of Hindu philosophy is that 'all of them accept the view of the great world rhythm. Vast periods of creation, maintenance and dissolution follow each other in endless succession. This theory is not inconsistent with belief in progress; for it is not a question of the movement of the world reaching its goal times without number, and being again forced back to its starting point . . . It means that the race of man enters upon and retravels its ascending path of realisation. This interminable succession of world ages has no beginning. It may also be said that all the systems of Hindu philosophy believe in rebirth and pre-existence. 'Our life is a step on a road, the direction and goal of which are lost in the infinite. On this road, death is never an end of an obstacle but at most the beginning of new steps.' Thus, it is clear that unlike other religions and religious creeds, Hindu religion is not tied to any definite set of philosophic concepts as such.

36. Do the Hindus worship at their temples the same set or number of gods? That is another question which can be asked in this connection; and the answer to this question again has to be in the negative. Indeed, there are certain sections of the Hindu community which do not believe in the worship of idols; and as

regards those sections of the Hindu community which believe in the worship of idols, their idols differ from community to community and it cannot be said that one definite idol or a definite number of idols are worshipped by all the Hindus in general. **In the Hindu Pantheon the first gods that were worshipped in Vedic times were mainly Indra, Varuna, Vayu and Agni. Later, Brahma, Vishnu and Mahesh came to be worshipped. In course of time, Rama and Krishna secured a place of pride in the Hindu Pantheon, and gradually as different philosophic concepts held sway in different sects and in different sections of the Hindu community, a large number of gods were added, with the result that today, the Hindu Pantheon presents the spectacle of a very large number of gods who are worshipped by different sections of the Hindus.**

37. **The development of Hindu religion and philosophy shows that from time to time saints and religious reformers attempted to remove from the Hindu thought and practices elements of corruption and superstition and that led to the formation of different sects.** Buddha started Buddhism; Mahavir founded Jainism; Basava became the founder of Lingayat religion; Dnyaneshwar and Tukaram initiated the Varakari cult; Guru Nank inspired Sikhism; Dayananda founded Arya Samaj; and Chaitanya began Bhakti cult; and as a result of the teachings of Ramakrishna and Vivekananda, Hindu religion flowered into its most attractive, progressive and dynamic form. If we study the teachings of these saints and religious reformers, we would notice an amount of divergence in their respective views; but underneath that divergence, there is a kind of subtle indescribable unity which keeps them within the sweep of the broad and progressive Hindu religion.

38. There are some remarkable features of the teachings of these saints and religious reformers. All of them revolted against the dominance of rituals and the power of the priestly class with which it came to be associated; and all of them proclaimed

their teachings not in Sanskrit, which was the monopoly of the priestly class, but in the languages spoken by the ordinary mass of people in their respective regions.

39. **Whilst we are dealing with this broad and comprehensive aspect of Hindu religion, it may be permissible to enquire what, according to this religion, is the ultimate goal of humanity? It is the release and freedom from the unceasing cycle of births and rebirths; Moksha or Nirvana, which is the ultimate aim of Hindu religion and philosophy, represents the state of absolute absorption and assimilation of the individual soul with the infinite.** What are the means to attain this end? On this vital issue, there is great divergence of views; some emphasise the importance of Gyan or knowledge, while others extol the virtues of Bhakti or devotion; and yet others insist upon the paramount importance of the performance of duties with a heart full of devotion and mind inspired by true knowledge. In this sphere again, there is diversity of opinion, though all are agreed about the ultimate goal. **Therefore, it would be inappropriate to apply the traditional tests in determining the extent of the jurisdiction of Hindu religion. It can be safely described as a way of life based on certain basic concepts to which we have already referred.**

Despite the rich theological literature on Hinduism, this judicial formulation will serve as the relevant view for the purpose of judicial approach to questions of religious import. In another matter relating to elections*, Justice J.S. Verma (as his Lordship then was) explored the idea of Hinduism and declared that seeking votes in the name of Hindutva did not amount to seeking votes in the name of religion:

---

* 'Dr Ramesh Yeshwant Prabhoo v Prabhakar Kashinath Kunte and Others', 1996, 1 SCC 130.

36. [. . .] In Unabridged Edition of Webster's Third New International Dictionary of the English language, the term 'Hinduism' has been defined as meaning 'a complex body of social, cultural and religious beliefs and practices evolved in and largely confined to the Indian subcontinent and marked by a caste system, an outlook tending to view all forms and theories as aspects of one eternal being and truth, a belief in ahimsa, karma, dharma, sanskara and moksha, and the practice of the way of works, the way of knowledge, or the way of devotion as the means of release from the bound of rebirths; the way of life and form of thought of a Hindu.'

In Encyclopaedia Britannica (15th Edition), the term 'Hinduism' has been defined as meaning:

'. . . the civilization of Hindus (originally, the inhabitants of the land of Indus River). It properly denotes the Indian civilization of approximately the last 2000 years, which gradually evolved from Vedism, the religion of the ancient Indo–European peoples who settled in India in the last centuries of the 2nd millennium B.C. Because it integrates a large variety of heterogeneous elements, Hinduism constitutes a very complex but largely continuous whole, and since it covers the whole of life, it has religious, social, economic, literary, and artistic aspects. As a religion, Hinduism is an utterly diverse conglomerate of doctrines, cults, and way of life . . . In principle, Hinduism incorporates all forms of belief and worship without necessitating the selection or elimination of any. The Hindu is inclined to revere the divine in every manifestation, whatever it may be, and is doctrinally tolerant, leaving others—including both Hindus and non-Hindus—whatever creed and worship practices suit them best. A Hindu may embrace a non-Hindu religion without ceasing to be a Hindu, and since the Hindu is disposed to think synthetically and to regard other forms of worship, strange gods, and divergent

> doctrines as inadequate rather than wrong or objectionable, he tends to believe that the highest divine powers complement each other for the well-being of the world and mankind. Few religious ideas are considered to be finally irreconcilable. The core of religion does not even depend on the existence or non-existence of God or on whether there is one god or many. Since religious truth is said to transcend all verbal definition, it is not conceived in dogmatic terms. **Hinduism is, then, both a civilization and a conglomerate of religions, with neither a beginning, a founder, nor a central authority, hierarchy, or organization. Every attempt at a specific definition of Hinduism has proved unsatisfactory in one way or another, the more so because the finest Indian scholars of Hinduism, including Hindus themselves, have emphasized different aspects of the whole.'**

In his celebrated treatise Gitarahasya,* B.G. Tilak has given the following broad description of the Hindu religion:

> Acceptance of the Vedas with reverence; recognition of the fact that the means or ways of salvation are diverse; and realisation of the truth that the number of gods to be worshipped is large, that indeed is the distinguishing feature of Hindu religion.

In Bhagwan Koer v. J.C. Bose it was held that Hindu religion is marvellously catholic and elastic. Its theology is marked by eclecticism and tolerance and almost unlimited freedom of private worship.

* * *

* *Shrimadh Bhagavad Gita Rahasya*, popularly also known as *Gita Rahasya* or *Karmayog Shashtra*.

This being the scope and nature of the religion, it is not strange that it holds within its fold men of divergent views and traditions which have very little in common except a vague faith in what may be called the fundamentals of the Hindu religion.

[. . .]

37.  **These Constitution Bench decisions, after a detailed discussion, indicate that no precise meaning can be ascribed to the terms 'Hindu', 'Hindutva' and 'Hinduism'; and no meaning in the abstract can confine it to the narrow limits of religion alone, excluding the content of Indian culture and heritage. It is also indicated that the term 'Hindutva' is related more to the way of life of the people in the sub-continent.** It is difficult to appreciate how in the face of these decisions the term 'Hindutva' or 'Hinduism' per se, in the abstract, can be assumed to mean and be equated with narrow fundamentalist Hindu religious bigotry . . .

38.  Bharucha, J. in M. Ismail Faruqui (Dr) v. Union of India , (Ayodhya case), in the separate opinion for himself and Ahmadi, J. (as he then was), observed as under:

[. . .]

. . . Hinduism is a tolerant faith. It is that tolerance that has enabled Islam, Christianity, Zoroastrianism, Judaism, Buddhism, Jainism and Sikhism to find shelter and support upon this land . . .

39.  **Ordinarily, Hindutva is understood as a way of life or a state of mind and it is not to be equated with, or understood as religious Hindu fundamentalism.** In Indian Muslims: The Need for a Positive Outlook by Maulana Wahiduddin Khan, (1994), it is said [. . .]:

The strategy worked out to solve the minorities problem was, although differently worded, that of Hindutva or Indianisation. This strategy, briefly stated, aims at developing a uniform culture by obliterating the differences between all of the cultures coexisting in the country. This was felt to be the way to communal harmony and national unity. It was thought that this would put an end once and for all to the minorities' problem.

**The above opinion indicates that the word 'Hindutva' is used and understood as a synonym of 'Indianisation', i.e., development of uniform culture by obliterating the differences between all the cultures coexisting in the country.**

* * *

Justice Verma relied on Maulana Waheedudin's work, which is not necessarily accepted amongst other Islamic scholars. Furthermore, the concept of a uniform culture and thus equating Indianization with Hindutva, though well-meaning, poses great difficulties and the problem of acceptability.

It appears that several years later, Chief Justice Verma publicly regretted having given the advocates of Hindutva that leeway and hoped that the court might review the finding. At one point, indications that a review by a larger bench of five judges was on the cards fructified into seven judges reviewing the technical requirement of appeals to religion during an election campaign,* but they felt that they were not required to look at the substantive issue of Hinduism vis-à-vis Hindutva. It remains to be seen if that issue will be reconsidered by a Constitutional Bench.

Yet another interesting attempt to define or describe Hinduism is to be found in 'M Chandra v M Thangamuthu & Anr':†

---

* 'Abhiram Singh v CD Commachen', 2017, 2 SCC 629.
† 'M. Chandra v M. Thangamuthu and Another', 2010, 9 SCC 712.

40. We must remember, as observed by this Court in Ganpat case,[*] Hinduism is not a religion with one god or one holy scripture. The practices of Hindus vary from region to region, place to place. The gods worshipped, the customs, traditions, practice, rituals, etc. they all differ, yet all these people are Hindus. The determination of the religious acceptance of a person must not be made on his name or his birth. **When a person intends to profess Hinduism, and he does all that is required by the practices of Hinduism in the region or by the caste to which he belongs, and he is accepted as a Hindu by all persons around him.**

41. **Hinduism appears to be a very complex religion. It is like a centre of gravity doll which always regains its upright position however much it may be upset.** Hinduism does not have a single founder, a single book, a single church or even a single way of life. Hinduism is not the caste system and its hierarchies, though the system is a part of its social arrangement, based on the division of labour. Hinduism does not preach or uphold untouchability, though the Hindu society has practised it, firstly due to reasons of public health and later, due to prejudices . . .

---

[*] 'Ganpat v Returning Officer', 1975, 1 SCC 589.

# Five

# Some Contestations at
# Home and around the Globe

Despite the long human history of violence and conflict, there have been relatively few occasions when people have engaged directly in fundamental contestation about the nature of God or the manifestations in everyday life of paying obeisance to the Unknown Ultimate we feel connected with. Pre-Islamic idol worship was the focus of the enlightenment brought on by Hazrat Muhammad as the Messenger of Allah. Interestingly, one of the idols removed was called Allah. But this was a case of an entire civilization being transformed in a lifetime.

Since the advent of Islam, there have been periodic changes in community relations based on shifting social dominance, but never again was there a similar fundamental questioning of the basic tenets of competing faiths. Even in Hinduism there are differences between sections of Hindus on idol worship. As we will see later in the chapter, the capture and destruction of a deity in battle had little to do with the essence of religious beliefs and more to do with the assertion of sovereignty.

It is often the case in history that prolonged disputes lead to people forgetting how and why they actually began. Consequential matters take on a contentious life of their own. Ayodhya, too, is no different, and therefore it is helpful to note the historical roots of the conflict and cut through narratives that caused misplaced feelings of historical wrongs, exploited for political reasons. While we are engaged in that exercise, it may be worth our while to look at the notion of historical wrongs, actual or perceived, in the story of mankind and how they have been attempted to be corrected or compensated by subsequent regimes trying to find closure.

Reparations are often talked about in the context of British rule in India and of the wartime exploitation of the Japanese 'comfort women' by the Chinese. America had to atone for the slaughter of Native Americans at the battle of Wounded Knee and elsewhere, and once again for dropping nuclear bombs on Hiroshima and Nagasaki. Germany remains conscious of the devastation caused by the Nazi Third Reich and has done its utmost to erase signs of Nazi power while preserving the reminders of human suffering. Nelson Mandela gave 'Truth and Reconciliation' a special place in the sad story of the apartheid. The Bishop of Canterbury, though not the British government, apologized for the Jallianwala Bagh massacre. In our own country, the prime minister and the president sought forgiveness from the Sikhs and the Akal Takht for the events connected with Operation Blue Star and the Khalistan movement. Pakistan has sought to placate Bangladesh for the massacres in Dhaka in 1971.

Yet many civil wars of Africa and Afghanistan have just melted into a gory history. History is replete with horrific massacres and genocides between different groups and ethnic divisions. Inevitably, places of religious significance get attacked, but there are other events in history that are centered on certain places for one reason or another.

## The Battle of Wounded Knee

In the United States, although there is no history of change of religious regime, and post the Civil War there has been an uninterrupted constitutional governance in the country, there have been historical events that call for reconciliation and reparation between the original inhabitants and the white settlers who came from across the seas. As white settlers advanced across north America, their military confronted the native populations, once described as 'Red Indians' in the mistaken belief that the explorers had reached India. The Battle of Wounded Knee or the Wounded Knee Massacre is remembered as the killing of several hundred people of the Lakota tribe, almost half of them women and children, by the soldiers of the United States Army. It happened on 29 December 1890, near Wounded Knee Creek on the Lakota Pine Ridge Indian Reservation in the state of South Dakota, following a failed attempt to disarm the natives in view of growing unrest in the reservations over unkept promises of the preservation of the natives' rights.

A detachment of the US 7th Cavalry Regiment, commanded by Major Samuel M. Whitside, escorted bands of the Lakota people from Porcupine Butte westward 8 km to the site of Wounded Knee, where they were encamped for the night. More troops of the 7th Cavalry Regiment, supported by heavy artillery, including Hotchkiss mountain guns, arrived to reinforce their colleagues, led by Colonel James W. Forsyth. With their arrival the US troops numbered 500 strong, in contrast to the 350 Lakota.

The next morning, the troops entered the camp on Colonel Forsyth's orders to disarm the Lakota. Accounts of what happened next seem to differ, with debate as to the trigger/spark that lit the powder keg. One account states that the US troops opened fire on account of one of the Lakota's rifles going off suddenly. One of the Lakota, Black Coyote, was deaf and spoke no English. He grappled with the soldiers attempting to wrestle his rifle away from him, not understanding their orders. In the struggle his rifle discharged accidentally, triggering the clash. According to other accounts, the tension during the disarming exercise was precipitated by one of the Lakota men performing a Ghost

Dance,* during which he threw dust in the air, at which point some of the Lakota men drew concealed weapons and attacked the soldiers, prompting a reprisal. Whatever the initial trigger, by many accounts the Lakota fought back with characteristic courage. However, they were outmatched and outnumbered, having already been mostly disarmed, apart from being a majority of women and children. Those who tried to escape were cut down by the gunfire. The US Army unceremoniously buried the fallen Lakota in a mass grave where the Hotchkiss guns had been placed, a location today known as Cemetery Hill.

This massacre marked the last major armed conflict between the United States and the indigenous Indians. Between 250 and 300 Lakota men, women and children were killed, and another fifty-one were wounded (four men and forty-seven women and children, some of whom died later). Twenty-five soldiers also died, and an equal number of soldiers were awarded the Medal of Honour. In 1990, both houses of the US Congress passed a resolution on the centennial of the event, formally expressing 'deep regret' for the massacre, and in 2001, the National Congress of American Indians passed two resolutions critical of the military awards and demanded that the US government rescind them. The Wounded Knee Battlefield, site of the massacre, has been designated as a National Historic Landmark by the US Department of the Interior.

## Ancient Indian History of Sovereign Assertion

Indian tradition has it that, in ancient times, Hindu kings who fought against each other sought to destroy or capture the presiding

---

* A rite performed by believers of the Ghost Dance religious movement, in which prophet–dreamers in western Nevada announced the return of the dead (hence 'ghost'), the ousting of the whites and the restoration of Native American lands, food supplies and way of life.

deity of the vanquished ruler. The deity would be carried to a suitable place in the conqueror's territory and installed for protection and as a reminder of the victory. Thus, it is not surprising that when the Muslims came to rule in India, they continued, in a sense, the same tradition. There are similar narratives from other parts of the world where established regimes were displaced by force and succeeded by the winner. In our own times, we have seen democratic assertions by the majority in the name of redressing the alleged wrongs of history. The calls for reparation by the British of their large-scale repatriation of Indian resources during their rule are expressions of a similar sentiment. My colleague Shashi Tharoor has written a brilliant, provocative book on the subject.* The only problem, is where does this stop? The demand for the Kohinoor to be returned to India and for the remains of Bahadur Shah Zafar to be brought from Yangon (Rangoon) and buried at Fatehpur Sikri in Delhi are similar sentimental demands. Interestingly, since the Indian Independence, statutes of former rulers have been removed and names of roads, and even cities, have been changed to reflect the new reality.

In ancient India, Hindu kings desecrated the temples of their rivals because of the close link between the deities worshipped and their own political authority. It was important for the victor to ensure complete annihilation of his defeated rival, and conquering the presiding deity sealed the matter beyond all doubt.

There are innumerable examples that validate the view. As early as 642 CE, the Pallava ruler Narasimhavarman I vanquished the Chalukyas and sacked their capital Vatapi, carrying the image of Lord Ganesha to his own kingdom in Tamil Nadu. The idol acquired the sobriquet of Vatapi Ganapati. Temple idols that passed from the defeated king to the victor were often known by inscriptions showing who the previous owners were. Similarly, in

---

* Shashi Tharoor, *Inglorious Empire: What the British Did to India* (reprint edition), Scribe, 2018.

950 CE, the Chandelle ruler Yashovarman built the Lakshman temple at Khajuraho to house the Vishnu Vaikunth, made of gold, to house the image of Lord Ganesha obtained from Mount Kailash by the 'Lord of Tibet', from whom the Sahi King of Orissa had wrested it. It was seized from the Sahis when they were defeated by the Pratihara ruler Herambapala. Yashovarman then overwhelmed Herambapala's son, Devapala, and carried the idol to Khajuraho.

Among the most fascinating stories of idol appropriation is the one narrated by the Buddhist chronicler Dhammakitti. According to him, the Pandyan ruler Srimara Srivallabha invaded Sri Lanka around 835 CE and routed the army of the Sinhala king, Sena I, who fled to the mountains. Srimara plundered the royal treasury and took away, among other things, 'the statue of the Teacher (Buddha)'.

Spirituality is the soul of India. Our country is a splendid land which embraced every religion, every faith that landed on its shores or across land borders. Not only did India adopt numerous religions, it is the birthplace of some of the oldest religions of the world—Hinduism, Sikhism, Jainism and Buddhism. It is this remarkable religious diversity, however, that has been used in modern times to cause strife and disquiet among Indians. Some of the most sacred sites and places of worship in the country have also been witness to heart-wrenching violence and bitter disputes but have not succeeded in destroying its composite culture.

## Mosque–Cathedral of Córdoba, Spain

The Mosque–Cathedral of Córdoba was an Islamic mosque in Andalusia, Spain, which was converted into a Roman Catholic cathedral in 1236. It is now officially known by its ecclesiastical name, the Cathedral of Our Lady of the Assumption. It is also known as the Great Mosque of Córdoba or the Mezquita.

The current structure originated in 784 under the Umayyad ruler Abd ar-Rahman I, though according to some accounts the site originally homed a Christian church dedicated to St Vincent of Saragossa, the Protomartyr of Spain, which was later demolished by Abd ar-Rahman I. The structure was expanded several times in the ninth and tenth centuries, making it one of the largest religious buildings in the Islamic world. It has been a World Heritage Site since 1984. When Christian forces re-invaded the city of Córdoba in the thirteenth century, they took back the site and built a cathedral altar within the structure of the mosque, reclaiming the site while maintaining its architecture and grandeur.

Since the early 2000s, Muslims have attempted to persuade the Roman Catholic Church to allow them to pray there as well. But their entreaties have been rejected both by the church authorities in Spain and by the Vatican. The great poet Iqbal wrote his long and beautiful poem 'The Mosque of Córdoba' in and around the monument; the poem is considered to be one of his greatest works.

## Toledo Cathedral, Spain

Beginning in the eighth century, the advance of Arab armies had captured vast parts of Europe, including the city of Toledo in Spain. In due course, as fortunes reversed, the city of Toledo was reclaimed by Alfonso VI, King of León and Castile, in 1085, from the Muslims of Al Andalusia. The Muslims of the city agreed to transfer power without bloodshed on the king's promise to protect their institutions of higher learning, as well as the customs and religion of the Muslim population, which had throughout coexisted with the larger Mozarabic population, particularly the preservation of the main mosque of the city. The king had clear intentions to keep this promise; however, soon after he departed the city on important matters of state, leaving his wife, Queen Constance, and Bernard of Sedirac, abbot of the Sahagun monastery, in charge of the city. The two conspired against the directions of the king, and on 25 October 1087, armed forces were sent in to seize the mosque by force. The armed men set to reclaim the site by installing a Christian altar within the building and hanging a bell in the minaret. The local Muslim population was terribly disturbed by this, and there was nearly an uprising in the city on account of it. The act shocked the conscience of the king when he came to know of it, and it is stated that in reprisal he ordered the execution of all involved.

The mosque–cathedral stood on the site until the thirteenth century, when the Vatican authorized the construction of a new cathedral. Archbishop Rodrigo Jiménex de Rada oversaw the construction of the new cathedral beginning in 1227 in the French gothic style, tearing away one of the most potent symbols of the region's Islamic past.

Ironically, though Muslims were once driven back from Spain. in recent decades, Arab oil has brought them back to the area of their past glory and once again changed the landscape through the building of new mosques.

## Hagia Sophia, Turkey

Next to the Blue Mosque, the Hagia Sophia dominates the landscape of Istanbul. The Holy Hagia Sophia Grand Mosque (formerly the Church of Hagia Sophia or the Church of the Holy Wisdom), the largest church of the Byzantine Empire, was built around 537 CE and remained a cathedral until 1453, when Constantinople fell to the Ottomans.

When the Ottomans, led by Emperor Fatih Sultan Mehmed— known as Mehmed the Conqueror—captured Constantinople, the Ottomans renamed the city Istanbul. Mehmed had the Church repurposed as a mosque and made several additions to the structure. As part of the conversion, the Ottomans covered many of the original Orthodox-themed mosaics with Islamic calligraphy designed by Kazasker Mustafa İzzet. Panels or medallions were hung on the columns in the nave, featuring the names of Allah, the Prophet Muhammad, the first four Caliphs and the Prophet's two grandsons, Hasan and Husain.

The mosaic on the main dome—believed to be an image of Christ—was also covered by gold calligraphy during the time it was used as a mosque. A *mihrab*, or nave, was installed in the wall, as is tradition in mosques, to indicate the direction towards Mecca, as per Islamic practice. The Ottoman Emperor Kanuni Sultan Süleyman (1520–1566) installed two bronze lamps on each side of the mihrab, and Sultan Murad III (1574–1595) added two marble cubes from the Turkish city of Bergama that date back to fourth century BC.

The four minarets of Hagia Sophia that define the Istanbul skyline were added to the original building during this period, partly for religious and aesthetic purposes, as well as to fortify the structure following earthquakes that struck the city.

In 1934, Turkish president Kemal Atatürk secularized the building, and in 1935 it was turned into a museum. In 1985, it was designated a component of a UNESCO World Heritage Site called the Historic Areas of Istanbul. The recent decision of the Turkish government to revert the building to a place of worship seems to indicate a repudiation of Atatürk's vision of modern Turkey.

The Hagia Sophia's symbolism in politics and religion remains a delicate issue—some 100 years after the fall of the Ottoman Empire. Since 1935, nine years after the Republic of Turkey was established by Atatürk and Khilafat was abolished,* the legendary structure has been a museum under the national government and reportedly attracts more than 3 million visitors annually.

---

* The Khilafat movement resonated in India as Mahatma Gandhi wove Indian nationalism into a greater challenge to the British imperialists with the help of Muslims.

However, since 2013, some Islamic religious leaders in the country have been trying to have the Hagia Sophia once again opened as a mosque. The debate maybe seen as purely a religious one but, given that Turkish society is witnessing a rise of nationalistic fervour, with a growing demand that the Ottoman era be given a prominent place in the country's history, the issue will not subside easily. The Ottomans' capture of Istanbul, and the Hagia Sophia, from the Orthodox Greeks is a high-water mark of that period, and the use of the building as a mosque, it is argued, will do justice to that history. The recent reconversion of the museum into a mosque was part of President Erdoğan's quest to be the leader of the contemporary Islamic world and perhaps the final repudiation of Turkey's attempt to be part of Europe.

## Al-Aqsa Mosque, Jerusalem

The decades-old conflict between Israelis and Arabs, since the Balfour Declaration of 1917 and the birth of the state of Israel, has largely focused on Jewish settlements on Palestinian Arab territory, on the status of Jerusalem and more particularly of the holy site of the Temple Mount Har HaBáyit, also known to Muslims as Al-Ḥaram Al-Šarīf, 'the Noble Sanctuary', or Al-Ḥaram Al-Qudsī Al-Šarīf, 'the Noble Sanctuary of Jerusalem'. The Al-Aqsa compound is a hill located in the Old City of Jerusalem that for thousands of years has been venerated as a holy site in Judaism, Christianity and Islam alike.

The present site is a flat plaza surrounded by retaining walls, including the Western Wall, which was built during the reign of Herod the Great for the expansion of the temple. The plaza is dominated by three monumental structures from the early Umayyad period: the Al-Aqsa Mosque, the Dome of the Rock and the Dome of the Chain, as well as the four minarets. Herodian walls and gates, with additions from the late Byzantine and early Islamic periods, cut through the flanks of the Mount. Currently, it can be reached through eleven gates, ten reserved for Muslims and one for non-Muslims, with guard posts of Israeli police in the vicinity of each.

According to Jewish tradition and scripture, the First Temple was built on the site by King Solomon, the son of King David, in 957 BC and destroyed by the Neo-Babylonian Empire in 586 BC—however, archaeological evidence has not satisfactorily verified this. The Second Temple was constructed under the auspices of Zerubbabel in 516 BC and destroyed by the Romans in 70 BC. Jewish tradition maintains it is here that a third and final temple will also be built. The location is the holiest site in Judaism and is the place Jews turn towards during prayer. Due to the site's extreme sanctity, many Jews will not walk on the Mount itself, to avoid unintentionally entering the area.

For Muslims, the Mount is the site of one of the three Sacred Mosques, the holiest sites in Islam. Revered as the Noble Sanctuary, the location of Prophet Muhammad's journey to Jerusalem and ascent to heaven from there, the site is also associated with Jewish biblical prophets who are also venerated in Islam. The Umayyad Caliphs commissioned the construction of the Al-Aqsa Mosque and Dome of the Rock (completed in 692 CE) on the site. The Al-Aqsa Mosque rests on the far southern side of the Mount, facing Mecca. The Dome of the Rock currently sits in the middle, occupying or close to the area where the Holy Temple previously stood.

It is one of the most contested religious sites in the world, with competing claims made by Judaism and Islam. Since the Crusades, the Muslim community of Jerusalem has managed the site as a Waqf. The Temple Mount within the Old City has been controlled by Israel since 1967. After the Six-Day War, Israel handed administration of the site back to the Waqf under Jordanian custodianship, while maintaining Israeli security control. It remains a major focal point of the Arab–Israeli conflict. In an attempt to keep the status quo, the Israeli government enforced a controversial ban on prayer by non-Muslims. Former US president Donald Trump's recognition of Jerusalem as the capital of Israel has added further complications.

## Quwwat-ul-Islam Masjid, Delhi

This mosque, whose name means the 'Might of Islam', is one of the oldest, most ancient mosques that survived the political vicissitudes across the centuries. Called by many as the Great Mosque of India and the Qutub Mosque, it stands within the imposing, ancient expanse of the Qutub Complex in south Delhi. It was built along with the Qutub Minar in 1193 AD and finished in 1197 AD by Sultan Qutb-ud-Din Aibak of the slave dynasty as a 'Jami Masjid' or 'Friday Mosque' of the royal city of Delhi, then situated in the vicinity.

There is speculation that the Qutub Minar was built as an exclusive minaret for the Quwwat-ul-Islam Mosque and hence is also known as the 'Minar of Jami Masjid', which means the 'Tower of Quwwat-ul-Islam Mosque', from where the muezzin might have given the call for prayer. The architecture and design of this mosque resembles that of the Adhai Din Ka Jhonpra mosque in Ajmer, Rajasthan, which was also constructed under the rule of Qutb-ud-Din Aibak. Here, too, are stories of the destruction of temples to make place for the mosque.

The Qutub Minar and the Quwwat-ul-Islam Mosque were reported to have used stones from an ancient Jain temple and, in typical Islamic style, a mixture of gravel and bricks for the building decorated with glazed tiles. The mosque was constructed on a raised platform that measures 141 by 105 feet, with two courtyards on the inner and outer portions, surrounded by colonnades and sanctuaries, and supported by pillars added sometime between 1210 and 1220 AD by Sultan Iltutmish. There are elaborately decorated shafts, which are believed to have been made from the temple remnants, which gives this mosque a typical blend of

Hindu and Islamic contours—in some ways syncretic assimilation but in another a reminder of an unpleasant past.

In 1196 AD, a 16-metre-tall screen made of stone and a pointed central arch, with two smaller pointed arches on either sides, carrying beautiful Arabic calligraphic inscriptions were erected to separate the courtyard from the main prayer hall on the western end of the mosque. The central arch, 6.15 metres high, is heavily decorated, with the finest carvings and designs that display a pure fusion of Hindu and Islamic architectures.

The entrance of the Quwwat-ul-Islam Mosque has an ornamental dome or mandap taken from Jain temples; it leads to a flight of steep steps into the interior, with a stunning view of the courtyard fringed with corbelled pillars on either side and carved ceilings, decorated with Hindu images, like floral motifs, bells, ropes, tassels, cows and leaves, etc.

In 1230 AD, Sultan Iltutmish, aka Altamash (successor of Qutb-ud-Din Aibak), reportedly added three more arches to extend the screen of the prayer hall, so that it could accommodate more worshippers. These additional three arches are products of true Islamic–Arabic architecture. They were specially made by craftsmen from Afghanistan, exquisitely carved with Islamic motifs in traditional geometric patterns.

The original five arches were carved by Hindu masons, unaware of the Islamic techniques used to make the 'keystone' that holds the arches in place. This technique was familiar to skilled Muslim craftsmen, who would cut each stone into a wedge-shaped semicircle that formed the centre of the arch described as a 'keystone' in Islamic architectural terms.

Later, in 1315 AD, Alauddin Khalji added the outer courtyard, to extend the area of the mosque, and the Alai Darwaza, made of red sandstone and white marble, on the eastern side, to create the royal entrance leading through an exterior pavement right into the mosque.

The story of the Qutub mosque is similar to that of the Gyanvapi mosque in Varanasi and Krishan Janmabhoomi in Mathura, except that in the case of the latter two, local adjustments and accommodations were made during the medieval period, permitting the places of worship of two religions to coexist side by side. The Places of Worship Act, upheld by the Supreme Court Constitutional Bench, ensures that the historical arrangement is not disturbed.

## ASI-Controlled Mosques in Delhi

There are nearly 600 mosques all over India, and fifty-three in Delhi alone, where Muslims cannot pray because they are notified as historical monuments under the control of the Archaeological Survey of India (ASI). The fifty-three mosques in the Indian capital include those located inside the seventeenth-century Red Fort, one across the road near Jama Masjid, one in the Safdarjung Tomb, one in Lodi Garden and one at the imposing Qutub Minar complex (Quwwat-ul-Islam). The Khairul Manazil mosque, opposite the Old Fort, is also out of bounds for worshippers. So are the mosques inside the Delhi Golf Club grounds and near the Wazirabad bridge over Yamuna River. Similar restrictions are in place at the mosque near the Feroz Shah Kotla ground in Delhi. Nevertheless, on major Islamic holidays, Muslims pray there in large numbers. Periodically, the police file cases against the prayer leaders, accusing them of intruding into protected monuments.

There are 1076 temples and 250 mosques of national importance under the ASI. Of these, 242 temples and thirty-six mosques are in the state of Karnataka, while 132 temples and sixty-two mosques in Uttar Pradesh fall under the same category. Madhya Pradesh has ninety-six temples and twenty mosques within the purview of the ASI.

The years of construction, with respect to the temples and mosques under the ASI, vary from fourth to nineteenth centuries for temples, and twelfth to nineteenth centuries for mosques.

An interesting dispute that surfaces periodically in the national capital concerns the claim of Muslims to pray at the mosques within the ASI-protected monuments. The late Syed Shahabuddin had pursued the matter vigorously, and some accommodation was made by the government from time to time. In 2013, the National Commission for Minorities (NCM) suggested a joint inspection of as many as thirty-one ASI-protected mosques across Delhi, following a demand to open them for prayers at least on Fridays. Officials from the commission, the ASI and the Waqf Board carried out the joint survey after a demand from the Jamiat Ulama-i-Hind, a Muslim organization.

As per the Ancient Monuments and Archaeological Sites and Remains (AMASR) Act, no religious activity can be allowed at a protected monument or site if the practice was not prevalent there at the time when the protection notification for that monument was issued.

The thirty-one monuments listed by the NCM come under two categories: mosques that are not presently being used for prayers but are situated near a habitation and hence should be opened for prayers; and mosques that are already being used for prayers. Among the thirty-one mosques were Mohammadi Masjid (near Siri Fort Auditorium), Masjid Jamali Kamali (Mehrauli Archeological Park), Masjid Begumpur (near Sarvapriya Vihar/ Malviya Nagar), Moti Masjid (Red Fort) and even Chauburji mosque (near Kamala Nehru Park, Delhi University).

'Although the commission was not very keen that heritage monuments should be opened for prayers, we nevertheless decided to suggest the joint survey for ascertaining the condition of these mosques,' said Wajahat Habibullah, NCM chairperson at the time. The NCM letter written in July 2012 to the Ministry of Culture stated, 'What needs to be noted is that such monuments, although declared protected, are, in fact, often in a state of disrepair, poor maintenance and even undesirable use.'* The survey considered

---

* Nivedita Khandekar, 'ASI, Minorities Panel to Survey Heritage Mosques', *Hindustan Times*, 26 August 2012, https://www.hindustantimes.

the following aspects: the status of maintenance of each of these thirty-one monuments and steps needed for better upkeep of those mosques which are in poor condition.

Interestingly, at times questions arise about people getting access to the Taj Mahal complex, which includes a mosque as well. Since the ASI claims to control the complex and has set fixed visiting hours, there is a problem about hosting late-night *taravi* prayers there during Ramazan, as indeed at other times when the complex is closed. This question, too, is before the Supreme Court.

The incremental expansion, since 1960, of the Bhagyalaxmi temple, cheek by jowl with the Charminar, another ASI monument in Hyderabad, is yet another sore that is slowly festering. For the present, the high court in Hyderabad has directed status quo.

## Kashi Vishwanath Temple, Varanasi

The Kashi Vishwanath Mandir, a temple dedicated to Lord Shiva, is located in what is the centre of Hindu spirituality: the city of Varanasi (Kashi) on the banks of River Ganga. Not only is this temple one of the twelve sacred Jyotirlingas, it is also the holiest Shiva temples, according to the Hindus. The history of this temple, however, is marred by numerous incidents of violence and religious persecution. In 1124, Muhammad Ghori pillaged and destroyed the temple. Even as the locals undertook the reconstruction, Qutb-ud-Din Aibak once again wrought havoc in 1194, having defeated the Raja of Kannauj, who was the commander under Mohammed Ghori. In 1351, the temple was destroyed again by the sultan of Delhi, Firuz Shah Tughlaq. In 1669, the temple was destroyed yet again by Mughal emperor Aurangzeb, who ordered the construction of the Gyanvapi mosque in its place.

The temple has been mentioned in the Puranas, including the Kashi Kanda section of the Skanda Purana. It was rebuilt by a Gujarati merchant during the reign of Delhi's Sultan Iltutmish (1211–1266). It was demolished again during the rule of either Hussain Shah Sharqi (1447–1458) or Sikandar Lodhi (1489–1517). Raja Man Singh built the temple during Mughal emperor Akbar's rule, but some Hindus boycotted it as Man Singh had let the Mughals marry within his family. Raja Todar Mal further rebuilt the temple, with Akbar's funding, at its original site in 1585. This was not the only case of Mughals assisting in the construction and preservation of religious places of Hindus.

In 1669, Emperor Aurangzeb destroyed the temple, which had been rebuilt during the reign of his great grandfather, and built the Gyanvapi mosque in its place. Some scholars see that as evidence of the last great Mughal's bigotry, but some credit accounts that the destruction was brought about by the reaction to enslaved women, or *devadasis*, kept in the basement of the temple, and to send a message to the local zamindars and Jai Singh I, grandson of Raja Man Singh, who were believed to have helped Shivaji escape from Aurangzeb's custody. The remains of the erstwhile temple can be seen in the foundation, the columns and at the rear part of the mosque.

In 1742, the Maratha ruler Malhar Rao Holkar's hope to demolish the mosque and reconstruct a Vishweshwar temple could not succeed, because of obstruction by the nawab of Awadh, who controlled the territory. Eight years later, in 1750, the Maharaja of Jaipur had the land around the site surveyed, hoping to acquire it for rebuilding the Kashi Vishwanath temple, but without any further steps. Finally, in 1780, Malhar Rao's daughter-in-law, Ahilyabai Holkar, constructed the present temple adjacent to the mosque.

Two petitions were filed over the years over the disputed site, by the Anjuman Intazamia Masjid, Varanasi and Uttar Pradesh Sunni Central Waqf Board, Lucknow. The Allahabad High Court directed for them to be placed before an appropriate bench. The Anjuman Intazamia Masjid moved court, challenging orders passed by additional district judge, Varanasi, in 1997 and 1998, whereby its application challenging a civil suit filed by the Kashi Vishwanath Mandir Trust had been turned down. The trust had filed a suit in 1991, claiming that a temple was constructed by Maharaja Vikramaditya more than 2000 years ago on the site where the mosque had been much later constructed. Alleging that the temple was demolished by Mughal emperor Aurangzeb in 1664 and a mosque constructed on a part of the land with materials of the razed place of worship, the trust has sought removal of the Gyanvapi Masjid from the site and possession of the entire land. The findings of the Ayodhya judgment, particularly on the Places of Worship Act, will have direct consequences for this dispute.

## Krishna Janmabhoomi, Mathura

The dust from the demolition of the Babri Masjid had barely settled in 1992 when the Shahi Idgah adjacent to the Krishna Janmabhoomi temple in Mathura was placed on the agenda of the Vishva Hindu Parishad (VHP), campaigning 'for the removal of the three mosques built by the marauders at Ayodhya, Mathura and Kasi'.

The Sri Krishna Janmabhoomi Trust made claim to the four-and-a-half-acre plot next to the mosque for a *rangamanch* for religious and cultural functions of the trust and temple authorities. Further, the recent demolitions in the vicinity to clear a passage to the Ganga have raised the spectre of a repeat of Ayodhya. The Sri Krishna Janmabhoomi Sangh (SKJS), which manages the affairs of the trust, has asked the Uttar Pradesh governor to remove the CRPF company deployed there to address any emergent eventuality. The trust's demand for the withdrawal of the CRPF shows that it intends to take possession of the land and fortify its claim over the idgah in the long run.

In addition to this, the issue has inevitably reached the courts as well. One Manohar Lal Sharma, a resident of Vrindavan, has filed a case in the Allahabad High Court, seeking a restraint on Muslims offering namaz five times a day, arguing that in the past namaz was offered only twice a year, on Id-ul-Fitr and Id-ul-Zoha. The petition also seeks the quashing of the Places of Religious Worship Act of 1992, which protects the status in situ of all shrines and places of worship as on 15 August 1947. Yet another strand to the controversy is a petition filed by one Abdul Haq, the principal of Islamic Inter College, claiming that the entire complex belongs to the Shahi Idgah Masjid Committee and not the temple.

The ownership of the 13.37 acres of land, on which the idgah and the shrine are located, was the subject of dispute until 1935. The Allahabad High Court upheld the Benaras king's ownership of the land on which Aurangzeb had built an idgah in 1669, next to the ruins of the Keshavnath temple—believed to be Lord Krishna's birthplace—which Aurangzeb is reported to have destroyed.

In 1968, the SKJS and the idgah committee reached an agreement, granting ownership of the land to the temple trust dominated by the VHP, including Vishnu Hari Dalmia, noted industrialist and the head of that outfit, even as the management rights of the masjid were left to the idgah committee. The agreement deprived the trust of the legal right to stake claim on the masjid. Meanwhile, Sharma has filed another petition in the Mathura District Court, challenging the 1968 agreement.

## Ram Janmabhoomi, Ayodhya

According to Hindu belief, Lord Ram, the avatar of Lord Vishnu and the king of Ayodhya, was born at the sacred site in Ayodhya some 9,00,000 years ago. Archaeological evidence corroborates the fact that a great city stood here in the seventh century AD, but it cannot be concluded if it was Buddhist or Hindu. In 1528, Mir Baqi, a general of Mughal emperor Babur, constructed a mosque at the spot. From time immemorial, the site has been at the centre of a deep conflict between the Hindu and Muslim communities. The 1992 clashes over Ram Janmabhoomi caused the worst instances of communal riots in the country. The courts were unable to deliver a verdict that could provide closure, till the recent Supreme Court judgment discussed in this book.

## Somnath Temple, Gujarat

The Somnath temple of Gujarat, dedicated to Lord Shiva, is one of the twelve Jyotirlinga sites of Shiva worship mentioned in the Rig Veda. The temple is believed to have been one of the holiest and wealthiest shrines of ancient India. Mahmud of Ghazni, who arrived to plunder the temple in 1025, looted an incredible amount of wealth and is also believed to have broken the Jyotirlinga. Thereafter, the temple saw one raid after another by invading forces. In 1299, Sultan Alauddin Khalji's troops raided and damaged the temple; in 1395, the temple was destroyed once again by Zafar Khan, the Delhi Sultanate's governor of Gujarat. In 1451, it was demolished once more by Mahmud Begada. Then, the Portuguese attacked and destroyed the temple in 1546, and Emperor Aurangzeb again destroyed it in 1665. Each time the temple was reconstructed by the faithful. After Independence, restoration of the temple was a top priority of the Congress government.

Having sorted out the Junagadh state issue, Sardar Patel, K.M. Munshi and other leaders of the Congress went to Mahatma Gandhi with their proposal to reconstruct the Somnath temple. But Gandhi suggested that the funds for the construction should be collected from the public, and that the temple should not be funded by the state. However, soon both Gandhi and Sardar Patel died, and the task of reconstruction of the temple continued under

Munshi, who was the minister for food and civil supplies under Prime Minister Jawaharlal Nehru.

The ruins were pulled down in October 1950, and the mosque at that site was shifted some distance away. In May 1951,President Rajendra Prasad participated in the installation ceremony and said, 'It is my view that the reconstruction of the Somnath Temple will be complete on that day when not only a magnificent edifice will arise on this foundation, but the mansion of India's prosperity will be really that prosperity of which the ancient temple of Somnath was a symbol.'

## Bodh Gaya, Bihar

Buddhism is known to be the religion of peace and tolerance, and inspired the warrior king Ashoka to give up violence. Bodh Gaya, the place where Lord Buddha gained enlightenment under the bodhi tree, is seen as the universal symbol of harmony. Yet in recent times, it too has been touched by violence and bloodshed. In July 2013, a series of low-intensity bomb blasts rocked the Mahabodhi Temple complex, injuring some monks. The Indian Mujahideen, a radical Islamist terrorist organization, is believed to have caused it, but it makes little sense as to why they would attack a symbol of peace that in no way represents a challenge to their world view.

Bodh Gaya is thus a religious place of pilgrimage associated with the Mahabodhi Temple complex in the Gaya district Bihar. Since antiquity, Bodh Gaya has remained the site of pilgrimage and veneration for both Hindus and Buddhists. For Buddhists, Bodh Gaya is the most important of the four main pilgrimage sites associated with the life of Gautama Buddha, the other three being Kushinagar, Lumbini and Sarnath. In 2002, Mahabodhi Temple became a UNESCO World Heritage Site.

Curiously, the complex remained under the control of non-Buddhists. In 1891, there was a campaign to return control of the temple to Buddhists, over the objections of the Hindu mahant. Edwin Arnold, author of *The Light of Asia*, started advocating for the renovation of the site and its return to Buddhist care. Arnold was directed towards this endeavour by Weligama Sri Sumangala Thera. In 1891, Anagarika Dharmapala was on a pilgrimage to the recently restored Mahabodhi Temple—where Siddhartha Gautama, the Buddha, had attained enlightenment at Bodh Gaya—and was shocked to find the temple in the hands of a Saivite priest. The Buddha image had been transformed into a Hindu icon and Buddhists were even barred from worship. To agitate the issue, the Mahabodhi Society was founded in 1891 in Colombo, but its offices were moved to Calcutta the following year.

One of the Mahabodhi Society's aims was the restoration of control of the Mahabodhi Temple at Bodh Gaya to Buddhists. Dharmapala initiated a lawsuit against the Brahmin priests who had held control of the site for centuries. There was a protracted struggle, and this was successful only after Indian Independence (1947) and sixteen years after Dharmapala's own death (1933), with the partial restoration of the site to the Mahabodhi Society in 1949. The temple management of Bodh Gaya was entrusted to a committee comprised of Hindus and Buddhists, and control passed from the Hindu mahant to the government of the state of Bihar, which established a Bodh Gaya Temple Management Committee (BTMC), vide the Bodh Gaya Temple Act of 1949.

The committee has nine members, the majority of whom, including the chairman, must by law be Hindus. Mahabodhi's first head monk under the management committee was Anagarika Munindra, a Bengali who had been an active member of the Mahabodhi Society. In 2013, the Bihar government amended the Bodh Gaya Temple Act 1949, enabling a non-Hindu to head the temple committee. However, in 2013, a thousand Indian Buddhists protested at the Mahabodhi temple to demand that complete control be given to Buddhists. The protestors included such leaders as Bhante Anand (president of the Akhil Bharatiya Bhikkhu Mahasangh, an influential body of monks as well as the president of the Bodh Gaya Mukti Andolan Samiti). The Japanese-born Surai Sasai and Bhante Anand emerged as the two main leaders of this campaign to free the temple from Hindu control.

At Independence, the Bihar government assumed responsibility for the protection, management of the temple and its properties. Pursuant to the Bodh Gaya Temple Act of 1949, such responsibilities are shared with the Bodhgaya Temple Management Committee and an advisory board. The committee, which serves for a three-year term, must by law consist of four Buddhist and four Hindu representatives, including the head of the Sankaracharya Math monastery as an ex-officio Hindu member. A 2013 amendment to the Bodhgaya Temple Management Act allows the Gaya district magistrate to be the chairman of the committee, even if he is not Hindu. The advisory board consists of the governor of Bihar and 20–25 other members, half of them from Buddhist countries.

## Shrine of Baba Budangiri, Karnataka

Deep in the beautiful Mullayangiri mountain ranges of Karnataka, the shrine of Baba Budangiri, near Chikmagalur, is a symbol of the shared heritage of Hindus and Muslims. It is named after Hazrat Dada Hayat Meer Qalandar, believed by Hindus to be God Dattatreya.

At the peak of the Ram Janmabhoomi movement, local units of organizations like the VHP and RSS demanded that the shrine be converted into a Hindu temple, making the issue into south India's Ayodhya. The RSS fought the case in the Supreme Court, which ordered status quo and thus it remains.

In December 2017, the Chikmagalur BJP MLA reportedly visited the shrine and made inflammatory statements. Minutes after his visit, devotees allegedly hoisted saffron flags at the site and even destroyed some graves of the Sufi saint's followers. Since then, the Datta Teertha, which is held annually in December, and the annual urs held every March, have been affected. However, people visiting the site are impressed to see Hindu women entering the cave after respectfully covering their heads, like their Muslim counterparts, and Muslims serve prasada water inside the cramped, narrow confines of the shrine. As with many similarly contested places, ordinary people have no problem in sharing the beneficence, but once political forces get involved, inevitable trouble breaks out.

## Last Resting Place of Sant Kabir

Kabir Das, the fifteenth-century Sufi and Bhakti poet, was born on the banks of the Ganga in Varanasi, to a poor Muslim weaver family. Having acquired considerable following for his syncretic literary work, his legend became unique when he chose to die at a place called Maghar, about 240 km from Lucknow, considered to be a passage to hell in contrast with holy Kashi. Sant Kabir departed his mortal body at Maghar in Januanry 1518, on Magh Shukl Ekadashi, according to the Hindu calendar in Vikram Samvat 1575. Kabir was deeply admired by Muslims and Hindus alike, and upon his death a dispute arose as to whether he was to be buried or cremated. Legend has it that while the two groups were engaged in a confrontation, Kabir's mortal remains disappeared, leaving behind a heap of rose petals. The chastised followers decided to build both a *mazaar* (tomb) and samadhi side by side. An annual festival is held here on Makar Sankranti. Kabir reportedly chose Maghar as his resting place above holy Kashi, where people go seeking salvation in death, on the banks of the holy Ganga, because as an enlightened soul he wanted to dispel the myth that anyone breathing his last in Maghar would be born a donkey in his next life or would be transported to hell.

Kabir was famous for his *dohas*, which contain innumerable nuggets of wisdom and sage advice for human beings:

> *Jab mai tha tab Hari nahin, ab Hari hai mai nahi,*
> *Sab andhiyara mit gaya, jab deepak dekhya mahi.*

> (When I had ego, there was no presence of God,
> Now, on realizing God, my ego is gone.
> There is no darkness now that I have seen light.)

> *Maati kahe kumhar se tu kya ronde mohe,*
> *Ik din aisa aiyega mai rondungi tohe.*

> (Earth says to the potter, you may now me knead,
> But a day will be when I shall thee knead.)

# Six

# The Saffron Sky

Whatever rationalization might have been offered, the Ayodhya saga was throughout about one faith trumping the methods of another. But the former faith itself was experiencing a contest of interpretation. Sanatan dharma and classical Hinduism known to sages and saints was being pushed aside by a robust version of Hindutva, by all standards a political version similar to the jihadist Islam of groups like ISIS and Boko Haram of recent years. Since the political content was clear, the term inevitably found place in election campaigns. One such election travelled to the Supreme Court, where Justice J.S. Verma considered, inter alia, the term 'Hindutva' in the context of use of religion for electoral purposes, giving it the benefit of the doubt.

Since Articles 25 and 26 guarantee the right to religion, the Supreme Court is periodically called upon to examine the very idea of religion. In a series of cases soon after Independence, Chief Justice P.B. Gajendragadkar defined Hinduism, in 'Yagnapurushadji vs Muldas'* known as the 'Satsangi case'. By

---

* 'Sastri Yagnapurushadji and Others vs Muldas Bhudardas Vaishya and Another', 1966, 3 SCR 242; AIR 1966 SC 1119.

virtue of the Bombay Harijan Temple Entry Act 1948, every Hindu temple was to be open to entry of Harijans. Satsangis, or followers of Swaminarayan, claimed that they represented a distinct religion and their temples were not of Hindu religion. But the court held, on the basis of material placed before it, that the Satsangis claiming their religion to be distinct from Hinduism could not be accepted. In the process, the chief justice inquired, '[W]hat are the distinctive features of Hindu religion?' and then proceeded to answer the question, 'When we think of Hindu religion, we find it difficult if not impossible, to define Hindu religion or inadequately describe it. Unlike other religions in the world, the Hindu religion does not claim any one prophet; it does not worship any one God; it does not subscribe to any dogma; it does not believe in one philosophical concept; it does not follow any one set of religious rites . . . It does not appear to satisfy the narrow traditional features of any religion or creed. It may broadly be described as a way of life and nothing more.'

Similarly, in deciding the Ramakrishna Mission matter* and reversing the Calcutta high court's judgment, the Supreme Court found that a traditional Hindu claims to be a Hindu and Hindu only, and believes in the Vedas only, and not in the scriptures of any other religion, whereas a follower of the cult/religion of Shri Ramakrishna, coming originally from the Hindu fold, though a Hindu claims to be something more at the same time. As a follower of Shri Ramakrishna's Religion Universal, along with the Vedas, he accepts also the Holy Koran, the Holy Bible and all other religious scriptures to be true.

The model of Hinduism that Chief Justice Gajendragadkar supported was essentially inclusive and propounded by Swami Vivekanand as well as Sarvepalli Radhakrishnan.

---

* 'Brahmachari Sideshwar Shai and Others vs State of West Bengal', 1995, 4 SCC 646.

Several decades later, Justice J.S. Verma (as his Lordship then was) used the 'way of life' description for Hindutva, without distinguishing it from Hinduism. In a group of cases related to Maharashtra assembly elections in 1990, and speeches by Bal Thackeray exhorting the people to vote for Prabhoo because he was a Hindu, the court held as follows:[*]

> Thus, it cannot be doubted . . . that the words 'Hinduism' and 'Hindutva' are not necessarily to be understood and confined only to the strict Hindu religious practices unrelated to the culture and ethos of the people of India, depicting the way of life of the Indian people. Unless the context of a speech indicates a contrary meaning and use, in the abstract these terms are indicative of a way of life of the Indian people and are not confined merely to describe persons practising the Hindu religion as a faith.

Many years later, after laying down his office, Chief Justice Verma regretted having given that judgment.[†] Efforts to persuade successive chief justices to have the matter examined by a constitutional bench have faltered on technical grounds, given that the case was supposed to have been referred to a bench of five judges, while another related issue was further referred to a bench of seven judges, who answered the reference limited to what 'his religion' means in Section 123 of the Representation of Peoples Act, 1951. In practical terms there is little doubt that the word 'Hindutva' is used as representing an aggressive and assertive

---

[*] 'Dr Ramesh Yeshwant Prabhoo vs Prabhakar Kashinath Kunte and Others', 1996, 1 SCC 130.
[†] Seema Chishti, 'Why, 22 Years On, the SC's "Hindutva Judgment" Remains Elephant in Room', *Indian Express*, 3 January 2017, https://indianexpress.com/article/explained/gujarat-riot-nhrc-religion-elections-vote-bank-supreme-court-why-22-years-on-the-scs-hindutva-judgment-remains-elephant-in-room-4456258/

version of political Hinduism rather than the description of it being a way of life.

The capturing of power at the Centre by the BJP and its allies in 2014, and then its further consolidation in 2019, has emboldened the right wing to speak out against what they describe as their centuries-long subjugation and to speak for the inevitable journey of this nation towards becoming a Hindu Rashtra. There is still lip service being paid to secularism, as it remains a prominent idea in the Preamble to the Constitution, but theirs is an assertive definition of secularism that describes all that the Right believes to be the true vision of Bharat or India.

As talk of Hindu Rashtra becomes more and more common, though without any official endorsement or indication of its contours, support for it, surprisingly, comes from unexpected quarters. For example, from Professor Faizan Mustafa.

Prof. Mustafa has an impressive academic record and the unique capacity to respond within hours, if not minutes, on any legal development, including Supreme Court judgments running into hundreds of pages. As head of the National Academy of Legal Studies and Research, Hyderabad (NALSAR) and former registrar of Aligarh Muslim University, Prof. Mustafa has, at a relatively young age, carved out a place for himself among constitutional lawyers. His contributions to debates on Triple Talaq and CAA–NPR–NRC have been salutary and rewarding. Yet his recent proposition is that many of our current political difficulties might be resolved if we opted to become a Hindu Rashtra. Curiously, he goes on to suggest that all it would take is a fifteen-judge constitutional bench of the Supreme Court to overrule the Kesavananda Bharti case and the doctrine of basic structure, so that Parliament could amend/omit one of the fundamental values of our Constitution—secularism. That, unfortunately, is an incorrect understanding of that judgment, but that is for another day.

What is interesting is that Prof. Mustafa believes that a Hindu Rashtra would recognize Hinduism to be the dominant religion (presumably he means *de jure* because de facto it already is), but people of other religions will have the freedom to practise their faiths and human rights will be protected. It is surprising that he believes the right to equality and freedom of conscience will not be impaired. Prof. Mustafa's confidence flows from his understanding of the systems in Sri Lanka (with Buddhism as state religion), Pakistan and Bangladesh (with Islam as state religion), the UK and USA (with Protestantism as the majority's religion) Ireland (with Catholicism, although the dominant position of the Church was deleted in 1972), Israel (with Judaism), etc. Curiously, he does not pause to distinguish the secularism practised in India from that in the West. India is arguably the only country in the world that practises 'inclusive secularism' (equal respect and regard to all religions) as opposed to the traditional 'exclusive secularism' (strict separation of the state and the church).

Prof. Mustafa's argument can be summarized as follows: 'The minorities, too, are now fed up with this facade of secularism, with all state institutions tilting towards one religion. Perhaps some kind of Hindu Rashtra can help bring peace and save the country from the path of self-destruction.'*

In world history, there have been innumerable souls who chose resistance over submission and supine calculation. Mahatma Gandhi, Emiliano Zapata, Che Guevara, Martin Luther King, Nelson Mandela, Lawrence of Arabia are but a few among the galaxy who stood their ground against social injustice and denial of human dignity. It was the great revolutionary Che who said, 'Better to die on your feet than to live on your knees.'

But all that happens during extraordinary times, we will be told, as though these are not such times. Depending on the stage and state of social development, the nature of the extraordinary can

---

* Faizan Mustafa, 'Minorities, Too, Are Fed up with This Facade of Secularism', *Indian Express*, 21 March 2020, https://indianexpress.com/article/opinion/columns/narendra-modi-govt-6324468/

vary. It is possible that we never imagined that politics could take such a turn in our country. But then, did we ever imagine that we would sit idle at our homes under official lockdown, with similar restrictions imposed in cities across the country? Ironically, the COVID-19 pandemic and our individual and collective responses seem to say a great deal about politics in times of the coronavirus. Experts and social scientists can rush back to their libraries to glean the similarities and contrasts with historical events, and to predict the path our politics will take even as virologists are charting the destructive path of the virus. The fact remains that like nuclear energy national unity of the kind displayed at 5 p.m. of 22 March 2020 can easily be manipulated from creativity to destruction. Today there can be no greater purpose than to destroy, or at least contain the COVID-19 virus. Inspiring a voluntary people's curfew is a powerful instrument in our battle with the virus but the beating of metal plates and dancing in the streets is about breaking the virus chain is extremely doubtful. It is more like putting us all in the chain of frenzy en route to fanaticism. We have been forced into relative isolation and that gives us the time to think, hard.

Prof. Faizan Mustafa, perhaps, needs to do a rethink. I can hardly imagine the likes of John Stuart Mill, Edward Said, Ronald Dworkin, John Rawls, Noam Chomsky, Upendra Baxi (placing Prof. Mustafa in exalted company) ever contemplating buying peace with fascist ideologues for the sake of survival. There is a struggle going on for the soul of India, and the women and men who came out across the country in protest against the CAA demonstrated their do-or-die spirit. We cannot let them down by negotiating peace on terms that are neither honorable for people nor compatible with the constitutional values bequeathed to us by the founding fathers.

The historical trajectories that culminated in the constitutional positions described by Prof. Mustafa are vastly different from our experience. There is no way to believe that a change such as contemplated by Prof. Mustafa will be innocuous as far as human rights are concerned, including the right to citizenship. The benign assumptions in this case have already come to grief in the Hindutva judgment by Justice J.S. Verma, when he described it as a way of life.

In my own party, the Congress, discussion often veers towards this subject. There is a section that, with growing assertiveness, regrets the fact that our image is that of a pro-minority party and advocates the *jeneu-dhari* credentials of our leadership; this section responded to the Ayodhya judgment with the declaration that a *bhavya* (grand) temple should be built on the site, bypassing any further politics over this issue. That position, of course, overlooked or sidestepped the part of the Supreme Court order, directing land to be given for a masjid as well. On one particular occasion, as senior leaders gathered for a cup of tea after flag hoisting, a colleague indulged in a refrain about the BJP's intention to create a Hindu Rashtra but was left speechless when the party president asked what a Hindu Rashtra would be.

The BJP must know what it intends, but its top leaders skirt the issue in their ambition to secure world recognition, while secular parties remain caught in a vortex of uncertainty and unreliable ideological moorings. One is reminded of 'the king is dead; long live the king'; and, 'If you 'can't beat them, join them.' This cannot, and must not, be our strategic position.

Seshadri Chari, former editor of *Organiser* and a rational communicator, has tried to explain Hindu Rashtra in remarkably comforting terms:

> The words Hindu, Hindutva and Hinduism have defied definition . . . The word dharma, as in 'Hindu dharma', cannot be equated with the Western concept of religion . . . In fact, the term 'Hindu dharma' itself is a misnomer.
>
> . . . 'Hindu' refers to a society, a group of people with a distinct cultural and civilisational character, a core set of beliefs, traditions, practices—and, yes, prejudices too. In the Indian

context, dharma forms the very basis of everyday life, it is about
ethics, values and social mores, not religion . . .*

Chari, the urbane face of the RSS (although not always thought to
be comfortable for the leadership), argues a well-structured brief
but without direct reference to Veer Sarvarkar's *Hindutva*, citing
Shri Madhavrao Sadashivrao Golwalkar:†

> We find that this great country of ours, extending in the north
> from the Himalayas with all its branches spreading north,
> south, east and west, and with the territories included in those
> great branches right up to the Southern Ocean inclusive of
> all islands, is one great natural unit. As the Child of this soil,
> our well-evolved society has been living here for thousands of
> years. This society has been known, especially in modern times,
> as the Hindu society. This also is a historical fact. For, it is the
> forefathers of the Hindu people who have set up standards and
> traditions of love and devotion for the motherland. They also
> prescribed various duties and rites with a view to keep aglow in
> the people's mind for all time to come, a living and complete
> picture of our motherland and devotion to it as a Divine
> Entity. And again it is they who shed their blood in defence
> of the sanctity and integrity of the motherland. That all this
> has been done only by the Hindu people is a fact to which
> our history of thousands of years bears eloquent testimony. It
> means that only the Hindu has been living here as the child
> of this soil . . .
>
> The common adoration for the motherland has made our
> people, in a way, related by blood to one another—from the
> man in Kashi to the man in Kanyakumari and from a forest-
> dweller to a city-dweller. All the various castes, the various ways

* Seshadri Chari, 'Decoding "Hindu Rashtra"', *India Today*, 8 November 2019.
† Madhavrao Sadashivrao Golwalkar, 'For a Virile National Life'.

of worshipping god, the various languages are all expressions of one great homogeneous solid Hindu people—the children of this motherland. Therefore, we say that in this land of ours, Bharat, the national life is of the Hindu People. In short, this is the Hindu nation.

The trouble is that by distinguishing dharma from religion and using that as the core content of Hinduism and Hindutva, by encasing it all as a way of life, we blind ourselves to the major cultural input of Muslims in the medieval age. I recall one RSS ideologue, many years ago, describing Muslims as Muslim Hindus, the latter being the pervasive category of person inhabiting the plains beyond the Indus River or the Sindhu (Hindu) River. But in that geographical definition, how does the land on the west bank of the river, as indeed Afghanistan, get included?

Even as celebrated champions of liberal secularism, like Jyotiraditya Scindia, take their 'mood of the people' strides and intellectuals like Prof. Faizan Mustafa rationalize choice in our times, the 100-day sit-in by women of various ages, octogenarians to little children, at Shaheen Bagh in south Delhi, sent a message across the globe, to the loud applause of lovers of democracy, that the Indian Constitution, and its Preamble of justice, liberty, equality and fraternity, is not negotiable at any cost.

Yet critics tell us that since we became free in 1947, any talk of freedom now is idle, misconceived, foolish or suspicious, if not patently seditious. Freedom is a bad word, even an ingredient of hate speech. That some people have persuaded courts to examine the alleged culpability of using the word 'freedom' in public speaks volumes for our system. Might it not be said that attempts to proscribe and impose sanctions on the use of the word is itself an extended form of violence against free speech? Getting the courts to collaborate, willingly or unwittingly, in that unwholesome enterprise itself is a sad dimension of our system.

Freedom, or *azadi*, is one word with multiple meanings. It was used in the national movement because of the illegitimate control and subjugation the British imposed on us. It has been used by some people in the North-east region and the Kashmir Valley to assert unwarranted claims of independence from the rest of us owing to an imagined sense of wrong. It has also been used by university students who seek to be unshackled from the restrictions and regulations they believe are unfairly imposed on them. Most recently, it has been used in the spontaneous anti-CAA/NPR/NRC protests to highlight constitutional values enshrined in the Preamble. Besides the fear and varying levels of social isolation that the COVID-19 pandemic has caused, it has left people with an urge to attain freedom from it. On a less serious note, the BJP leadership seeks similar freedom from the presence of the Congress on the political map of India!

Freedom, then, is essentially getting rid of things one believes to be bad or restrictive towards one's endeavour to realize the full potential of their personal attributes and aspirations. But one person's meat is another's poison; the freedom fighter for some is a secessionist or even a terrorist for others. Many such conundrums get resolved by one side winning and the other losing. But where in the nature of things winning and losing cannot be absolute or permanent, we need to find ways of accommodating and learning to live together; to accept defeat or disappointment till fortunes and tables can be turned.

But of course, majority verdicts cannot be the control moderator for the extent and quality of one's freedom, or else that cherished right will mean nothing. Electoral majorities cannot decide what people's rights are; it is the Constitution which does. Lest we forget, rights must belong to all, and they become even more meaningful when they are denied. It is natural that this happens more often where minority rights are involved, and that is the reason that liberal constitutions have a separate section on minority rights. As a category, minority is not necessarily limited to religion but includes language, subcultures, political opinions, etc.

The Preamble speaks of justice, liberty, equality and fraternity. For what it's worth, liberty comes even before equality (strikingly resonant of Rawls's principles of justice). Furthermore, what is liberty but freedom or azadi? People who question the right to freedom are surely defying and denigrating, even desecrating, our noble Constitution. Having the audacity to bring such unwholesome propositions to court, they are also abusing the legal process and deserve an appropriate reprimand from the court.

The tragedy is that they are ignorant of the essence of our Independence movement. We might we tell them of Josh Malihabadi (1894–1982), who, as *shayar-e-inqilaab* or the poet of revolution, wrote:

*Kaam hai mera taghayyar, naam hai mera shabab,*
*Mera naara, inqilaab o inqilaab o inqilaab.*

(My work is change, my name is youth,
My slogan is revolution, revolution, revolution.)

Or of the great Altaf Hussain (1837–1914), who adopted the pen name of Hali (the contemporary) and whose poem 'Hub-e-Watan' (Patriotism) was very popular with children:

*Teri ek musht-e-khaak ke badle,*
*Luun naa hargis agar bahisht mile.*

(In exchange of one fistful of your dust,
Even paradise would I inevitably refuse.)

Bismil Azimabadi's verse, written in 1921, became the cry of a generation of revolutionaries, like Bhagat Singh, Raj Guru and Sukhdev, even as they marched to the gallows:

*Sarfaroshi ki tamanna ab hamaare dil mein hai,*
*Dekhna hai zor kitna baazu-e-qatil mein hai.*

(In my heart I nurse the desire to sacrifice my life,
To see what power the hand of executioner holds.)

Then came Chandrashekhar Azad's (1906–1931) unforgettable lines that stir the soul even today:

*Dushman ki goliyon ka hum saamna karenge,*
*Azaad hi rahe hain, azaad hi rahenge.*

(The enemy's bullets we shall resolutely face,
Free we were and free we shall remain.)

'Inquilab Zindabad', coined by the poet Hasrat Mohani (1875–1951) in 1921, as a call against the British, became an anthem for the freedom struggle. As did these lines:

*Rasm-e-jafa kaamyaab dekhiye kab tak rahe,*
*Hubb-e-watan mast-e-khwaab kab tak rahe,*
*Daulat-e-Hindustan qabzah-e-aghyar mein*
*Be adad o be hisaab dekhiye kab tak rahe!*

(How long will the norm of tyranny prevail, let us see,
Till when will love for our land remain a dream,
Hindustan's bounties are in the clutches of adversaries
But let us see how long unaccountable they will be!)

Brij Narain Chakbast (1882–1926) used his pen to inculcate patriotism in his fellow countrymen:

*Yeh khaak-e-Hind se paida hain josh ke aasaar,*
*Himalaya se uthe jaise abr-e-daryabaar.*

(Hark, from the dust of India is born this sense of passion,
As if from the Himalayas has risen a cloudburst.)

These words, and many more like these, are part of our identity
and self-esteem. People who do not know this need to be chastised
for their ignorance and betrayal of India's ethos. Better still, they
might be sent for re-education to relieve the country of the burden
of their vacuous thinking.

# Seven

# The Law of Unforgiven Past, Unforgiving Present

Everyone knows that the Babri Masjid was built during the reign of Emperor Babur around 1528, although there is some ambiguity about which of the generals actually built it. Although the court found that no evidence was produced of namaz having been performed at the mosque between 1528 and 1856, it seems difficult to believe that this would have been the case during the successive reigns of several Mughal emperors, including Akbar and Aurangzeb (the two ends of the ideological spectrum).

It is another matter that, with Mughal rule on the wane and Oudh under the British, disputes arose between the Hindu and Muslim communities. The court made note of the first such clash, which happened in 1857. It is ironic that the most divisive conflict of recent times should be situated in this high point of Hindu–Muslim unity, during what is described as the First War of Independence, under the ageing Mughal emperor Bahadur Shah Zafar. The definitive recent history of the disputed structure is captured in the Ayodhya judgment:

53.    **In 1856–7, a communal riot took place**. Historical accounts indicate that the conflagration had its focus at Hanumangarhi and the Babri mosque. Some of those accounts indicate that prior to the incident, Muslims and Hindus alike had access to the area of the mosque for the purpose of worship . . . The incident led to the setting up of a railing made of a grill-brick wall outside the mosque . . . The **setting up of the railing was not a determination of propriety rights over the inner and outer courtyards**, the measure having been adopted to maintain peace between the communities . . .

53.1.  On 28-11-1858 a report was submitted by Sheetal Dubey who was the Thanedar, Oudh. The report spoke of an incident during which Hawan and Puja was organised inside the mosque by a Nihang Sikh who had erected a religious symbol. The report states:

Today Mr. Nihang Singh Faqir Khalsa resident of Punjab, organised Hawan and Puja of Guru Gobind Singh and erected a symbol of Sri Bhagwan, within the premises of the Masjid. At the time of pitching the symbol, 25 Sikhs were posted there for security . . .

[. . .]

53.9.  Aggarwal, J. has alluded to the . . . documentary evidence including in particular, the application of the Moazzin dated 30-11-1858 . . . Justice Agarwal has noted that the genuineness of this document has not been disputed by the plaintiff in the suit or of it having been written by a person whose identity was not disputed. The learned Judge held that the document contains admissions which prove that Hindus had continuously offered prayers inside the disputed building including the inner courtyard and at Ramchabutra and Sita Rasoi in the outer courtyard. However, during the course of the proceedings Mr Mohd. Nizamuddin Pasha, learned counsel for the plaintiffs in Suit 4 has challenged the translation of the exhibit.

[. . .]

53.12. On 29-11-1885, a suit was instituted in the court of the Munsif, Faizabad by Mahant Raghubar Das, describing himself as 'Mahant Janmasthan at Ayodhya' . . .

53.13. The . . . suit was dismissed by the Sub-Judge on 24-121885. The Trial Court held that:

(a) The Chabutra was in possession of the plaintiff, which was not disputed by the second defendant;

[. . .]

(d) **The divide was made to so that Muslims could offer prayers inside and the Hindus outside;**

[. . .]

This was a critical finding of the court that played an important role in its reasoning. Essentially, this provided the basis for distinguishing the possessory rights of the Hindu party from those of the Muslims.

The court had earlier given the historical backdrop that is useful if we want to understand the context of the dispute:

2. **This Court is tasked with the resolution of a dispute whose origins are as old as the idea of India itself. The events associated with the dispute have spanned the Mughal empire, colonial rule and the present constitutional regime. Constitutional values form the cornerstone of this nation and have facilitated the lawful resolution of the present title dispute through forty-one days of hearings before this Court . . .**

[. . .]

8. These suits [i.e. Suit Nos 1, 3, 4, the leading suit, while No. 2 was withdrawn on 18 September 1990] together with a separate suit by Hindu worshippers [i.e. Suit No. 5] were transferred by the Allahabad High Court to itself for trial from the civil court at Faizabad [on 10 July 1989 to be heard by a bench of three judges]. The High Court rendered a judgment in original proceedings arising out of the four suits and these appeals arise out of the decision of a Full Bench dated 30 September 2010. The High Court held that the suits filed by the Sunni Central Waqf Board and by Nirmohi Akhara were barred by limitation. Despite having held that those two suits were barred by time, **the High Court held in a split 2:1 verdict that the Hindu and Muslim parties were joint holders of the disputed premises. Each of them was held entitled to one third of the disputed property. The Nirmohi Akhara was granted the remaining one third. A preliminary decree to that effect was passed in the suit brought by the idol and the birth-place of Lord Ram through the next friend.**

[. . .]

10. The disputed site has been a flash point of continued conflagration over decades. In 1856–57, riots broke out between Hindus and Muslims in the vicinity of the structure. The colonial government attempted to raise a buffer between the two communities to maintain law and order by setting up a grill-brick wall having a height of six or seven feet. This would divide the premises into two parts: the inner portion which would be used by the Muslim community and the outer portion or courtyard, which would be used by the Hindu community . . .

[. . .]

24. The Central Government acquired an area of about 68 ac, including the premises in dispute, by a legislation called the

Acquisition of Certain Area at Ayodhya Act 1993 ('Ayodhya Acquisition Act 1993'). Sections 3 and 4 envisaged the abatement of all suits which were pending before the High Court . . .

25. [. . .] The decision of a Constitution Bench of this Court, titled Dr M Ismail Faruqui v Union of India held Section 4(3), which provided for the abatement of all pending suits as unconstitutional. The rest of the Act of 1993 was held to be valid. The Constitution Bench declined to answer the Presidential reference and, as a result, all pending suits and proceedings in relation to the disputed premises stood revived . . . The conclusions arrived at by the Constitution Bench are extracted below:

[. . .]

(2) **Irrespective of the status of a mosque under the Muslim law applicable in the Islamic countries, the status of a mosque under the Mahomedan Law applicable in secular India is the same and equal to that of any other place of worship of any religion;** and it does not enjoy any greater immunity from acquisition in exercise of the sovereign or prerogative power of the State, than that of the places of worship of the other religions.

[. . .]

(4) The vesting of the said disputed area in the Central Government by virtue of Section 3 of the Act is limited, as a statutory receiver with the duty for its management and administration according to Section 7 requiring maintenance of status quo therein . . .

[. . .]

(6) The vesting of the adjacent area, other than the disputed area, acquired by the Act in the Central Government by virtue of Section 3 of the Act is absolute with the power of management and administration thereof in accordance with sub-section (1) of Section 7 of the Act, till its further vesting in any authority or other body or trustees of any trust in accordance with Section 6 of the Act . . .

(8) Section 8 . . . does not apply to the disputed area, title to which has to be adjudicated in the suits and in respect of which the Central Government is merely the statutory receiver as indicated, with the duty to restore it to the owner in terms of the adjudication made in the suits.

[. . .]

[. . .]

28. On 30-9-2010, the Full Bench of the High Court comprising of Justice S.U. Khan, Justice Sudhir Agarwal and Justice D.V. Sharma delivered the judgment, which is in appeal. Justice S.U. Khan and Justice Sudhir Agarwal held—all the three sets of parties—Muslims, Hindus and Nirmohi Akhara—as joint holders of the disputed premises and allotted a one third share to each of them in a preliminary decree.

Justice Sudhir Aggarwal and Justice S.U. Khan, in effect, and for practical purposes, agreed on the aforementioned demarcation, even if their description varies somewhat:

28.2. Sudhir Aggrawal, J. . . . concluded with the following directions:

[. . .]

4566. [. . .] (i) It is declared that the area covered by the central dome of the three domed structure, i.e., the disputed structure being the deity of Bhagwan Ram Janamsthan and place of birth of Lord Rama as per faith and belief of the Hindus, belong to plaintiffs (Suit No. 5) and shall not be obstructed or interfered in any manner by the defendants . . .

(ii) The area within the inner courtyard . . . (excluding (i) above) belong to members of both the communities, i.e., Hindus (here plaintiffs, Suit No. 5) and Muslims since it was being used by both since decades and centuries. It is, however, made clear that for the purpose of share of plaintiffs, Suit No. 5 under this direction the area which is covered by (i) above shall also be included.

(iii) The area covered by the structures, namely, Ram Chabutra . . . Sita Rasoi . . . and Bhandar . . . in the outer courtyard is declared in the share of Nirmohi Akhara . . . and they shall be entitled to possession thereof in the absence of any person with better title.

(iv) The open area within the outer courtyard . . . (except that covered by (iii) above) shall be shared by Nirmohi Akhara . . . and plaintiffs (Suit No. 5) since it has been generally used by the Hindu people for worship at both places

(iv-a) It is however made clear that the share of Muslim parties shall not be less than one-third (1/3) of the total area of the premises and if necessary it may be given some area of outer courtyard. It is also made clear that while making partition by metes and bounds, if some minor adjustments are to be made with respect to the share of different parties, the affected party may be compensated by allotting the requisite land from the area which is under acquisition of the Government of India.

(v)    The land which is available with the Government of India acquired under Ayodhya Act 1993 for providing it to the parties who are successful in the suit for better enjoyment of the property shall be made available to the above concerned parties in such manner so that all the three parties may utilize the area to which they are entitled to, by having separate entry for egress and ingress of the people without disturbing each other's rights. For this purpose the concerned parties may approach the Government of India who shall act in accordance with the above directions and also as contained in the judgment of Apex Court in Ismail Farooqi.

(vi)   A decree, partly preliminary and partly final, to the effect as said above . . . is passed. Suit No. 5 is decreed in part to the above extent. The parties are at liberty to file their suggestions for actual partition of the property in dispute in the manner as directed above by metes and bounds by submitting an application to this effect to the Officer on Special Duty, Ayodhya Bench at Lucknow or the Registrar, Lucknow Bench, Lucknow, as the case may be.

[. . .]

Justice S.U. Khan found the three parties, i.e., Muslims, Hindus and Nirmohi Akhara, to be joint title-holders of the property, to the extent of one-third, but with the Hindu party to be allotted the portion below the central dome and the Nirmohi Akhara the part with the Ram Chabutra and Dita Rasoi.

Justice D.V. Sharma dissented from the view of his fellow judges and held that[*]:

---

[*] D.V. Sharma, judgment in OOS No. 5/1989 (RS No. 2–50), High Court of Judicature at Allahabad, Lucknow Bench, Lucknow.

> It is manifestly established by public record, gazetteers, history
> accounts and oral evidence that the premises in dispute is the
> place where Lord Ram was born as son of Emperor Dashrath of
> Solar Dynasty. According to the traditions and faith of devotees
> of Lord Ram, the place where He manifested Himself has ever
> been called as Sri Ram Janmabhumi by all and sundry through
> ages.

The high court judgments have now merged with the Supreme
Court judgment, but it is important to keep in mind that the
Supreme Court steered carefully through the copious findings in
partially accepting or rejecting them. In the process, a great deal
of attention was given to the analysis of Justice Sudhir Agarwal,
known for his strong opinions. It therefore merits a serious look.

To begin with, Justice Agarwal could not persuade himself
that the disputed structure was built by or under instructions of
Emperor Babur, as recorded in the judgment of the Allahabad
High Court:*

1645. The building in dispute, therefore, not constructed in 1528 AD
or during the reign of Babar, the preponderance of probability lie
in favour of the period when Aurangzeb was the Emperor since it
is again nobody's case that such an action could have been taken
during the reign of Humaun, Akbar or Shahjahan. Without entering
into the wild goose chase on this aspect suffice it to say that the
building in dispute must have come into existence before 1707 AD
when the reign of Aurangzeb ended on his death. Tieffenthaler's visit
to Ayodhya is 35–55 years thereafter and this gave sufficient time in
which the things as we have indicated above could have happened.
The inscription on the disputed building either inside or outside
was not there otherwise there was no occasion that the same could

---

* Judgment in OOS No. 4/1989 (RS No. 12/1961), 'Sunni Board of Waqfs and
Ors vs Shri Gopal Singh Visharad and Ors'.

not have been noticed and seen by Tieffenthaler who himself was quite conversant with the language in which these inscriptions were written and found subsequently.

[. . .]

1679. **In the above facts and circumstance, it is difficult to record a finding that the building in dispute was constructed in 1528 AD by or at the command of Babar since no reliable material is available for coming to the said conclusion.** On the contrary the preponderance of probability shows that the building in dispute was constructed some later point of time and the inscriptions thereon was fixed further later but exact period of the two is difficult to ascertain.

[. . .]

1682. It is a matter of further probe by Historians and others to find out other details after making an honest and independent inquiry into the matter. The three issues, therefore, are answered as under:

[. . .]

    (B) **Issue No. 1(a) (Suit-4) is answered in negative.** The plaintiffs have failed to prove that the building in dispute was built by Babar. Similarly defendant no.13 has also failed to prove that the same was built by Mir Baqi. The further question as to when it was built and by whom cannot be replied with certainty since neither there is any pleadings nor any evidence has been led nor any material has been placed before us to arrive at a concrete finding on this aspect. However, applying the principle of informed guess, we are of the view that the building in dispute may have

been constructed, probably, between 1659 to 1707 AD i.e.
during the regime of Aurangzeb.

[. . .]

2104. **We have no hesitation in holding and recording our finding
that under the central dome of the disputed building, idols were
kept in the night of 22nd/23rd December, 1949.**

* * *

Justice Agarwal then digressed into the area of faith and how the
absence of concrete evidence does not come in the way of accepting
that something existed in ancient times.

4382. May be on account of non availability of the reliable feedback
some of the aspects of Hindu scriptures are termed by others as
Myth, legend, epic etc., doubting its historicity, ignoring the fact
that the common people are so deep embedded in blood that it
is beyond imagination for them to even think of a situation where
those faith and belief can be termed as a mere fiction and not a
matter of historicity. For example, the two of the world's biggest
works known as 'Ramayana' and 'Mahabharatha' of Hindu scriptures,
other people started to call it 'Epic' and that we have followed since
the days of British India and now also. Initially the European writers
in their own understanding find it unthinkable even the existence of
such an antique society and culture and that too so perfect and so
well defined, sophisticated, but complicated in different facets. With
the passage of time the thoughts and approach have undergone a
sea of change and now we find quite a sectionable intelligentsia who
is changing its views and that is not merely on some kind of altered
hypothesis etc., but due to the cemented, reliable information,
they have collected in the meantime. In brief, it can be said that
merely because I am not able to trace my history of succession it will
not mean that I do not have a chain of succession. One's inability

in finding something cannot result in a conclusion that actually nothing existed. There has to be much more. The mathematical, astronomical calculation of the learned people in ancient India have been found to be reasonably correct though they are presumed to lack so called advanced technology for arriving at such conclusions. It is easy to discard something at the threshold but difficult to find reason and logic behind its existence. Difficulty cannot be a reason to opt for an easier method instead of the cumbersome one. If Indian culture and society could have survived for such a long time even though other ancient cultures, whether Egyptian, Greek or Roman have lost behind the time, then one has to find out the reason for its sustenance. It cannot be brushed aside loosely. This is a kind of approach, thoughts, faith and belief of one part of the litigants before us and their contemporary opponent wants in existence of positive material irrespective of the time and antiquity [the] matter relates to. The reason being that the issue has been brought in a Court of law which is presently governed by the system we have inherited from a totally different culture i.e. British legacy where they have told us to decide the dispute only on getting evidence and not otherwise. The issues relating to faith and belief and that too, which had continued from generations to generations, from hundreds and thousands [of] years neither depend on the so called existence of evidence nor one can shake such custom which they have received by tradition for want of evidence. It is not totally a different concept and notion, independent in its own ways. In the erstwhile territory of India, before entry of the far east people or from other parts of world it appears that natives had their own traditions, system, faith and belief, and the society had different kinds of religious concept. The subsequent scholars tried to bifurcate this religious system of ancient India into that of Aryan and Dravidian but what we find is that barring a few differences in the matter of system of worship etc., the core belief and faith remained same. The entire society remained connected with a common thread of religious faith. This difference, more or less, was political. It is in this system, where we find the people in ancient India believed in the Avtaars of God which found mention in Vedic texts. All these Avtaars in one or the other way we find had a specific objective and ultimately helped to save the world, human being[s] and other creatures and also to guide the living being in lives, some are to attract the people back to the spiritual domain.

[. . .]

4388. If history as written about construction of the disputed structure by Mir Baki in 1528 AD can depend solely on two inscriptions, which nobody knew whether installed by Mir Baki himself or came into being as a result of any subsequent manipulation, we fail to understand why something written almost two and half century ago by a person who was well conversant in the local languages at that time, whose motive in writing those facts is not doubted, ought not to be believed. Further it may be considered in the light that some facts were written by different people after about 40 or 50 years from the visit of Tieffenthaler having no knowledge of his work. They also repeated except of the distinction that this time they refer to an inscription also relying whereon the local belief was discarded by them, i.e., Martin's Eastern India (supra).

[. . .]

4410. In other words, the precise issue, in terms of the 'birthplace', as we could understand, is in the following terms:

I.   According to faith and belief of Hindus, a particular smallest area in Ayodhya which they treat as the sanctum sanctorum i.e. 'Garbh Grah' that is where Lord Rama was born.

II.  A temple constructed in the area which included sanctum sanctorum and the place covered by that temple which is termed as 'Janam Bhumi temple' or 'Ram Janam Bhumi temple.

III.  There is a complete unanimity amongst all Hindu parties
      as also deposed by their witnesses that under the central
      dome lie the sanctum sanctorum, i.e. 'Garbh-Grah' since
      lord Rama was born thereat and it was part of a bigger holy
      structure, i.e., a temple, which was constructed and known
      as 'Janam Bhumi temple' or 'Ram Janam Bhumi temple'
      which included the rest of the area occupied by the disputed
      structure.

[. . .]

4521. We have already held that there existed a religious place of
[n]on-Islamic character before the construction of the disputed
structure. From the travel account of William Finch it is also evident
that Hindus were worshipping in the Fort of Lord Rama, as he called
it, when he visited Ayodhya between 1608 to 1611 AD. It is not the
case of the Muslim parties that in that Fort of Lord Rama, besides
the place in dispute, there was any other place known as place of
birth of Lord Rama which the people used to worship at that time or
thereafter also. The disputed structure, as we have already noticed,
came into being after the visit of William Finch but before the visit of
[F]ather Joseph Tieffenthaler. He (Tieffenthaler) has also mentioned
about the worship at the premises in dispute by Hindus during his
visit, and, from the description he has given, we are satisfied that the
said worship must have been near the structure itself. The cumulative
effect of these facts as also the discussion we have already made in
respect of various issues above, leaves no doubt in our mind that
even before the construction of the building in dispute, the place
which the Hindus believed the place of birth of Lord Rama, used to
be worship[ped]. We have also held that according to faith, belief
and tradition amongst Hindus it is the area covered under the central
dome of the disputed structure which they believe to be the place of
birth of Lord Rama and worship thereat continuously. Therefore, in
the absence of anything otherwise, it can safely be said that only this

was the part of the property in dispute which was used as a place of worship by Hindus immediately prior to the construction of the building in question. To this extent the first part of the issue under consideration is answered in affirmative.

[. . .]

4541. Be that as it may, before us, firstly, neither any evidence has been placed to show that Mir Baqi in fact existed during the regime of Babar, and, then nothing is there to prove about his religion, what it was. Some observations here and there by some writers and that too on sheer guess work would not be sufficient for this Court to investigate into this factual position which relates back to an alleged event of almost 500 years back. Moreover, we have already held that the building in question has not been proved to have been constructed in 1528 AD by Mir Baqi. Therefore the question, whether it was a Sunni waqf or Shia waqf becomes redundant. Moreover, the rights of Hindus would in no manner be affected whether the building in dispute, if mosque, constitute a 'Sunni Waqf' or 'Shia Waqf' since the consequence, if any, would flow in the same way and would be equal in both the cases.

[. . .]

4559. Plaintiffs have sought a declaration that the entire premises described vide Annexures- 1, 2 and 3 belonged to the plaintiffs' deities and also a permanent injunction against the defendants prohibiting them from interfering with or raising any objection to or placing any restriction on the construction of the new temple at Sri Ram Janambhumi Ayodhya. We have already held that the area under the central dome of the disputed construction believed and worshipped by the Hindu people as the place of birth of Lord Rama and they were worshiping thereat since time immemorial. This part of the land constitutes deity, 'Sri Ram Janamsthan', and a place of special significance for Hindus. Therefore it has to be treated In a manner where the very right of worship of Hindus of place of birth of Lord Rama is not extinguished or otherwise interfered with. We have simultaneously held that so far as other land within the inner courtyard of the disputed structure is concerned, this open land had been continuously used by members of both the communities for their respective prayers and worship for decades and centuries.

\* \* \*

Although the governments of Uttar Pradesh and the Centre were very nervous on the eve of the high court's judgment on 30 September 2010, there was virtually no reaction in any camp. Gradually, as expected, appeals were filed by all parties. It seemed the best solution in the circumstances, even if there were questions as to how the court could have partitioned property when there were no pleadings to that effect or relief claimed. It is anyone's guess whether that would have worked, but as we will see with the Supreme Court judgment, the basis for the high court relief was unsustainable in the eyes of the law.

# Eight

# Lord Ram in Their Lordships' Temple of Justice

Even as the Supreme Court assembled for hearing the Ayodhya case, Dr Rajiv Dhawan sought to have the matter heard by five judges, in view of paragraph 82 of the Ismail Faruqui judgment holding that mosques were not integral to Islam.[*] A three-judge bench, by a majority of two to one,[†] rejected the plea that the appeals against the impugned judgment be referred to a larger bench. The issue raised was about the essential features of religion, and who could decide upon such a question? Furthermore, the court had to decide whether the earlier decision was per curiam and yet affected the decision in the suits under appeal.

Dr Dhawan based his arguments on the following propositions:

The observations about the essential character of a mosque to Islam have been widely relied upon by the high court and

---

[*] 'Dr M. Ismail Faruqui and Others vs Union of India and Others', AIR 1995 SC 605A; (1994) 6 SCC 360.

[†] 'M Siddiq (D) Thr Lrs vs Mahant Suresh Das & Ors', 2019, 18 SCC 631.

therefore must be placed in correct perspective before the appeals are heard.

The Shirur Mutt case* does not make a distinction between essential and integral part of religion that has crept in the two judgments that follow the Mutt case.

The findings in Ismail Faruqui are not res judicata because they were not on the identical issues framed in the suits.

The majority of Chief Justice Dipak Misra and Justice Ashok Bhushan (with Justice S. Abdul Naseer partly dissenting) while looking at the issue before it stated[†]:

143.  At this juncture, it is also pertinent to note the observations in Sri Adi Visheshwara of Kashi Vishwanath Temple, Varanasi v. State of U.P., (1997) 4 SCC 606, at paragraph 28, where it is stated:

'. . . The concept of essentiality is not itself a determinative factor. It is one of the circumstances to be considered in adjudging whether the particular matters of religion or religious practices or belief are an integral part of the religion. It must be decided whether the practices or matters are considered integral by the community itself. Though not conclusive, this is also one of the facets to be noticed. The practice in question is religious in character and whether it could be regarded as an integral and essential part of the religion and if the court finds upon evidence adduced before

---

* 'Commissioner, Hindu Religious Endowments, Madras vs Sri Lakshmindra Thirtha Swamiar of Sri Shirur Mutt', 1954, SCR 1005; AIR 1954 SC 282. This landmark case first laid down the test of Essential Religious Practices, holding that what constitutes the essential part of a religion is primarily to be ascertained with reference to the doctrines of that religion itself.
† 'Ismail Faruqui' (supra), [143], p. 706.

it that it is an integral or essential part of the religion, Article 25 accords protection to it.'

The court further noted that in paragraph 82 of the judgment of Ismail Faruqui. the constitutional bench summarized the position as under:*

82. **The correct position may be summarised thus. Under the Mahomedan Law applicable in India, title to a mosque can be lost by adverse possession (See Mulla's Principles of Mahomedan Law, 19th Edn., by M. Hidayatullah - Section 217; and Shahid Ganj v. Shiromani Gurdwara. If that is the position in law, there can be no reason to hold that a mosque has a unique or special status, higher than that of the places of worship of other religions in secular India to make it immune from acquisition by exercise of the sovereign or prerogative power of the State. A mosque is not an essential part of the practice of the religion of Islam and namaz (prayer) by Muslims can be offered anywhere, even in open.** Accordingly, its acquisition is not prohibited by the provisions in the Constitution of India. Irrespective of the status of a mosque in an Islamic country for the purpose of immunity from acquisition by the State in exercise of the sovereign power, its status and immunity from acquisition in the secular ethos of India under the Constitution is the same and equal to that of the places of worship of the other religions, namely, church, temple etc. It is neither more nor less than that of the places of worship of the other religions. Obviously, the acquisition of any religious place is to be made only in unusual and extraordinary situations for a larger national purpose keeping in view that such acquisition should not result in extinction of the right to practise the religion, if the significance of that place be such. Subject to this condition, the power of

---

* 'M. Siddiq', 2019, (supra), [129], at p. 700.

acquisition is available for a mosque like any other place of worship of any religion. The right to worship is not at any and every place, so long as it can be practised effectively, unless the right to worship at a particular place is itself an integral part of that right.

The majority further noted the petitioners' contention that the **'law laid down in Ismail Faruqui case in relation to praying in a mosque not being an essential practice is contrary to the law relating to essential practice and the process by which essential practice is to be considered'.** In response the court stated that:

> [T]he observations as made by the constitution bench in paragraphs 78 and 82 which have been questioned by the petitioners are observations made in reference to acquisition of place of worship and has to confine to the issue of acquisition of place of worship only and the observation need not be read broadly to hold that a mosque can never be an essential part of the practice of the religion of Islam.[†]

Counsel for some of the parties argued that '[t]he case being very important and appeals having been filed by all the sides, the case [was] of such a magnitude that it [was] appropriate that matter be referred to a Bench of a larger strength to consider the case'.[‡] The court, before dealing with these submissions, noted the constitutional provision regarding reference of a case for hearing by the constitution bench, more specifically the proviso to Article 145(3):

> Provided that, where the Court hearing an appeal under any of the provisions of this Chapter other than Article 132

---

* Ibid., at [10], p. 650.
† Ibid., at [61], p. 671.
‡ Ibid., at [99], p. 688.

consists of less than five judges and in the course of the hearing
of the appeal the Court is satisfied that the appeal involves a
substantial question as to the interpretation of this Constitution
the determination of which is necessary for the disposal of the
appeal, such Court shall refer the question to a Court constituted
as required by this clause for the purpose of deciding any case
involving such a question and shall on receipt of the opinion
dispose of the appeal in conformity with such opinion.

Finally, the majority decided against referring the matter to a
constitutional bench:

> **Normally appeals arising out of suits are placed before a
> bench of two judges but looking to the importance of the
> matter, the present appeals have already been placed before
> three judge bench. Reference to constitution Bench of five
> judges to reconsider the constitution bench judgment in
> Ismail Faruqui case cannot be accepted.***

Justice Naseer took a somewhat different view and held:

> **150.  Hence, it is clear that the questionable observations in Ismail
> Faruqui have certainly permeated the impugned judgment.
> Thus, the impugned judgment can be claimed to be both
> expressly and inherently affected by the questionable
> observations made in Ismail Faruqui. Further, Ismail Faruqui
> prima facie leads a different approach regarding the
> application of essential and/or integral test which also needs
> to be resolved as a matter of constitutional significance. In
> my view, Ismail Faruqui needs to be brought in line with
> the authoritative pronouncements in Shirur Mutt and other**

---

* Ibid., at [114], p. 696.

decisions referred to in paragraphs 14 to 18 and 20 of this judgment.*

155.   Considering the Constitutional importance and significance of the issues involved, the following need to be referred to a larger Bench:

155.1 Whether in the light of Shirur Mutt and other aforementioned cases, an essential practice can be decided without a detailed examination of the beliefs, tenets and practice of the faith in question?

155.2 Whether the test for determining the essential practice is both essentiality and integrality?

155.3 Does Article 25 only protect belief and practices of particular significance of a faith or all practices regarded by the faith as essential?

155.4 Do Articles 15, 25 and 26 (read with Article 14) allow the comparative significance of faiths to be undertaken?

[. . .]

155.6 The Registry is directed to place this matter before the Hon'ble Chief Justice of India for appropriate orders.†

His lordship, in arriving at this opinion, was mindful of several other matters where the importance of a view on Nikah Halala and female genital mutilation was held to require examination by a constitutional bench.

In the Shirur Mutt case, the court had held that 'what constitutes the essential part of religion is primarily to be as ascertained with the reference to the doctrines of that religion itself'.‡ It also observed that:

---

* Ibid., at [150], p. 716.
† Ibid., at [155], p. 718.
‡ Shirur Mutt Case (supra), at [20].

17. [. . .] A religion undoubtedly has its basis in a system of beliefs or doctrines which are regarded by those who profess that religion as conducive to their spiritual well being, but it would not be correct to say that religion is nothing else but a doctrine or belief.

[. . .]

23. [. . .] Under article 26(b), therefore, a religious denomination or organization enjoys complete autonomy in the matter of deciding as to what rites and ceremonies are essential according to the tenets of the religion they hold and no outside authority has any jurisdiction to interfere with their decision in such matters.[*]

Despite the judgment that the matter need not be placed before five judges the new chief justice, Ranjan Gogoi, by an administrative order dated 8 January 2019, made pursuant to the provisions of Order VI Rule 1 of the Supreme Court Rules, 2013, constituted a five-judge bench to hear the appeals. On 10 January 2019, the registry was directed to inspect the records and, if required, engage official translators. On 8 March 2019, a panel of mediators—comprising (i) Justice Fakkir Mohamed Ibrahim Kalifulla, a former judge of this court; (ii) Sri Sri Ravi Shankar; and (iii) Sriram Panchu, senior advocate—was constituted in the hope that a settlement will be reached.

The mediation process was moved away from the politically hot national capital to Ayodhya where five sessions took place before the scene shifted back to Delhi for another three sessions. At one point it seemed that a settlement was imminent, and it was assumed that Maulana Arshad Madani, of the Majlis-e-Ulema-e-Hind, would support it. But under pressure from other

---

[*] Ibid.

quarters, he finally opted to fall back on court proceedings and the mediation failed.

When the Allahabad High Court judgment was delivered, there was an indication that by and large all parties were happy, or equally unhappy, about the outcome. The preparations made to prevent untoward public reactions seemed unnecessary as silence greeted the judgment. Appeals were inevitable and, finally, several were filed. Although this was an unprecedented first appeal from the high court as trial court and was being heard by a bench of three judges instead of two, it was finally heard by five judges, despite the fact that the court under Chief Justice Dipak Misra, speaking through Justice Ashok Bhushan, had rejected the arguments of the 'Muslim side' to have it heard by five judges. As noted above, the argument to have it heard by five judges was made by Dr Rajeev Dhawan to try and overcome the hurdle of the findings in the Faruqui case that a mosque is not an essential part of Islam.

Interestingly, although the court laboured to emphasize that it was dealing with a title suit and had nothing to do with religion, the backdrop of essential features of religion and therefore our understanding of religion might well have influenced the final decision, particularly if the addenda are to be taken seriously. We may therefore take a detour here to consider the law on this issue.

To consider the essential features of a religion it is important to understand the concept of religion to begin with. Since Articles 25 and 26 guarantee religious freedom, the Supreme Court has had to deal with the issue for decades. The Constitution does not define 'religion' and leaves it to concerned entities to rely upon their instincts. Discussion, as reflected in the various judgments, focuses on distinguishing religion per se from a religious denomination. This is all a far cry from scholarship on the subject in the West, such as the provocative book *Religion without God*, published by Ronald Dworkin just before his untimely death.[*] The book is described thus by the publisher: 'The conviction that God underwrites value presupposes a prior commitment to the independent reality of that value—a commitment that is available to nonbelievers as well. So theists share a commitment with some atheists that is more fundamental than what divides them. Freedom of religion should flow not from a respect for belief in God but from the right to ethical independence.' If this thesis were to be accepted by the Supreme Court, the approach to Articles 25 and 26 might be radically modified.

An erudite exposition of the meaning of religion is to be found in the case of S.P. Mittal v Union of India.[†] Justice Chinnappa Reddy (partly dissenting on other issues) held:

2.   Quite a considerable part of the hearing of the petitions was devoted to a debate on the question, **what is Religion?** Religion: Everyone has a religion, or at least, a view or a window on religion, be he a bigot or simple believer, philosopher or pedestrian, atheist or agnostic. **Religion, like 'democracy' and 'equality' is an elusive expression,** which everyone understands according to his preconceptions. What is religion to some is pure dogma to others and what is religion to others is pure superstition to some others. Karl Marx in his contribution to the Critique of Hegel's Philosophy of Law described religion as the 'Opium of the people'. He said further, 'Basically religion is a very convenient sanctuary for bourgeois thought to flee to in times of stress'. Bertrand Russell, in his essay 'Why I Am Not a Christian', said, 'Religion is based, I think, primarily and mainly upon fear. It is partly the terror of the unknown and partly, as I have said, the wish to feel that you have a kind of elder brother, who will stand by you in all your troubles and disputes.

---

[*] Ronald Dworkin, *Religion without God*, Harvard University Press, 2013.
[†] 'S.P. Mittal vs Union of India and Others', 1983, *1 SCC 51*.

Fear is the basis of the whole thing – fear of the mysterious, fear of defeat, fear of death. Fear is the parent of cruelty, and, therefore, it is no wonder if cruelty and religion have gone hand in hand. As a worshipper at the altar of peace, I find it difficult to reconcile myself to religion, which throughout the ages, has justified war calling it a dharma yuddha, a jehad or a crusade. I believe that by getting mixed up with religion, ethics has lost 'much of its point, much of its purpose and a major portion of its spontaneity'. I apprehend I share the views of those who have neither faith nor belief in religion and who consider religion as entirely unscientific and irrational. Chanting of prayer appears to me to be mere jingoism and observance of ritual, plain superstition. But my views about religion, my prejudices and my predilections, if they be such, are entirely irrelevant. So are the views of the credulous, the fanatic, the bigot and the zealot. **So also the views of the faithful, the devout, the acharya, the moulvi, the padre and the bhikshu, each of whom may claim his as the only true or revealed religion. For our present purpose, we are concerned with what the people of the Socialist, Secular, Democratic Republic of India, who have given each of its citizens freedom of conscience and the right to freely profess, practise and propagate religion and who have given every religious denomination the right to freely manage its religious affairs, mean by the expressions 'religion' and 'religious denomination'.** We are concerned with what these expressions are designed to mean in Articles 25 and 26 of the Constitution. Any freedom or right involving the conscience must naturally receive a wide interpretation and the expression 'religion' and 'religious denomination' must therefore, be interpreted in no narrow, stifling sense but in a liberal, expansive way.

3.   Etymology is of no avail. Religion is derived from 'religare' which means 'to bind'. Etymologically, therefore, every bond between two people is a religion, but that is not true. To say so is only to

indulge in etymological deception. Quite obviously, religion is much more than a mere bond uniting people.

4.  **Quite obviously, again, religion is not to be confined to the traditional, established, well-known or popular religions like Hinduism, Mahomedanism, Buddhism and Christianity. There may be and, indeed, there are, in this vast country, several religions, less known or even unknown except in the remote corners or in the small pockets of the land where they may be practised.** A religion may not be widespread. It may have little following. It may not have even a name, as indeed most tribal religions do not have. We may only describe them by adding the suffix 'ism' to the name of the founder–teacher, the tribe, the area or the deity. The nomenclature is not of the essence. Again, a band of persons, large or small, may not be said to be adherents of a religion merely because they share some common beliefs and common interests and practise common rites and ceremonies; nor can pietistic recitation and solemn ritual combine to produce religion, on that account only. Secret societies dedicated to secular tasks and indulging in queer oaths and observances, guilds and groups of persons who meet but to dine and wine but who subject their members to extravagant initiation ceremonies, village and tribal sorcerers and coven of witches who chant, rant and dance in the most weird way possible are all far removed from religion. They appear to lack the 'spiritual connection'. But, all this is unsatisfactory. **We are not arriving at any definition of religion. We are only making peripheral journeys and not getting any nearer to the core of the problem presented to us.**

5.  Let us examine the relevant provisions of the Constitution for such light as they may throw on the meaning of the expressions 'religion' and 'religious denomination'. They are not defined. The word 'religion' does not occur in the Preamble to the Constitution, but the Preamble does promise to secure to its citizens 'Liberty of thought, expression, belief, faith and worship'. The freedom

of conscience and the right to profess, propagate and practise religion, flow out of the idea so expressed in the Preamble. In Part III of the Constitution, under the head 'Right to Freedom of Religion', there are four Articles. Article 25(1) guarantees to all persons, subject to public order, morality and health and to the other provisions of Part III of the Constitution, freedom of conscience and the right freely to profess, practise and propagate religion. Freedom of conscience is not to be separated from the right to profess, practise and propagate religion. They go together and together they form part of the Right to Freedom of Religion. Clause (2) of Article 25, however, stipulates that the freedom and the right guaranteed by Clause (1) shall not prevent the State from making any law regulating or restricting, any economic, financial, political or other secular activity which may be associated with religious practice, or to provide for social welfare and reform or to throw open Hindu religious institutions of a public character to all classes and sections of Hindus. So, the Article makes it clear that secular activity may be associated with religion, though the guarantee of the article does not extend to such activity. Article 26 guarantees that every religious denomination or any section thereof shall have the right, subject to public order, morality and health, to establish and maintain institutions for religious and charitable purposes, to manage its own affairs in matters of religion, to own and acquire moveable and immovable property and to administer such property in accordance with law. Article 27 prohibits compulsion for payment of taxes for promotion of any particular religion. Article 28 bars religious instruction in any institution wholly maintained out of State funds and prevents compulsion to attend any religious instruction or religious worship in educational institutions recognised by the State or receiving aid out of State funds.

6. **Apart from Articles 25 to 28, the word 'religion' occurs in Articles 15(1), 15(2), 16(2), 16(5), 23(2), 29(2) and 30 of the Constitution.**

7. Article 15(1) prescribes that the State shall not discriminate against any citizen on grounds only of religion, race, caste, sex, place of birth or any of them. Article 15(2) provides, in particular, that no citizen shall, on grounds only of religion, race, caste, sex, place of birth or any of them, be subject to any disability, liability, restriction or condition with regard to access to shops, public restaurants, hotels and places of public entertainment; or the use of wells, tanks, bathing ghats, roads and places of public resort maintained wholly or partly out of State funds or dedicated to the use of the general public.

8. Article 16(2) guarantees that no citizen shall, on grounds only of religion, race, caste, sex, descent, place of birth, residence or any of them, be ineligible for, or discriminated against in respect of, any employment or office under the State. Article 16(5) exempts from the right guaranteed under Article 16 the operation of any law which provides that the incumbent of an office in connection with the affairs of any religious or denominational institution or any member of the governing body thereof shall be a person professing a particular religion or belonging to a particular denomination.

9. Article 23(2), while enabling the State to impose compulsory service for public purposes, prohibits the State from making any discrimination on grounds only of religion, race, caste or class or any of them.

10. Article 29(2) provides that no citizen shall be denied admission to any educational institution maintained by the State or receiving aid out of State funds on grounds of religion, race, caste, language or any of them.

11. Article 30(1) guarantees to all minorities, whether based on religion or language the right to establish and administer educational institutions of their choice. Article 30(2) further provides that the State shall not, in granting aid to educational institutions, discriminate against any educational institutions on the ground that it is under the management of a minority, whether based on religion or language.

12. It is readily seen that the several provisions of the Constitution where the expressions 'religion' and 'religious denomination' are used are either those which are concerned with equality and equal opportunity or those which are concerned with freedom of religion. Article 15(1), Article 16(2), Article 23(2), Article 29(2) are the several equality and equal opportunity clauses of the Constitution which bar discrimination on the ground of religion, and they place religion in equation with race, caste, sex, place of birth, residence and language for the purposes of the various aspects of equality dealt with by them. Article 30 recognises the existence of minority groups based on religion along with minority groups based on language. Articles 25 to 28 deal with the Right to Freedom of Religion which, as we said earlier is traceable to the idea of 'Liberty of thought, expression, belief, faith and worship' in the Preamble to the Constitution. Article 25 guarantees freedom of conscience and the right freely to profess, practise and propagate religion, but saves laws regulating or restricting any economic, financial, political or other secular activity which may be associated with religious practice. Reading Article 25 in the background of the proclamation regarding Liberty in the Preamble to the Constitution, we may safely conclude that the Constitution views religion, as comprising thought, expression, belief, faith or worship, as involving the conscience and as something which may be professed, practised and propagated and which is any man's attribute in the same manner as race, sex, language, residence etc. We also see that economic, financial, political or other secular activity may be associated with religious practice though such activity is not covered by the guarantee of freedom of conscience and the right freely to profess, practise and propagate religion. **So, the Constitution considers religion as a matter of thought, expression, belief, faith and worship, a matter involving the conscience and a matter which may be professed, practised and propagated by anyone and which may even have some**

**secular activity associated with it.** We have already said that any freedom or right involving the conscience must naturally receive a wide interpretation and the expressions 'religion' and 'religious denomination' must, therefore, be interpreted in no narrow, stifling sense but in a liberal, expansive way.

[. . .]

20. **It is obvious that religion, undefined by the Constitution, is incapable of precise judicial definition either.** In the background of the provisions of the Constitution and the light shed by judicial precedent, we may say religion is a matter of faith. It is a matter of belief and doctrine. It concerns the conscience, i.e. the spirit of man. It must be capable of overt expression in word and deed, such as, worship or ritual. So, religion is a matter of belief and doctrine, concerning the human spirit, expressed overtly in the form of ritual and worship. Some religions are easily identifiable as religions; some are easily identifiable as not religions. There are many in the penumbral region which instinctively appear to some as religions and to others as not religions. There is no formula of general application. There is no knife-edge test. Primarily, it is a question of the consciousness of the community, how does the fraternity or sodality (if it is permissible to use the word without confining it to Roman Catholic groups) regard itself, how do others regard the fraternity or sodality. A host of other circumstances may have to be considered, such as, the origin and the history of the community, the beliefs and the doctrines professed by the community, the rituals observed by the community, what the founder, if any, taught, what the founder was understood by his followers to have taught, etc. In origin, the founder may not have intended to found any religion at all. He may have merely protested against some rituals and observances, he may have disagreed with the interpretation of some earlier religious tenets. What he said, what he preached

and what he taught, his protest, his dissent, his disagreement might have developed into a religion in the course of time, even during his lifetime. He may be against religion itself, yet, history and the perception of the community may make a religion out of what was not intended to be a religion and he may be hailed as the founder of a new religion. **There are the obvious examples of Buddhism and Jainism and for that matter Christianity itself. Neither Buddha, nor Mahavira, nor Christ ever thought of founding a new religion, yet three great religions bear their names.**

21. *If the word* 'religion' is once explained, though with some difficulty, the expression 'religious denomination' may be defined with less difficulty. As we mentioned earlier Mukherjea, J., borrowed the meaning of the word 'denomination' from the Oxford Dictionary and adopted it to define religious denomination as 'a collection of individuals classed together under the same name, a religious sect or body having a common faith and organisation and designated by a distinctive name'. The followers of Ramanuja, the followers of Madhwacharya, the followers of Vallabha, the Chishtia Soofies have been found or assumed by the Court to be religious denominations. It will be noticed that these sects possessed no distinctive name except that of their founder–teacher and had no special organisation except a vague, loose-un-knit one. The really distinctive feature about each one of these sects was a shared belief in the tenets taught by the teacher–founder. We take care to mention here that whatever the ordinary features of a religious denomination may be considered to be, all are not of equal importance and surely the common faith of the religious body is more important than the other features. It is, perhaps, necessary to say that judicial definitions are not statutory definitions; they are mere explanations, every word of which is not to be weighed in golden scales. Law has a tendency to harden with the passage of time and judicial pronouncements are made to assume the form

of statutory pronouncements. So soon as a word or expression occur in the statute is judicially defined, the tendency is to try to interpret the language employed by the judges in the judicial definition as if it has been transformed into a statutory definition. That is wrong. Always, words and expressions to be interpreted are those employed in the statute and not those used by judges for felicitous explanation. Judicial definition, we repeat, is explanatory and not definitive. One remark requires to be added here. Religious denomination has not to owe allegiance to any parent religion. The entire following of a religion may be no more than the religious denomination. This may particularly be so in the case of small religious groups or 'developing' religions, that is, religions in the formative stage.

* * *

Justice R.B. Misra wrote the main judgment (on behalf of Chief Justice Y.V. Chandrachud, Justice P.N. Bhagwati and Justice V. Balakrishna Eradi, J.J. and himself). The majority held as under:

39. The first two petitions under Article 32 of the Constitution of India filed in this Court and the third under Article 226 of the Constitution filed in the Calcutta High Court and later on transferred to this Court, seek to challenge the vires of the Auroville (Emergency Provisions) Ordinance, 1980 (Ordinance 19 of 1980), later on replaced by the Auroville (Emergency Provisions) Act, 1980 (Act 59 of 1980). The fourth is an appeal by special leave against the order of the Division Bench of the Calcutta High Court dated November 21, 1980 vacating the interim order passed by a Single Judge in the writ petition. All these cases raise common questions of constitutional importance and, therefore, they were posted before the Constitution Bench.

[. . .]

76. *In order to appreciate the contentions of the parties, it is necessary to know the implication of the* words 'religion' and 'religious denomination'. **The word 'religion' has not been defined in the Constitution and indeed it is a term which is hardly susceptible of any rigid definition. In reply to a question on Dharma by Yaksha, Dharmaraja Yudhisthira said thus:**

**'Tarko pratiṣṭhaḥ śrutayo vibhinnā**
**nāsau munir yasya matam na bhinnam**
**dharmasya tattvam nihitam guhāyām**
**mahājano yena gataḥ sa panthāḥ'**
**Mahabharata—Aranyakaparvan 313.117.**

(Formal logic is vacillating. Srutis are contradictory. There is no single rishi whose opinion is final. The principle of Dharma is hidden in a cave. The path of the virtuous persons is the only proper course.)

77. *The expression* 'Religion' has, however, been sought to be defined in Words and Phrases, Permanent Edn., 36-A, p. 461 onwards, as given below:

Religion is morality, with a sanction drawn from a future state of rewards and punishments.

The term 'religion' and 'religious' in ordinary usage are not rigid concepts.

**'Religion' has reference to one's views of his relations to his Creator and to the obligations they impose of reverence for his being and character, and of obedience to his will.**

**The word 'religion' in its primary sense (from 'religare', to rebind, bind back), imports, as applied to moral questions, only a recognition of a conscious duty to obey restraining principles of conduct. In such sense we suppose there is no one who will admit that he is without religion.**

**'Religion' is bond uniting man to God, and virtue whose purpose is to render God worship due him as source of all being and principle of all government of things.**

'Religion' has reference to man's relation to divinity; to the moral obligation of reverence and worship, obedience, and submission. It is the recognition of God as an object of worship, love and obedience; right feeling toward God, as highly apprehended.

'Religion' means the service and adoration of God or a god as expressed in forms of worship; an apprehension, awareness, or conviction of the existence of a Supreme Being; any system of faith, doctrine and worship, as the Christian religion, the religions of the Orient; a particular system of faith or worship.

The term 'religion' as used in tax exemption law, simply includes: (1) a belief, not necessarily referring to supernatural powers; (2) a cult, involving a gregarious association openly expressing the belief; (3) a system of moral practice directly resulting from an adherence to the belief; and (4) an organization within the cult designed to observe the tenets or belief, the content of such belief being of no moment.

While 'religion' in its broadest sense includes all forms of belief in the existence of superior beings capable of exercising power over the human race, as commonly accepted it means the formal recognition of God, as members of societies and associations, and the term, 'a religious purpose', as used in the constitutional provision exempting from taxation property used for religious purposes, means the use of property by a religious society or body of persons as a place for public worship.

'Religion' is squaring human life with superhuman life. Belief in a superhuman power and such an adjustment of human activities to the requirements of that power as may enable the individual believer to exist more happily is common to all 'religions'.

The term 'religion' has reference to one's views of his relations to his Creator, and to the obligations they impose of reverence for his being and character, and of obedience to his will. With man's relations to his Maker and the obligations he may think they impose, and the manner in which an expression shall be made by him of his belief on those subjects, no interference can be permitted, provided always the laws of society, designed to secure its peace and prosperity, and the morals of its people, are not interfered with.

78. These terms have also been judicially considered in Commissioner, Hindu Religious Endowments, Madras v. Lakshmindra Thirtha Swamiar of Sri Shirur Mutt where in the following proposition of law have been laid down:

    (1) Religion means 'a system of beliefs or doctrines which are regarded by those who profess that religion as conducive to their spiritual well-being'.
    (2) A religion is not merely an opinion, doctrine or belief. It has its outward expression in acts as well.
    (3) Religion need not be theistic.
    (4) 'Religious denomination' means a religious sect or body having a common faith and organisation and designated by a distinctive name.
    (5) A law which takes away the rights of administration from the hands of a religious denomination altogether and vests in another authority would amount to violation of the right guaranteed under clause (d) of Article 26.

[. . .]

80. *The words* 'religious denomination' in Article 26 of the Constitution must take their colour from the word 'religion' and if this be so, the expression 'religious denomination' must also satisfy three conditions:

    (1) It must be a collection of individuals who have a system of beliefs or doctrines which they regard as conducive to their spiritual well-being, that is, a common faith;

(2)  common organisation; and

(3)  designation by a distinctive name.

In the case of A.S. Narayana Deekshitulu vs State of AP,[*] Justice
K. Ramaswamy held as under:

3.  Religion is inspired by ceaseless quest for truth which has many
    facets to release and free the soul from ceaseless cycle of birth
    and death to attain salvation. Hindus believe that worship
    consists of four forms of which idol worship is one such form.
    Mode of worship varies among persons of different faiths. It is
    an assimilation of the individual soul with the infinite. For its
    attainment diverse views and theories have been propounded
    and one of them is idol worship. Hindu creed believes that the
    Supreme Being manifests Himself with three aspects as Brahma,
    the Creator, Vishnu, the Preserver and Shiva, the Destroyer and
    Renovator. Those who believe and are devoted to the worship
    of Vishnu are known as Vaishnavas and those who worship Shiva
    are called Shaivites.

4.  Vaishnavas believe that God had manifested Himself in different
    incarnations. In other words, manifesting Himself into flesh
    and the very contrary of Avatara which is expressive, absolute
    and immaculate. The finite forms of His Avatara are not forms
    of material impurity but of imperium purity, the purity of
    Suddhasattva. Vaishnavas believe in Deity Vishnu who has
    manifested Himself in 10 Avataras. Lord Vishnu descends in one
    Avatara 'Archavatar'. It is a Deity in the form of idols in the temple.

[. . .]

**28. The concept of Hindu religious faith and practice referred to in
the judgments in the narration of the facts needs preface with**

---

[*] 'A.S. Narayana Deekshitulu vs State of AP and Others', 1996, *9 SCC 548.*

**inner depth of religion as revealed by (1) Swami Vivekananda's scholastic concepts in his *The Complete Works*, Vol. I, at p. 124; and (2) broad spectrum of self-realisation by Shri Aurobindo.** Swami Vivekananda had stated that:

'Each soul is potentially divine. The goal is to manifest this divinity within by controlling nature, external and internal. Do this either by work, or worship, or psychic control, or philosophy— by one, or more, or all of these—and be free. This is the whole of religion. Doctrines, or dogmas, or rituals, or books, or temples, or forms, are but secondary details.

Religion is based upon faith and belief, and, in most cases, consists only of different sets of theories, and that is the reason why there is difference in form.'

Thereafter, at p. 341 he had stated that:

'Get rid, in the first place, of all these limited ideas of God and see Him in every person—working through all hands, walking through all feet, and eating through every mouth. He lives, through all minds of his thinking. He is self-evident, nearer unto us than ourselves. To know this is religion, is faith, and may it please the Lord to give us this faith.'

29. Shri Aurobindo, one of the illustrious revolutionary patriots and philosophers of Bharat, in his *The Human Cycle, the Ideal of Human Unity War and Self-Determination* had in Chapter XVII 'Religion as the Law of Life' elucidated its real content and purpose thus:

'The absolute and transcendent, the universal, the One is the secret summit of existence and to reach the spiritual consciousness and the Divine the ultimate goal and aim of our being and therefore of the whole development of the individual and the collectivity in all its activities, reason cannot be the last and highest guide; culture as it is understood ordinarily, cannot be the directing light or find out the regulating and harmonising principle of all our life and action. For religion is that instinct, idea, activity, discipline in man which aims directly at the Divine, while all the rest seem to aim at it only indirectly and reach it with difficulty after much wandering and stumbling in the pursuit of the outward and imperfect appearances of things. The whole root of the historic insufficiency of religion as a guide and control of human society lies in confusion of religion with liberty, creed, sect, cult, religious society are (sic) as such.'

At p. 166 he elaborated that:

'It is true in a sense that religion should be dominant thing in life, its light and law, but religion as it should be and is in its inner nature, its fundamental law of being, a seeking after God, the cult of spirituality, the opening of the deepest life of the soul to the indwelling Godhead, the eternal Omnipresence. On the other hand, it is true that religion when it identifies itself only with a creed, a cult, a church, a system of ceremonial forms, may well become a retarding force and there may therefore arise a necessity for the human spirit to reject its control over the varied activities of life. There are two aspects of religion, true religion and religionism. True religion is spiritual religion, that which seeks to live in the spirit, in what is beyond the intellect, beyond the aesthetic and ethical and practical being of man, and to inform and govern these members of our being by the higher light and law of the spirit. Religionism, on the contrary, entrenches itself in some narrow pietistic exaltation of the lower members or lays exclusive stress on intellectual dogmas, forms and ceremonies, on some fixed and rigid moral code, on some religio-political or religio-social system. Not that these things are altogether negligible or that they must be unworthy or unnecessary or that a spiritual religion need disdain the aid of forms, ceremonies, creeds or systems. On the contrary, they are needed by man because the lower members have to be exalted and raised before they can be fully spiritualised, before they can directly feel the spirit and obey its law.'

At pp. 168–69 he added that:

'Only by the light and power of the highest can the lower be perfectly guided, uplifted and accomplished. The lower life of man is in form undivine, though in it there is the secret of the divine, and it can only be divinised by finding the higher law and the spiritual illumination . . . The spiritual man who can guide human life towards its perfection is typified in the ancient Indian idea of the Rishi, one who has lived fully the life of man and found the world of the supra-intellectual, supra-mental, spiritual truth.'

In Chapter XXXIV at pp. 541–42, he opined that:

'Humanitarianism has been its most prominent emotional result. Philanthropy, social service and other kindred activities have been its outward expression of good works. Democracy, socialism, pacificism are to a great extent its by-products or at least owe much of their vigour to its inner presence.

The fundamental idea is that mankind is the godhead to be worshipped and served by man and that the respect, the service, the progress of the human being and human life are the chief duty and chief aim of the human spirit. No other idol, neither the nation, the State, the family nor anything else ought to take its place; they are only worthy of respect so far as they are images of the human spirit and enshrine its presence and aid its self-manifestation. But where the cult of these idols seeks to usurp the place of the spirit and makes demands inconsistent with its service, they should be put aside. No injunctions of old creeds, religious, political, social or cultural, are valid when they go against its claim.'

At p. 543, he mentioned that:

'One has only to compare human life and thought and feeling a century or two ago with human life, thought and feeling in the pre-war period to see how great an influence this religion of humanity has exercised and how fruitful a work it has done. It accomplished rapidly many things which orthodox religion failed to do effectively, largely because it acted as a constant intellectual and critical solvent, an unsparing assailant of the thing that is and an unflinching champion of the thing to be, faithful always to the future, while orthodox religion allied itself with the powers of the present, even of the past, bound itself by its pact with them and could act only at best as a moderating but not as a reforming force. Moreover, this religion has faith in humanity and its earthly future and can therefore aid its earthly progress, while the orthodox religions looked with eyes of pious sorrow and gloom on the earthly life of man and were very ready to bid him bear peacefully and contentedly, even to welcome its crudities, cruelties, oppressions, tribulations as a means for learning to appreciate and for earning the better life.'

At pp. 546–47, he concluded his thoughts on brotherhood thus:

'Yet is brotherhood the real key to the triple gospel of the idea of humanity. The union of liberty and equality can only be achieved by the power of human brotherhood and it cannot be founded on anything else. But brotherhood exists only in the soul and by the soul; it can exist by nothing else. For this brotherhood is not a matter either of physical kinship or of vital association or of intellectual agreement. When the soul claims freedom, it is the freedom of its self-development, the self-development of the divine in man in all his being. When it claims equality, what it is claiming is that freedom equally for all and the recognition of the same soul, the same godhead in all human beings. When it strives for brotherhood, it is founding that equal freedom of self-development on a common aim, a common life, a unity of mind and feeling founded upon the recognition of this inner spiritual unity. These three things are in fact the nature of the soul; for freedom, equality, unity are the eternal attributes of the Spirit. It is the practical recognition of this truth, it is the awakening of the soul in man and the attempt to get him to life from his soul and not from his ego which is the inner meaning of religion, and it is that to which the religion of humanity also must arrive before it can fulfil itself in the life of the race.'

At p. 594, he stated as under:

'Later religions gave a name and some body of form and quality to the one unknown Godhead and proclaimed an ideal law which they gave out as his word and scripture. But the dogmatism of a partial and unlived knowledge and the external tendencies of the human mind darkened the illuminations of religion with the confusions or error and threw over its face strange masks of childish and cruel superstitions. Religion too by putting God far above in distant heavens made man too much of a worm of the earth, little and vile before his Creator and admitted only by a caprice of his favour to a doubtful salvation in superhuman words. Modern thought seeking to make a clear riddance of these past conceptions had to substitute something else in its place, and what it saw and put there was the material law of Nature and the biological law of life of which human reason was to be the faithful exponent and human science the productive utiliser and profiteer. But to apply the mechanical blindness of the rule of physical Nature as the sole guide of thinking and seeing man is to go against the diviner law of his being and maim his higher potentiality. Material and vital Nature is only a first form of our being and to overcome and rise beyond its formula is the very sense of a human evolution. Another and greater Power than hers is the master of this effort, and human reason or human science is not that Godhead, but can only be at best one and not the greatest of its ministers.'

[. . .]

34. **The very attempt to define religion to find some distinct or possible unique essence or set of qualities that distinguish religion from the remainder of human life, is primarily a Western speculative, intellectualistic and scientific disposition. It is also the product of the dominant Western religious mode or custom of religious people. Even the Western thinkers recognise their cultural bias in the concept of religious assumptions of theism permeating their thought. *Encyclopaedia of Religion* by Mircea Eliasde (Vol. 12) states that religion is the organization of life around the deep dimensions of experience—varied in form, completeness, and clarity in accordance with the environing culture. If religiousness is a depth-awareness coming to distinctive expression in the forms we call religion, how is religiousness distinguished from various other types of awareness such as the aesthetic and ecstatic—what Abraham Maslow (1964) calls 'peak experiences' and Marghanita Laski (1961) terms 'non-religious ecstasy'—and the states of 'altered consciousness' produced by various psychosomatic techniques or drugs? On Hindu religion, at p. 290 it is stated that**

'yet deep within ritualism there is inherent the concern for accuracy and faithfulness. This is the essentially sacramental nature of ritual that arises from its nature as an ordered symbol system. Thus both symbol and ritual are perceived as intrinsic embodiments of the sacred essence, the supersensible and indescribable ultimacy of a religion. Thus ritual and symbol bring the real presence of the religious depth-dimension into the lives of its experiments and in so doing become incredibly precious.'

35. At p. 292, it is further stated under the caption 'Religion and Modernity' that 'the question whether religion, at least, in its traditional forms, will survive the ongoing cultural changes of modern times is often discussed. Certainly many traditional and current formulations, and perhaps entire traditions, will radically change or even disappear. Yet it also seems that as soon as one form of religion disappears, another rises to take its place.' Without asserting a religious instinct in mankind, it may perhaps be said that man is incessantly religious in one way or another and that the human situation and human nature make it inevitably so. The immense mysteries and uncertainties of the world and man's own inquiring and evaluating self-consciousness make inevitable a reaching out for some sort of ultimate values and realities—which is yet another name for the religious quest.

36. Religion is thus eternal and in development is in search of God throughout history, building into a fuller religious life. The eternal religion remains unchanging but the form and content keep changing with the change of times with the experience of the past keeps to preserve to the fullest religious life. But as Shri Aurobindo put it, the religiousness of man descends him into lower levels and due to confusion predominance is given to forms like rituals etc. So John Macmurray in *Reason and Emotion* (Faber and Faber Publication) at p. 40 states thus:

'. . . religion is also the consciousness of life in God; that which we seek for is also there always eternally in us. It is this eternal aspect of religion which is expressed in the religious recognition of equality in all human life at any stage of its development; in the knowledge that all distinction of superiority and inferiority are relative distinctions; and that ultimately all persons and all personal experience are of equal, because of eternal or infinite, worth. Just so in love between two persons, if it is a real love, there is a sense in which it is always perfect and complete, and this, as we know very well, is not in contradiction with the fact of development in that love; it is indeed, the condition of the development.'

[. . .]

39. *Swami Vivekananda in his lecture on* 'Religion and Science' incorporated in *The Complete Works (Vol. VI, 6th* Edn.) had stated at p. 81 thus:

'Experience is the only source of knowledge. In the world, religion is the only science where there is no surety, because it is not taught as a science of experience. This should not be. There is always, however, a small group of men who teach religion from experience. They are called mystics, and these mystics in every religion speak the same tongue and teach the same truth. This is the real science of religion. As mathematics in every part of the world does not differ, so the mystics do not differ. They are all similarly constituted and similarly situated. Their experience is the same; and this becomes law.'

In Vol. II, 9th Edn. at p. 432, Swamiji said that:

'There are two worlds: the microcosm and the macrocosm, the internal and the external. We get truth from both these by means of experience. The truth gathered from internal experience is psychology, metaphysics and religion; from external experience, the physical sciences. Now a perfect truth should be in harmony with experience in both these worlds. The microcosm must bear testimony to the macrocosm and the macrocosm to the microcosm; physical truth must have its counterpart in the internal world, and internal world must have its verification outside;'

Swami Vivekananda in his *The Complete Works*, Vol. 1, 11th Edn. at p. 366 said that:

'The foundations have all been undermined; and the modern man, whatever he may say in public, knows in the privacy of his heart that he can no more "believe", believing because it is written in certain books, believing because people like him to believe, the modern man knows it to be impossible for him. There are, of course, a number of people who seem to acquiesce in the so-called popular faith but we also know for certain that they do not think. Their idea of belief may be better translated as "non-thinking carelessness". This fight cannot last much longer without breaking to pieces all the buildings of religion.

\* \* \*

Is religion to justify itself by the discoveries of reason, through which every other science justified itself? Are the same methods of investigation, which we apply to sciences and knowledge outside, to be applied to the science of religion? In my opinion this must be so, and I am also of opinion that the sooner it is done the better. If a religion is destroyed by such investigation, it was then all the time useless, unworthy superstition; and the sooner it goes the better. I am thoroughly convinced that its destruction would be the best thing that could happen. All that is dross will be taken off, no doubt, but the essential parts of religion will emerge triumphant out of this investigation. Not only will it be made scientific—as scientific, at least, as any of the conclusions of physics or chemistry—but will have greater strength, because physics or chemistry has not internal mandate to vouch for its truth, which religion has.'

Swami Vivekananda in his *The Complete Works*, Vol. VI, 6th Edn. at p. 81 said that:

'Religion deals with the truths of the metaphysical world just as chemistry and the other natural sciences deal with the truth of the physical world. The book one must read to learn chemistry is the book of (external) nature. The book from which to learn religion is your own mind and heart. The sage is often ignorant of physical science because he reads the wrong book—the book within; and the scientist is too often ignorant of religion because he, too, reads the wrong book—the book without.'

Again in his *The Complete Works*, (Vol. V, 8th Edn.) pp. 192–93, he says that:

'The basis of all systems, social or political, rests upon the goodness of men. No nation is greater or good because Parliament enacts this or that, but because its men are great and good . . . Religion goes to the root of the matter. If it is right, all is right . . . One must admit that law, government, politics are phases not final in any way. There is a goal beyond them where law is not needed . . . All great masters teach the same thing. Christ saw that the basis is not law, that morality and purity are the only strength.'

[. . .]

41. According to Hindu belief, Vishnu as preserver is stated to take five forms, viz., Para, Vyuha, Vibhava, Arca and Antaryamin.

Para Is the transcendental form. Vibhava includes the ten divine descends (avatara) and also thirty-nine forms which He takes from time to time. Arca represents God in the form of idol, which He though formless, takes this finite form to show favour to His devotees. The form of Antaryamin is to remain within the self and control it by directing it to lead a virtuous way of life, in accordance with the residues of the deeds done by it. Temple, therefore, forms an integral part of Hindu religion and the idol installed therein forms the main symbol of religious worship manifesting the dignity of God.

[. . .]

72. Religion became identified with untested beliefs and dogmas and got shattered in the progress of scientific enquiry. But the mental make-up of Indians proceeds from our long cultural experience; therefore, our spiritual religious experience is not hostile to scientific spirit but sympathetic and hospitable to it. Science will have no opposition from philosophy or religion in India. Human welfare partly depends upon the knowledge and control of human environment, natural and social. Vedantha has always given an honoured place to science as also to politics in this period of human welfare. Man is more than a political animal. He is also more than an intellectual being. He has depth and heights which cannot be compressed in a purely materialistic or positivistic philosopher. Swamy Ranganathananda further stated as under:

'. . . democracy should have a content of universal value which is something more than the merely political, social, or national. It is obvious that value is the ethical and spiritual content. Without that content, our democracy will be nothing more than a mere carbon copy of what obtains in the mediocratic countries of the West.

In the background of these agitating questions lies the great spiritual heritage of India. Those who are acquainted with its vitality hold the hope that India can yet show the world how to understand, assimilate, and express human values which form the theme of democracy everywhere. India's spirituality can enable Indians and the peoples of the world to digest the formidable forces that are being generated and placed in man's hands today. India's ancient and modern seers—in other words, the religion of the spiritual oneness of humanity has to be revived and reactivated in men's thinking and day-to-day living, and its powerful influence brought to bear on these new and ever newer forms of scientific and social power, thereby giving them a higher direction and a loftier spiritual and human purpose.

This is the central message of religion. It is a message which requires to be specially emphasised in the world in which we are living today. The "religion" carries to some at least of the modern world a bit of bad odour. It is unfortunate. It is due to the fact that religion became identified with untested beliefs and dogmas. And these got shattered in the progress of scientific enquiry. [. . .]

. . . [N]either science nor politics can give man peace or happiness, joy or sense of fulfilment. These non-utilitarian values proceed from religion and morality. Science and politics can create only conditions for their emergence, but cannot create them directly. Without this spiritual direction, the forces generated by science and politics nourish the low self of man and become sources of sorrow and discord, division and instability for man and society. A knowledge which leads to the increase of sorrow is not knowledge but ignorance, the offspring of spiritual blindness. It is spiritual awareness alone that transforms all knowledge into wisdom, and into forms of peace and happiness, love and service.

The transformation of the world which science and politics seek is powerless to ensure human welfare without the transformation of human nature itself, which religion seeks through a discipline of the whole personality. It is only such spiritually disciplined individuals and groups that can ensure for humanity at large the values of life, liberty, and the pursuit of happiness, of liberty, fraternity, and equality. The peace and happiness of man and the stability and ordered progress of civilizations depend entirely upon the intensification of the spiritual awareness of humanity. With this spiritual awareness for foundation, the structure of civilization raised by science and democracy becomes strong and steady; without it, it sways in periodic crises to topple down eventually. Without the inspiration of religion, civilization shall ever remain an unstable structure.

Besides the integral unity of man and his interests, Vedanta also proclaims the unity and solidarity of all existence. The objective of Vedanta is the happiness and welfare of man; not man as divided into sects, creeds, castes, and classes, but man as man wherever he may be found. Based on this unitary and universal view of man upheld in her philosophy, religion in India taught that man, in the course of his development, in the course of his self-expression, generates various forces, physical or mental, social or political, and that the development of these forces needs to be matched by a corresponding development of his inner spiritual resources, which alone can provide the factors of stability to an evolving personality or social system.

True democracy is inconsistent with a narrow self-sufficient nationalism or sectarianism; it must tend to reach out to the universal. Breaking the barriers of caste and creed, race and sects, high and low, the democratic ideas, deriving its sustenance from the divinity in man, marches on, without obstruction, to the realization of the universal. Swami Vivekananda desired India to uphold this ideal of the universal in her religion and politics, science, and literature. He desires India to strive for the evolution of a Vedantic civilization where science and politics would be utilized to lead man to higher and higher levels of self-expression; not merely desired it, but he also demonstrated that India, among all the nations, had the requisite historically acquired capacity to make that contribution to world civilization.'

[. . .]

85. Articles 25 and 26 deal with and protect religious freedom. Religion as used in these articles must be construed in its strict and etymological sense. Religion is that which binds a man with his Cosmos, his Creator or super force. It is difficult and rather impossible to define or delimit the expressions 'religion' or 'matters of religion' used in Articles 25 and 26. Essentially, religion is a matter of personal faith and belief of personal relations of an individual with what he regards as Cosmos, his Maker or his Creator which, he believes, regulates the existence of insentient beings and the forces of the universe. Religion is not necessarily theistic and in fact there are well-known religions in India itself like Buddhism and Jainism which do not believe in the existence of God. In India, Muslims believe in Allah and have faith in Islam; Christians in Christ and Christianity; Parsis in Zoroastrianism; Sikhs in Guru Granth Sahib and teachings of Guru Nanak Devji, its founder, which is a facet of Hinduism like Brahmo Samaj, Arya Samaj etc.

86. A religion undoubtedly has its basis in a system of beliefs and doctrine which are regarded by those who profess religion to be conducive to their spiritual well-being. A religion is not merely an opinion, doctrine or belief. It has outward expression in acts as well. It is not every aspect of religion that has been safeguarded by Articles 25 and 26 nor has the Constitution provided that every religious activity cannot be interfered with. Religion, therefore, cannot be construed in the context of Articles 25 and 26 in its

strict and etymological sense. Every religion must believe in a conscience and ethical and moral precepts. Therefore, whatever binds a man to his own conscience and whatever moral or ethical principles regulate the lives of men believing in that theistic, conscience or religious belief that alone can constitute religion as understood in the Constitution which fosters feeling of brotherhood, amity, fraternity and equality of all persons which find their foothold in secular aspect of the Constitution. Secular activities and aspects do not constitute religion which brings under its own cloak every human activity. There is nothing which a man can do, whether in the way of wearing clothes or food or drink, which is not considered a religious activity. Every mundane or human activity was not intended to be protected by the Constitution under the guise of religion. The approach to construe the protection of religion or matters of religion or religious practices guaranteed by Articles 25 and 26 must be viewed with pragmatism since by the very nature of things, it would be extremely difficult, if not impossible, to define the expression religion or matters of religion or religious belief or practice.

87. In pluralistic society like India, as stated earlier, there are numerous religious groups who practise diverse forms of worship or practise religions, rituals, rites etc.; even among Hindus, different denominants and sects residing within the country or abroad profess different religious faiths, beliefs, practices. They seek to identify religion with what may in substance be mere facets of religion. It would, therefore, be difficult to devise a definition of religion which would be regarded as applicable to all religions or matters of religious practices. To one class of persons a mere dogma or precept or a doctrine may be predominant in the matter of religion; to others, rituals or ceremonies may be predominant facets of religion; and to yet another class of persons a code of conduct or a mode of life may constitute religion. Even to different

persons professing the same religious faith some of the facets of religion may have varying significance. It may not be possible, therefore, to devise a precise definition of universal application as to what is religion and what are matters of religious belief or religious practice. That is far from saying that it is not possible to state with reasonable certainty the limits within which the Constitution conferred a right to profess religion. Therefore, the right to religion guaranteed under Article 25 or 26 is not an absolute or unfettered right to propagating religion which is subject to legislation by the State limiting or regulating any activity—economic, financial, political or secular which are associated with religious belief, faith, practice or custom. They are subject to reform on social welfare by appropriate legislation by the State. Though religious practices and performances of acts in pursuance of religious belief are as much a part of religion as faith or belief in a particular doctrine, that by itself is not conclusive or decisive. What are essential parts of religion or religious belief or matters of religion and religious practice is essentially a question of fact to be considered in the context in which the question has arisen and the evidence—factual or legislative or historic—presented in that context is required to be considered and a decision reached.

[. . .]

92. The basis of Hindu dharma is twofold. The first is the Vedas and the second are the Agamas. Vedas, in turn, consist of four texts, namely, Samhitas, Brahmanas, Aranyakas and Upanishads.

93. Samhitas are the collections of mantras. Brahmanas explain the practical aspects of the rituals as well as their meanings. They explain the application of the mantras and the deeper meanings of the rituals. Aranyakas go deeper into the mystic meanings of the rituals, and Upanishads present the philosophy of the Vedas.

94. From the point of view of content, they are viewed as Karma Kanda (sacrificial portion) and Jnana Kanda which explain the philosophical portion. The major portion of the Vedic literature enunciates the Vedic sacrifices or the rituals which inevitably culminate in the philosophy of the Upanishads. That is why the Upanishads are called Vedantha or culmination of the Vedas.

95. The essence of the Vedic religion lies in Vedic sacrifices which not only purify the mind and the heart of those who participate in the sacrifices but also reveal the true and unfragmented nature of the Karma (Action). Erroneously, Western scholars explained the Vedic sacrifices in terms of either sympathetic magic or an act of offering fire to Gods emulating the mundane act of offering gifts. Thus, for them Vedic religion is a primitive religion and Vedic Gods are simply representing insentient departments of Nature; but it is not so. On the contrary, the term used for Vedic Gods is 'Deva' which literally means 'the shining ones', the adorable ones—bestowing grace on the worshippers. The root 'Div' also means that Devas are the embodiment of unfragmented consciousness, which is ultimately one and non-dual. Likewise, the Vedic sacrifice is an act of re-enactment of the cosmic creation in our mundane life. Our life of action is simply a life of fragmented acts. This is because of Raga and Dvesha whereby the perception is limited. The fragmented acts emanate from our deep-rooted attraction and hatefulness. The Vedic sacrifice moves towards 'Poorna', i.e., plenitude and thus overcoming the problem of fragmented action in our lives. Onwards, the seeker moves towards the knowledge of self or the Brahman. So many Upasanas are taught in the Vedas but not elaborated. The Agamas have elaborated these Upasanas such as Madhu Vidya and Dahra Vidya.

96. Upanishads speak of Para Vidya and Apara Vidya. Apara Vidya deals with Jnana through various methods. Agamas explain these Para Vidyas. The Agamic texts contain four parts, namely, Vidya Pada, Kriya Pada, Charya Pada and Yoga Pada.

97. Each text of the Agamas has the first portion, called 'Samhita' which contains the four parts namely the Vidya Pada, Kriya Pada, Charya Pada and Yoga Pada. Vidya Pada offers an elaborate enunciation of the philosophy, whereas Kriya Pada deals elaborately with the act of worship. Worship is viewed as Samurta Archana. In other words, the Gods are endowed with form and this form of worship culminates into Amurta or Nishkala Archana by which one worships and realises the formless. These are the steps to be treated upon one after another.

98. *The temples are taken to be sanctified space where entire* unfragmented Space and Time, in other words, the entire 'Universe' are deposited and the image of the Deity is worshipped symbolising the 'Supreme'. Although the Deities appear to be many, each and every Deity is again viewed as the Supreme One and, therefore, the Supreme Reality is one and non-dual. The multiplicity of the Gods has been effected in order to offer the paths which are required according to the entitlement and evolution of each and everyone. That is why the progress towards the ultimate evolutionary goal of man depends upon his level of comprehension and his capacity to learn. This is the whole concept of a Guru who knows precisely the extent of spiritual evolution of the seeker and would know what is the stage from which the seeker has to proceed.

99. *Hinduism cannot be defined in terms of Polytheism or Henotheism or Monotheism. The nature of Hindu religion ultimately is* Monism/Advaita. This is in contradistinction to Monotheism which means only one God to the exclusion of all others. Polytheism is a belief of multiplicity of Gods. On the contrary, Monism is a spiritual belief of one Ultimate Supreme and manifests Himself as many. This multiplicity is not contrary to non-dualism. This is the reason why Hindus start adoring any Deity either handed down by tradition or brought by a Guru or Swambhuru and seek to attain the Ultimate Supreme.

Justice Ranjan Gogoi, who presided over the Ayodhya bench as chief justice, had already dealt with the idea of religion in the case of Adi Saiva Sivachariyargal Nala Sangam vs Government of Tamil Nadu:*

1.  Religion incorporates the particular belief(s) that a group of people subscribe to. Hinduism, as a religion, incorporates all forms of belief without mandating the selection or elimination of any one single belief. It is a religion that has no single founder; no single scripture and no single set of teachings. It has been described as Sanatan Dharma, namely, eternal faith, as it is the collective wisdom and inspiration of the centuries that Hinduism seeks to preach and propagate. It is keeping in mind the above precepts that we will proceed further.

[. . .]

32. Before we go on to deliberate on the validity of the impugned G.O. dated 23-5-2006 **it will be useful to try to understand what is Hinduism?** A broad answer is to be found in the preface to this Report but, perhaps, we should delve a little deeper into the issue. The subject has received an in-depth consideration of the country's philosopher President Dr S. Radhakrishnan in the celebrated work *The Hindu View of Life*. The said work has been exhaustively considered in *Shastri* Yagnapurushdasji v. Muldas Bhundardas *Vaishya* in the context of the question as to whether Swaminarayan sect is a religion distinguishable and separate from the Hindu religion and consequently the temples belonging to the said sect fell outside the scope of Section 3 of the Bombay Hindu Places of Public Worship (Entry Authorisation) Act, 1956. The aforesaid Section 3 of the Act inter alia provided that every

---

* 'Adi Saiva Sivachariyargal Nala Sangam and Others vs Government Of Tamil Nadu and Another', 2016, 2 SCC 725.

temple to which the Act applied shall be open to the excluded classes for worship in the same manner and to the same extent as other Hindus in general. While the eventual decision of the Court which answered the question raised is in the negative, namely, that the sect in question was not a distinguishable and different religion, it is the very learned discourse that is to be found in the Report with regard to the true tenets of Hinduism that would be of interest so far the present case is concerned.

33. The following passages from the Report are truly worthy of reproduction both for the purpose of recapitulation and illumination: (Shastri Yagnapurushdasji *case* [Shastri Yagnapurushdasji v. Muldas Bhundardas *Vaishya*, AIR 1966 SC 1119 : (1966) 3 SCR 242], AIR pp. 1128–31, paras 29–33, 36–37 & 40)

29. **When we think of the Hindu religion, we find it difficult, if not impossible, to define Hindu religion or even adequately describe it. Unlike other religions in the world, the Hindu religion does not claim any one prophet; it does not worship any one God; it does not subscribe to any one dogma; it does not believe in any one philosophic concept; it does not follow any one set of religious rites or performances; in fact, it does not appear to satisfy the narrow traditional features of any religion or creed. It may broadly be described as a way of life and nothing more.**

30. The Hindu thinkers reckoned with the striking fact that the men and women dwelling in India belonged to different communities, worshipped different gods, and practiced different rites (Kurma Purana). (The Hindu View of Life by Dr Radhakrishnan, p. 12.)

31. . . . It presents for our investigation a complex congeries of creeds and doctrines which in its gradual accumulation may be compared to the gathering together of the mighty volume of the Ganges, swollen by a continual influx of

tributary rivers and rivulets, spreading itself over an ever-increasing area of country, and finally resolving itself into an intricate delta of tortuous streams and jungly *marshes* . . . The Hindu religion is a reflection of the composite character of the Hindus, who are not one people but many. It is based on the idea of universal receptivity. It has ever aimed at accommodating itself to circumstances, and has carried on the process of adaptation through more than three thousand years. It has first borne with and then, so to speak, swallowed, digested, and assimilated something from all creeds. (*Religious Thought and Life in India* by Monier Williams, p. 57.)

32. [. . .] The history of Indian thought emphatically brings out the fact that the development of Hindu religion has always been inspired by an endless quest of the mind for truth based on the consciousness that truth has many facets. Truth is one but wise men describe it differently . . . *The Indian mind has, consistently through the ages, been exercised over the problem of the nature of godhead*, the problem that faces the spirit at the end of life, and the interrelation between the individual and the universal soul. 'If we can abstract from the variety of opinion,' says Dr Radhakrishnan, 'and observe the general spirit of Indian thought, we shall find that it has a disposition to interpret life and nature in the way of monistic idealism, though this tendency is so plastic, living and manifold that it takes many forms and expresses itself in even mutually hostile teachings.' (Indian Philosophy by Dr Radhakrishnan, Vol. 1, p. 32.)

33. . . . Though philosophic concepts and principles evolved by different Hindu thinkers and philosophers varied in many ways and even appeared to conflict with each other in some particulars, they all had reverence for the past and accepted the Vedas as sole foundation of the Hindu philosophy. Naturally enough, it was realised by Hindu religion from the

very beginning of its career that truth was many-sided and different views contained different aspects of truth which no one could fully express . . .

* * *

36. Do the Hindus worship at their temples the same set or number of gods? That is another question which can be asked in this connection; and the answer to this question again has to be in the negative. Indeed, there are certain sections of the Hindu community which do not believe in the worship of idols; and as regards those sections of the Hindu community which believe in the worship of idols, their idols differ from community to community and it cannot be said that one definite idol or a definite number of idols are worshipped by all the Hindus in general. In the Hindu Pantheon the first gods that were worshipped in Vedic times were mainly Indra, Varuna, Vayu and Agni. Later, Brahma, Vishnu and Mahesh came to be worshipped. In course of time, Rama and Krishna secured a place of pride in the Hindu Pantheon, and gradually as different philosophic concepts held sway in different sects and in different sections of the Hindu community, a large number of gods were added, with the result that today, the Hindu Pantheon presents the spectacle of a very large number of gods who are worshipped by different sections of the Hindus.

37. The development of Hindu religion and philosophy shows that from time to time saints and religious reformers attempted to remove from the Hindu thought and practices elements of corruption and superstition and that led to the formation of different sects. Buddha started Buddhism; Mahavir founded Jainism; Basava *became the founder of Lingayat religion*; Dhyaneshwar *and Tukaram initiated the*

Varakari *cult; Guru Nanak inspired Sikhism; Dayananda founded Arya* Samaj, and Chaitanya began Bhakti cult; and as a result of the teachings of Ramakrishna and Vivekananda, Hindu religion flowered into its most attractive, progressive and dynamic form. If we study the teachings of these saints and religious reformers, we would notice an amount of divergence in their respective views; but underneath that divergence, there is a kind of subtle indescribable unity which keeps them within the sweep of the broad and progressive Hindu religion.

\* \* \*

40. Tilak faced this complex and difficult problem of defining or at least describing adequately Hindu religion and he evolved a working formula which may be regarded as fairly adequate and satisfactory. Said Tilak: 'Acceptance of the Vedas with reverence; recognition of the fact that the means or ways to salvation are diverse; and realisation of the truth that the number of gods to be worshipped is large, that indeed is the distinguishing feature of Hindu religion' . . . *This definition brings out succinctly the broad distinctive features of Hindu religion. It is somewhat remarkable that this broad sweep of Hindu religion has been eloquently described by Toynbee. Says Toynbee: 'When we pass from the plane of social practice to the plane of intellectual outlook, Hinduism too comes out well by comparison with the religions on ideologies of the South-West Asian group. In contrast to these Hinduism has the same outlook as the pre-Christian and pre-Muslim religions and philosophies of the Western half of the old world. Like them, Hinduism takes it for granted that there is more than one valid approach to truth and to salvation and that these different approaches are not only compatible with each other, but are complementary' (The*

*Present day Experiment in Western Civilisation* by Toynbee,
pp. 48-49).

(emphasis supplied)

34. The fact that reference to Hindus in the Constitution includes
persons professing the Sikh, Jain and Buddhist religions and the
statutory enactments like the Hindu Marriage Act, the Hindu
Succession Act, etc. also embraces Sikhs, Jains and Buddhists
within the ambit of the said enactments is another significant
fact that was highlighted and needs to be specially taken note of.

35. What is sought to be emphasised is that all the above
would show the wide expanse of beliefs, thoughts and
forms of worship that Hinduism encompasses without any
divergence or friction within itself or amongst its adherents.
It is in the backdrop of the above response to the question
posed earlier 'What is Hinduism?' that we have to proceed
further in the matter.

36. Image worship is a predominant feature of Hindu religion.
The origins of image worship is interesting and a learned
discourse on the subject is available in a century-old
judgment of the Madras High Court in Gopala Moopanar
v. Dharmakarta Subramaniya Iyer [Gopala Moopanar v.
Dharmakarta Subramaniya Iyer. In the said Report the
learned Judge (Sadasiva Aiyar, J.) on the basis of accepted
texts and a study thereof had found that in the 'first stage'
of existence of mankind God was worshipped as immanent
in the heart of everything and worship consisted solely
in service to one's fellow creatures. In the second stage,
the spirit of universal brotherhood lost its initial efficacy
and notions of inferiority and superiority amongst men
surfaced, leading to a situation where the inferior man was
asked to worship the superior man who was considered

as a manifestation of God. Disputes arose about the relative superiority and inferiority which were resolved by the wise sages by introducing image worship to enable all men to worship God without squabbles about their relative superiorities. With passage of time there emerged rules regulating worship in temples which came to be laid down in the treatises known as Agamas and the Thantras. Specifically in Gopala Moopanar it was noticed that the Agamas prescribed rules as regards 'what caused pollution to a temple and as regards the ceremonies for removing pollution when caused'.

As we can see, the court had a difficult task in defining religion, largely because most of the time it had spent grappling with Hinduism. We have seen elsewhere that the amorphous character of Hinduism, and its capacity to absorb innovative interpretations of the human condition, had earned it the description of it being a way of life. To borrow from the wisdom of Forrest Gump, 'Hinduism is as Hinduism does.' Similarly, religion is what we choose to see as religion. But as the court pointed out, religious denomination is easier to put a finger on, because it is a sort of subset of the whole.

# Nine

# In the Wake of the Devastation

The immediate shock of the unthinkable happening gradually settled down to a kind of numbness. The demolition happened on 6 December 1992, a Sunday. After the devastating weekend, on Monday morning, 7 December, the Council of Ministers was gathered in a crowded ground-floor room at Parliament House. Understandably, most were at a loss for words, but Madhavrao Scindia broke the ice to say how we all felt for Prime Minister Narasimha Rao. The reaction of the embattled PM took us by surprise when he retorted, 'Please spare me your sympathy.' I do not recall the meeting having lasted long or indeed any substantive further steps being discussed. The Uttar Pradesh government had been dismissed on 6 December itself and a week thereafter, the BJP governments in Himachal Pradesh, Rajasthan and Madhya Pradesh were dismissed by the President, as advised by the cabinet. That decision led to the challenge in the Supreme Court in the S.R. Bommai* case—a bench of nine judges heard the challenge along with other Article 356 matters and upheld the dismissal on the grounds of violation of secularism. As becomes clear in the

---

* 'S.R. Bommai and Others vs Union of India and Others', 1994, 3 SCC 1.

188

Ayodhya judgment as well, S.R. Bommai has become a bulwark against any attempt to encroach upon the territory of secularism in the constitution.

Meanwhile, the Narasimha Rao government gave clear signals of its intention to rebuild the demolished mosque and the attorney general repeated that before the Supreme Court. In due course it would have dawned on them that such a step would rekindle the ambers that were still smouldering. On the other hand, as the minister of state, Ministry of External Affairs, I was dispatched to the West Asian countries to reassure our friends.

Madhav Godbole, an outstanding officer and Union home secretary at the time of the demolition, resigned and subsequently took voluntary retirement after thirty-three years as an IAS officer. In his book *The Babri Masjid–Ram Mandir Dilemma*,* he wrote,

> Wherever in an act of communal violence any place of worship of any religion is damaged or destroyed it must be rectified and repaired by the government at its own cost. That is the only way you can give a sense of confidence to the minorities and affected communities that there is a government which will protect your rights . . .

Such outstanding men of the steel frame of Indian democracy may have faded away and their words become hidden in the dust of the years since 1992, but their memory must remain the cherished sentinel of the future.

## Findings of the Liberhan Commission

As is customary in India, every adverse event is quickly contained by the setting up of a commission of inquiry. Despite the

---

* M. Godbole, *Babri Masjid–Ram Mandir Dilemma: An Acid Test for India's Constitution*, Konark Publishers, 2020.

originally stated intent to get a commission to complete its work quickly, extensions of time are inevitably sought. Reports are submitted with great fanfare and swiftly put into cold storage. The Liberhan Ayodhya Commission of Inquiry was a long-running inquiry commissioned and set up by the Government of India to investigate the destruction of the Babri Masjid. The commission comprised a sitting justice, M.S. Liberhan of the Punjab and Haryana High Court, and was set up on 16 December 1992, soon after the demolition of the Babri Masjid in Ayodhya on 6 December and the subsequent riots that followed. The terms of reference required the commission to inquire into:

(a) The sequence of events leading to, and all, the facts and circumstances relating to, the occurrences in the Ram Janma Bhoomi–Babri Masjid complex at Ayodhya . . .
(b) The role played by the Chief Minister, Members of the Council of Ministers, officials of the Government of Uttar Pradesh and by the individuals, concerned organizations and agencies in, or in connection with, the destruction . . .

The commission was originally mandated to submit its report within three months, but extensions were given forty-right times, and after a delay of seventeen years, it finally submitted its report to Prime Minister Manmohan Singh on 30 June 2009.

The commission worked through changes of government that included the years under Prime Minister Atal Bihari Vajpayee, when L.K. Advani was home minister. In our system it is not easy to hold an inquiry against a person in a position of power. The work done by the special investigation team (SIT), formed in March 2008 to investigate the Gujarat riots, was very disappointing, despite close scrutiny by the Supreme Court. The Liberhan Commission proceedings, too, witnessed considerable disquiet from within—the assisting counsel Anupam Gupta expressed dissatisfaction at the laxity the commission had showed towards L.K. Advani. Gupta resigned in September 2007.

Once the report was presented to Parliament, there was precious little done or indeed could be done with the criminal proceedings against the main protagonists already in progress. Even as the Supreme Court speeded up the hearing of the appeals, at the time there was no knowing how speedily the criminal prosecutions would culminate. Now, the report has little more than historical value but will help to be kept in mind for a better understanding of the developments:

158.10. The theory or the claim made by the leaders of the movement or the icons, from political or social organisations, does not carry conviction to conclude that the demolition was carried out by the karsevaks spontaneously out of sheer anger or emotions. The mode of assault, the small number of karsevaks who carried out the demolition and the constraints of the space to accommodate the number of people, veiling of the identity of the karsevaks entering the domes, the removal of the idols and the cash box from under the dome and the subsequent reinstallation in the make-shift temple, construction of the make-shift temple, availability of instruments and material for demolition and for the swift construction of the make-shift temple categorically leads to the conclusion and finding that the demolition was carried out with great painstaking preparation and preplanning. The involvement of quite a number of karsevaks for carrying out the demolition ordinarily could not have been kept secret from people like the Chief Minister who admittedly has a number of sources of information; or from KS Sudershan who was heading the RSS while their Swayamsevaks were detailed on the spot for each and every act required to be carried out; or local leaders like Vinay Katiyar or Ashok Singhal or the persons present at the spot prior to December 6th, 1992.

[. . .]

159.5. The factual matrix also yields indisputable evidence that lured by the prospect of power or wealth, a rank of leaders emerged within the BJP, RSS, VHP, Shiv Sena, Bajrang Dal etc. who were neither guided by any ideology nor imbued with any dogma nor restrained by any moral trepidation. These leaders saw the 'Ayodhya Issue' as their road to success and sped down this highway mindless of the casualties they scattered about. These leaders were the executioners wielding the sword handed to them by the ideologues.

[. . .]

160.4. The BJP's claim that it was carrying out the people's mandate makes it inexplicable why it had to resort to subterfuge in order to effect the destruction of the disputed structure. The very fact that the Chief Minister of the state of Uttar Pradesh, its ministers and its mandarins supported the destruction with tacit, open, active and material support at every step, but did not make it part of the officially stated agenda lends overwhelming credence to the fact that they were aware of the gross illegality and impropriety they were guilty of. It would be reasonable to conclude that they were conscious of their acts and conduct ensuring the achievement of their concealed intent to demolish the disputed structure.

160.5. Kalyan Singh, his ministers and his handpicked bureaucrats created man-made and cataclysmic circumstances which could result in no consequences other than the demolition of the disputed structure and broadened the cleavage between the two religious communities resulting in massacres all over the country. They denuded the state of every legal, moral and statutory restraint and wilfully enabled and facilitated the wanton destruction and the ensuing anarchy.

160.6. While dealing with the role of the administration in detail in my report, I have dilated on the role of specific members of the de jure and the de facto government of Uttar Pradesh at the time. The parallel government run by the RSS has also been exposed and analysed in my report. There is no manner of doubt admissible in the culpability and responsibility of the Chief Minister, his ministers and his cohorts who were handpicked to occupy selected posts. Paramhans Ramchander Das, Ashok Singhal, Vinay Katiyar, Vishnu Hari Dalmia, Vamdev, KS Sudarshan, HV Sheshadari, Lalji Tandon, Kalraj Mishra, Govindacharya and others named in my report formed this complete cartel lead by Kalyan Singh and supported by the icons of the movement like LK Advani, MM Joshi, AB Vajpayee.

[. . .]

161.4. The Chief Minister Kalyan Singh on assuming office embarked on a focused mission to replace the administrative and police officers who were inclined to resist a change in the status quo or who demonstrated the slightest hesitation in conniving, supporting or collaborating with the new de facto leadership which was gradually taking control in Ayodhya and Faizabad. In my report I have quoted instances of senior officers peremptorily being posted to other parts of the state and pliant officers being nominated to fill their positions.

[. . .]

161.11. By far, the worst sin of omission of the State Government was leaking into the public domain the information that the police personnel had been hobbled and would not react or retaliate under any circumstances. Emboldened by the self-confessed handicap of the law enforcement agencies of the state, the karsevaks were not constrained by any concerns of self-preservation or personal safety and enjoyed a free hand. All the categories of karsevaks—whether they were present because of political, monetary or religious considerations—were aware that they were at zero risk from the state's agencies.

161.12. The only non-manageable variable, from the Sangh Parivar's point of view—was the possible deployment of central forces in the state, either at the behest of the Central Government or sanctioned by the Supreme Court. This threat was also neutralized by senior and well-respected individuals stating blatant lies on oath before the Supreme Court, apart from protesting against even the stationing of central paramilitary forces sent for the specific purpose of providing sufficient numbers of forces to be deployed by the state for the security of the disputed structure.

[. . .]

161.15. To sum up, December 6th 1992 saw a state of Uttar Pradesh unwilling and unable to uphold the majesty of the law. The ennui flowed from the very office of the Chief Minister downwards and infected the state's minions down till the bottom. The state had become a willing ally and co-conspirator in the joint common enterprise to announce the revival of a rabid breed of Hindutva, by demolishing the structure they had denounced as a symbol of Islam.

[. . .]

162.16. The government of Uttar Pradesh was guilty and it had abdicated its responsibility to the media just as they had abdicated governance and forsaken the very rule of law. By their sins of omission as well as commission, they incited, facilitated and organised the assault on the free press.

162.17. The media was consciously targeted by the karsevaks on the directions of their leaders. It was a preplanned enterprise and closely coordinated by those who ensured the demolition of the structures that Mir Baqi allegedly erected.

[. . .]

165. The Sangh Parivar

165.1. The blame or the credit for the entire temple construction movement at Ayodhya must necessarily be attributed to the Sangh Parivar. As already discussed elsewhere in this report, the Sangh Parivar is an extensive and widespread organic body which encompasses organisations which address and assimilate just about every type of social, professional or other demographic grouping of individuals.

165.2. The Parivar is a highly successful and corporatized model of a political party and as the Ayodhya campaign demonstrates, has developed a highly efficient organizational structure. Each time a new demographic group has emerged, the Sangh Parivar has hived off some of its RSS inner-core leadership to harness that group and bring it within the fold, enhancing the voter base of the Parivar.

165.3. While the structure or the methods of the Sangh Parivar for aggregating a substantial public base may neither be illegal nor strictly objectionable, the use of this gargantuan whole for the purpose of the Ayodhya campaign was clearly against the letter and spirit of Indian law and ethos.

165.4. The Sangh Parivar had spent long years and mobilized its immense media clout to numb the sensibilities of the masses, and at the very least to ensure the complete absence of resistance to its designs. The attempts by the pseudo-moderate elements even within the Parivar were predictably of little significance and were destined to fail, whether by design or otherwise.

165.5. As the inner core of the Parivar, the top leadership of the RSS, VHP, Shiv Sena, Bajrang Dal and the BJP bear primary responsibility.

[. . .]

166.2. On one hand, the leaders like AB Vajpayee, Murli Manohar Joshi and LK Advani, who are the undeniable public face and leaders of the BJP and thus of the Parivar, constantly protested their innocence and denounced the events of December 1992. Appearing as a witness before the Commission, Advani sought to reiterate his anguish at the demolition of the disputed structure and was at pains to state that he had never made any inflammatory statement, even during his Rath Yatras.

166.3. On the other hand it stands established beyond doubt that the events of the day were neither spontaneous nor unplanned nor an unforeseen overflowing of the people's emotions, nor the result of a foreign conspiracy as some overly imaginative people have tried to suggest.

166.4. In such a case, the logical questions that beg to be answered are whether the pseudo-moderates knew what was going on, whether they were in fact the prime movers of the show, whether they were in control of the Parivar and finally, could they have done anything to prevent the demolition and subsequent violence?

[. . .]

167. The Muslim Organizations

167.1. Selective communal Muslim leaders, obsessed with building personal or individual influence or following for enhancing their political influence and for self-gain, were merely bystanders during this entire period and put forth dismal performance. While the RSS, VHP, Shiv Sena, Bajrang Dal and the BJP brought the temple construction movement to the front burner and caused it to boil over, the fanatic Muslim leadership making the counterclaim were either completely complacent and had no substantial or effective leadership or were simply incompetent in projecting their own lopsided counter view to the people throughout the half century leading up to the 6th of December 1992. Their feeble attempts after

1983 to present a blinkered view of history were without researched substance and therefore possibly incapable of being believed.

167.2. The BMAC and later the AIBMAC* never set up or presented any claim to the disputed structure in any negotiation with the intervention of any person or at any time and their stand was a merely simplicitor denial of the claims of the Sangh Parivar which too underwent changes and shifts and articulation with the passage of time. The Muslim and Hindu leadership's shrill cries echoed the divisive and mischievous sentiments which had been heard around 1947, and which continue to cast a dark shadow on the age-old ethos of this great land.

167.3. The Muslim leadership did little to counter the latent fears stoked up by the RSS and VHP leadership and instead provided it with the opportunity to embark on what started out as a defensive strategy. Unfortunately a sizable number of Indians still feel that the Muslims of India should be treated as a deprived class despite the centuries-long Mughal–Muslim rule in India.

167.4. The Muslim leadership provided the rabid Hindu ideologues sufficient cause to instill fear into the common citizen of India. Whether the political Muslim leadership represented the views of the average Muslim citizen of India is highly doubtful. The elite political Muslim leadership constituted a class by itself and was neither responsible to, nor caring for the welfare of those they purported to champion.

[. . .]

168.5. The police and civil servants in Uttar Pradesh were the product of the degradation in the civil services which has become even more

---

* The Babri Masjid Action Committee and the All India Babri Masjid Action Committee.

pronounced in recent times. The administrative officers, the police and selective sections of the bureaucracy was a part and parcel of the cartel of the BJP Chief Minister and willingly helped it achieve its election manifesto, propagate the caste and communal oriented politics and in his attempt to perpetuate the rule of the political party in power. They failed to discharge their solemn duties as a counterbalance to the political executive in the administration. They could have at least attempted to stem the tide of communalism and the rape of democracy. But they chose to remain deaf, dumb and blind throughout and instead became a willing part of the cartel.

168.6. The police and the bureaucrats of the state not just turned a blind eye to the misadventures of the polity but actively connived and curried favour with the Chief Minister and the Sangh Parivar by systematically paralyzing the state machinery. Their sins are highlighted by their being rewarded with plum postings after the demolition as well as tickets for contesting elections.

[. . .]

170.8. It is also established by the evidence on the record that Karsevaks attacked the media personnel at the same time as the commencement of the assault on the disputed structure. There was no provocation offered by the media which was sought to be stated as the cause of these attacks. There were some suggestions that the media, in particular a German TV crew had earlier offended the Karsevaks by staging humiliating scenes etc. There is little substance in these allegations and none that can form the basis for justifying the subsequent attacks on December the 6th. Even the top leadership like KS Sudarshan went to the other extreme by propounding the imaginative theory about the alleged provocation of karsevaks by a German television crew. It was brought to his attention specifically by a reputed journalist like Mark Tully that journalists were being beaten up and he gave an assurance that he would bring it to the notice of Ashok Singhal. I cannot conclude other than that he was one of the main authors of the demolition.

170.9. The evidence also shows that the attacks were targeted primarily against journalists who were carrying recording equipment. The cameras, video recorders and the audio recorders were smashed up and even the exposed films and used tapes were systematically destroyed. The intent and effect of these attacks thus become crystal clear.[*]

## Criminal Proceedings in Parallel

The Liberhan Commission report seems to have been consigned to the racks in the home ministry but hopefully not to the dustbin. Meanwhile, the prosecutions filed against those deemed responsible told a story of their own and continued at a snail's pace. Most of the accused have moved on in life and held high political or constitutional office. Parliament used to perform the ritual of expressing deep regret on every 6 December, but now even that seems relegated to history.

The first FIR was registered even as the dust had barely settled over the demolition of the Babri Masjid. At 5.15 p.m. on 6 December 1992, FIR no. 197/92 was registered under various sections of the penal code (sections 395, 397, 332, 337, 338, 295, 297 and 153A of the IPC, and section 7 of the Criminal Law Amendment Act) against unknown 'kar sevaks' (someone who freely offers their services to a dharmic cause). Shortly thereafter, FIR no. 198/92 was registered, this time naming among the accused the well-known names and faces that had been present at the scene, who had allegedly taken part in making hateful and

---

[*] Report of the Liberhan Ayodhya Commission of Inquiry, published in 2009, available at https://www.mha.gov.in/about-us/commissions-committees/liberhan-ayodhya-commission

inciting speeches—L.K. Advani, Murli Manohar Joshi, Uma Bharti, Ashok Singhal, Sadhvi Rithambara, Vinay Kumar, Giriraj Kishore, Vishnu Hari Dalmia and Vinay Katiyar. Initially, FIR 197 was given to the UP Police for investigation (under the supervision of the court of Lucknow), while FIR 198 was investigated by the CBI (under the supervision of the court in Raebareli). One could question why two different investigations had to be conducted, by two different bodies, in relation to the same sequence of events. Was there some design behind this? Unfortunately, in India it is often difficult to separate or draw a distinction between institutional malice and institutional incompetence. In time both investigations came under the purview of the CBI, which filed a joint chargesheet before the district trial court in Lucknow.

Apart from the two main FIRs framing the criminal proceedings that followed the demolition, over the next few days scores of other FIRs were registered with the police at the Ram Janmabhoomi Thana (police station), encompassing several offences against the members of the media present, including assault and looting/theft of their property.

To most who read the final chargesheet filed by the CBI it would have seemed like a grave indictment against the top guns of the BJP and RSS, as well as outspoken proponents of the Ram temple movement, many of whose names were added to the already illustrious list of names mentioned in the second FIR. The CBI's investigations pointed squarely towards a larger malevolent conspiracy involving the deliberate demolition of the Babri Masjid, unlike the earlier narrative that the same was a result of a spur-of-the-moment movement. The chargesheet included firm evidence of a concerted, planned effort on the part of the accused, and thus charges under Section 120B, relating to criminal conspiracy, were added to the list. To those looking for justice, the chargesheet was a definitive step. However, even before the trail of the accused began, events began to unfold, entangling the proceedings in a legal quagmire.

An interim order was passed by the special judge presiding over the criminal trial on 9 September 1997, finding that a prima facie case was made out against the accused. The order read:

> From the above discussion this conclusion is drawn that in the present case the criminal conspiracy of felling down of the disputed structure of Ram Janam Bhumi/Babri Masjid was commenced by the accused from 1990 and it was completed on 06.12.1992. Sri Lal Krishan Advani and others at different times and at different places made schemes of criminal conspiracy of demolishing the above disputed structure.

Some of the accused wasted little time in approaching the hon'ble High Court of Allahabad against the trail court's directions to frame formal charges. The result may be viewed as a mixed bag for some of them, a significant win for others. The Lucknow bench of the high court, through Justice Jagdish Bhalla, passed a detailed order against the accused on 12 February 2001, after lengthy hearings on the matter. The court did not find any illegality in a joint chargesheet being filed in multiple FIRs, since each offence related to several acts that were part of/in execution of the same larger criminal conspiracy. However, the court went on to find that the state government of UP had not followed proper procedure in issuing the 8 October 1993 notification, which said that FIR no. 198 was to be tried with all the forty-nine cases in this special Lucknow court. In light of the same, the court refused to uphold the framing of charges against the accused in FIR no. 198 under the joint chargesheet and directed that the two FIRs would have to be tried separately. Yet, the court did leave an opening for the prosecution, indicating that the irregularity was curable.

The CBI wrote to the state government to issue a fresh notification so that the trial court could resume the case against the accused in FIR 198. But the consent from the state government for fresh notification for clubbing the FIRs was not forthcoming.

In light of the refusal from the then chief minister Rajnath Singh's government, the CBI even filed a petition seeking directions from the special designated court of Raebareli to revive and proceed with the trial of Advani and the twenty others. What was to follow was a surreal process of the dropping and reframing of charges, delaying any substantive trial for years. In September 2003, the special magistrate in Raebareli discharged Advani in the hate speech case, stating that the prosecution had not adduced sufficient evidence to support the charge against him in the supplementary chargesheet filed by the CBI after the de-clubbing of the FIRs, though charges were formally framed against the others. In 2005, the hon'ble high court set aside this order and directed reframing of charges against Advani and others, restarting the trial without the criminal conspiracy charges. The trial finally proceeded, with the first witness being examined in 2007. In 2010, the CBI once again failed to have the high court's 2001 decision revisited, with the high court upholding its earlier directions that the two FIRs had to be tried separately, as there were two classes of accused in the FIRs—the leaders and the members of the crowd—with no larger conspiracy charge, and their actions could not be clubbed under the same act/transaction.

It was only in the first quarter of 2011, during the tenure of the UPA-2 government headed by Prime Minister Manmohan Singh, that the CBI finally made it to the hon'ble Supreme Court of India, where it attempted to renew its stand for a common trial. The CBI fervently pressed its argument that each of the forty-nine cases lodged in the immediate aftermath of the demolition in 1992 was the direct fallout of a pre-planned conspiracy involving each of the accused; that each of the accused had acted in concert towards the goal of illegally demolishing the mosque, and thus all of the accused, including those who were not at the time facing any prosecution (having been discharged by lower courts/the high court), were equally culpable under the conspiracy. It was another five years before the highest court in the land gave its verdict—but it was a significant one. The apex court overturned the decisions of the Allahabad High Court, deciding that criminal conspiracy charges should be framed against many of the accused, including L.K. Advani, and further that the trials of all the cases were to be clubbed together. Thus, more than two decades after the inciting event, the so-called guilty parties were all to face criminal trials in the Lucknow court.

Since the legal case began, the course of justice in the Babri Masjid saga has run anything but smooth. Many of the accused enjoyed protection from prosecution under the orders of the court. In the end, the apex court sent them to face due process of law. Others were protected through their office, such as Kalyan Singh, against whom trial was stopped on his taking oath as governor of Rajasthan. But his relief lasted only as long as his position, and his trial resumed once he demitted office. In the end, as we know, the accused walked free. Some pre-emptively escaped any final justice by leaving the mortal world behind—Bal Thackeray, Ashok Singhal and Giriraj Kishore, among others. In the extensive trial over 300 witnesses were examined; many of them, too, did not live to see the end of the trial. The record of the matter is significant, encompassing volumes upon volumes of pleadings, statements, orders and reports. And although the Supreme Court judgment as to the title of the land had no legal effect on the criminal proceedings, at the time it felt there was little purpose left in the criminal proceedings after the judgment in 2019—the accused must have rejoiced in its light. And as if to put an emphasis on the futility of it all, eventually the accused were let off, found not guilty of any culpability in the destruction.

During the build-up to the D-Day of 6 December 1992, hectic activities to prepare for all eventualities, as indeed to prevent any major incident, were underway in Delhi and Lucknow political circles, not to mention the repeated hearings in the Supreme Court. The precautionary steps taken turned out to be inadequate and futile, as did the measures taken to seek some sort of resolution for those wronged. What actually happened was that the criminal cases filed against several senior BJP leaders, with a convoluted history of their own, came to an anti-climactic conclusion twenty-seven years later.

Until the day of the demolition, the Supreme Court was constantly engaged in keeping a close watch on the political pot as it neared boiling point. The Supreme Court had consistently passed orders with directions to maintain the law-and-order situation, as late as 1 December, five days before the karsevaks were to congregate in Ayodhya. Between its orders and the repeated assurances provided by the BJP players, the court seemed confident that the situation was not untenable. Hindsight is 20/20.

The vulnerability of the archaeological edifice was tested once before the final assault of 6 December. Mulayam Singh Yadav, then chief minister of UP, had proclaimed that '*parinda par nahi mar sakta*' (not a bird can take flight) in his state, without his say-so. In October 1990, the karsevaks were driven back, but not before doing damage to the mosque and in the process suffering casualties to police firing. Those were the heady days of 'Maulana' Mulayam, when human rights were put on the back burner and UP Police let loose to discipline, among others, karsevaks and protesters of the Uttarakhand movement at the Rampur Chouraha.

To date 6 December 1992 is described as a black day. Even for leaders of the BJP it was, avowedly, a sad day. The Supreme Court, which had reposed faith in the solemn assurance given by Kalyan Singh, chief minister of Uttar Pradesh, that no harm would come to the Babri Masjid if the karsevaks were allowed to assemble near the site, was shocked. Initially, the court reacted by asking the state to rebuild the destroyed mosque, but on second thought proceeded to order status quo and issue contempt notices to Kalyan Singh and others.

On the night of 6 December, some young ministers, including this author, gathered at the residence of Rajesh Pilot to take stock, and then proceeded together to C.K. Jaffer Sharief—thus two bold voices in the government were roused. Calls were made to Principal Secretary A.N. Verma, who suggested that we speak to the PM. We got through to the PM and suggested to him that Rajesh Pilot be included in the group that was flying to Faizabad. He in turn asked us to speak to A.N. Verma again, and thus the chase continued for a while, until we were told that the PM would not be available, having turned in for the night. The urgency was for a senior functionary of the government to intervene before the idols, which had been shifted during the demolition of the mosque, were reinstalled on the site. The reinstallation was eventually done, but when it appeared the next morning that a roof would be placed above the idols, the government moved to disperse the conspicuously reduced crowd of karsevaks.

The dazed Central government of Narasimha Rao reacted by issuing an ordinance acquiring the land around the disputed site and seeking assistance from the Supreme Court through a presidential reference. On Monday morning, after the shattering weekend, the Council of Ministers gathered in a small room in Parliament. The mood was sombre, and a pall of gloom hung on the gathering. Madhavrao Scindia spoke a few words to show support and solidarity with PM Narasimha Rao, who, as has been mentioned before, surprised us all with a curt response, 'Please spare me the sympathy.' There was no further opportunity for discussing the subject again, but a few days later I was sent to West Asia to reassure Arab countries about the future of Muslims in India.

The government issued a white paper that included, inter alia, an 'Overview' in Chapter I, which stated:

1.1. Ayodhya situated in the north of India is a township in District Faizabad of Uttar Pradesh. It has long been a place of holy pilgrimage because of its mention in the epic Ramayana as the place of birth of Sri Ram. The structure commonly known as Ram Janma Bhoomi–Babri Masjid was erected as a mosque by one Mir Baqi in Ayodhya in 1528 AD. It is claimed by some sections that it was built at the site believed to be the birth spot of Sri Ram where a temple had stood earlier. This resulted in a long-standing dispute.

1.2. The controversy entered a new phase with the placing of idols in the disputed structure in December 1949. The premises were attached under Section 145 of the Code of Criminal Procedure. Civil suits were filed shortly thereafter. Interim orders in these civil suits restrained the parties from removing the idols or interfering with their worship. In effect, therefore, from December 1949 till 6-12-1992 the structure had not been used as a mosque.

[. . .]

6.  The movement to construct a Ram Temple at the site of the disputed structure gathered momentum in recent years which became a matter of great controversy and a source of tension. This led to several parleys the details of which are not very material for the present purpose. These parleys involving the Vishwa Hindu Parishad (VHP) and the All India Babri Masjid Action Committee (AIBMAC), however, failed to resolve the dispute. A new dimension was added to the campaign for construction of the temple with the formation of the Government in Uttar Pradesh in June 1991 by the Bhartiya Janata Party (BJP) which declared its commitment to the construction of the temple and took certain steps like the acquisition of land adjoining the disputed structure while leaving out the disputed structure itself from the acquisition. The focus of the temple construction movement from October 1991 was to start construction of the temple by way of kar sewa on the land acquired by the Government of Uttar Pradesh while leaving the disputed structure intact. This attempt did not succeed and there was litigation in the Allahabad High Court as well as in

this Court. There was a call for resumption of kar sewa from 6-12-1992 and the announcement made by the organisers was for a symbolic kar sewa without violation of the court orders including those made in the proceedings pending in this Court. In spite of initial reports from Ayodhya on 6-12-1992 indicating an air of normalcy, around midday a crowd addressed by leaders of BJP, VHP, etc., climbed the Ram Janma Bhumi–Babri Masjid (RJM–BM) structure and started damaging the domes. Within a short time, the entire structure was demolished and razed to the ground. Indeed, it was an act of 'national shame'. What was demolished was not merely an ancient structure; but the faith of the minorities in the sense of justice and fair-play of majority. It shook their faith in the rule of law and constitutional processes. A five-hundred-year-old structure which was defenceless and whose safety was a sacred trust in the hands of the State Government was demolished.

[. . .]

9.   A brief reference to certain suits in this connection may now be made. In 1950, two suits were filed by some Hindus; in one of these suits in January 1950, the trial court passed interim orders whereby the idols remained at the place where they were installed in December 1949 and their puja by the Hindus continued. The interim order was confirmed by the High Court in April 1955. On 1-2-1986, the District Judge ordered the opening of the lock placed on a grill leading to the sanctum sanctorum of the shrine in the disputed structure and permitted puja by the Hindu devotees. In 1959, a suit was filed by the Nirmohi Akhara claiming title to the disputed structure. In 1981, another suit was filed claiming title to the disputed structure by the Sunni Central Wakf Board. In 1989, Deoki Nandan Agarwal, as the next friend of the Deity filed a title suit in respect of the disputed structure. In 1989, the aforementioned suits were transferred to the

Allahabad High Court and were ordered to be heard together. On 14-8-1989, the High Court ordered the maintenance of status quo in respect of the disputed structure (Appendix-I to the White Paper). As earlier mentioned, it is stated in para 1.2 of the White Paper that:

... interim orders in these civil suits restrained the parties from removing the idols or interfering with their worship. In effect, therefore, from December 1949 till 6-12-1992 the structure had not been used as a mosque.

5.  As a result of the happenings at Ayodhya on 06.12.1992, the President of India issued a proclamation under Article 356 of the Constitution of India assuming to himself all the functions of the Government of Uttar Pradesh, dissolving the U.P. Vidhan Sabha. As a consequence of the events at Ayodhya on 06.12.1992, the Central Government decided to acquire all areas in dispute in the suits pending in the Allahabad High Court. It was also decided to acquire suitable adjacent area, which would be made available to two Trusts for construction of a Ram Temple and a Mosque respectively. The Government of India has also decided to request the President to seek the opinion of the Supreme Court on the question whether there was a Hindu temple existing on the site where the disputed structure stood. An ordinance was issued on 07.01.1993 namely 'Acquisition of Certain Area at Ayodhya Ordinance' for acquisition of 67.703 acres of land in the Ram Janam Bhumi–Babri Masjid complex. A reference to the Supreme Court under Article 143 of the Constitution was also made on the same day, i.e. 07.01.1993. The Ordinance No. 8 of 1993 was replaced by the Acquisition of Certain Area at Ayodhya Act, 1993 (No. 33 of 1993). A Writ Petition Under Article 32 was filed in the Supreme Court challenging the validity of the Act No. 33 of 1993. Several writ petitions at Allahabad High Court were also filed challenging various aspects of the Act, 1993.

The Supreme Court exercising its jurisdiction under Article 139A transferred the writ petitions, which were pending in the High Court. The Writ Petitions under Article 32, transferred cases from High Court of Allahabad as well as Reference No. 1 of 1993 made by President under Article 143 were all heard together and decided by common judgment dated 24.10.1994, where the Constitution Bench upheld the validity of the Act with certain additional findings.

Thus, it was hoped that the dust of demolition would finally settle, passions would subside and all parties, political or otherwise, would await the process of law to play out to its logical (or illogical) end.

# Ten

# The President and the Justices

The first reactions had already come from the Supreme Court bench of the chief justice that had been led up the garden path by the assurances given by the chief minister of Uttar Pradesh, Kalyan Singh. The judges initially indicated that nothing less than the reconstruction of the mosque would satisfy them, but were ultimately prevailed upon by the attorney general, Milon Bannerjee, to preserve status quo and proceed for contempt against the chief minister. Ultimately, Kalyan Singh was pronounced guilty of contempt and directed to remain in custody till the rising of the court.

In response to the demolition of 6 December 1992, the Central government acquired an area of about 68 acres, including the premises in dispute, under the Ayodhya Acquisition Act (the Acquisition of Certain Area at Ayodhya Act, 1993). Sections 3 and 4 envisaged the abatement of all suits which were pending before the high court. Simultaneously, the President of India made a reference to this court under Article 143 of the Constitution, which empowers the President to pose questions to the Supreme Court that are deemed important for public welfare. Under presidential reference, the court was asked, '. . . whether a Hindu temple or any

Hindu religious structure existed prior to the construction of the Ram Janam Bhoomi and Babari Masjid (including the premises of the inner and outer courtyards on such structure) in the area on which the structure stands . . .'

Writ petitions that were filed before the Allahabad High Court and the Supreme Court, challenging the validity of the act of 1993 and the reference by the President, were heard together and decided by a judgment dated 24 October 1994 of a constitution bench of this court, titled 'Dr M. Ismail Faruqui vs Union of India'.*

The bench comprised M.N. Venkatachaliah, chief justice and justices A.M. Ahmadi J.S. Verma, G.N. Ray and S.P. Bharucha. (All the hon'ble justices, except Justice G.N. Ray, went on to become chief justice.) They were to meet again thereafter to consider the steps taken by the government. The conclusions arrived at by the majority on the constitution bench—comprising Chief Justice Venkatachaliah, and justices J.S. Verma and G.N. Ray—in which the court also often cited the government's white paper, are excerpted below:

6.  [. . .] There was a call for resumption of kar sewa from 6-12-1992 and the announcement made by the organisers was for a symbolic kar sewa without violation of the court orders including those made in the proceedings pending in this Court. In spite of initial reports from Ayodhya on 6-12-1992 indicating an air of normalcy, around midday a crowd addressed by leaders of BJP, VHP, etc., climbed the Ram Janma Bhumi–Babri Masjid (RJM–BM) structure and started damaging the domes. Within a short time, the entire structure was demolished and razed to the ground. Indeed, it was an act of 'national shame'. What was demolished was not merely an ancient structure; but the faith of the minorities in the sense of justice and fair play of majority.

---

* 'Ismail Faruqui' (supra).

It shook their faith in the rule of law and constitutional processes. A five-hundred-year-old structure which was defenceless and whose safety was a sacred trust in the hands of the State Government was demolished.

[. . .]

13. [. . .] Chapter VIII relating to the 'action taken by the central government' is as under:

'8.11 Mention has been made above (Overview) of the decisions taken on 7th December by the Government to ban communal organizations, to take strong action for prosecution of the offences connected with the demolition, to fix responsibilities of various authorities for their lapses relating to the events of December 8, to rebuild the demolished structure and to take appropriate steps regarding new Ram temple. The last two decisions were further elaborated on 27th December as follows:

The Government has decided to acquire all areas in dispute in the suits pending in the Allahabad High Court. It has also been decided to acquire suitable adjacent area. The acquired area excluding the area on which the disputed structure stood would be made available to two Trusts which would be set up for construction of a Ram Temple and a Mosque respectively and for planned development of the area.

The Government of India has also decided to request the President to seek the opinion of the Supreme Court on the question whether there was a Hindu temple existing on the site where the disputed structure stood. The Government has also decided to abide by the opinion of the Supreme Court and to take appropriate steps to enforce the Court's opinion. Notwithstanding the acquisition of the disputed area, the Government would ensure that the position existing prior to the promulgation of the Ordinance is maintained until such time as the Supreme Court gives its opinion in the matter. Thereafter the rights of the parties shall be determined in the light to the Court's opinion.'

[. . .]

14. [. . .]

'Special Reference

Whereas a dispute has arisen whether a Hindu temple or any Hindu religious structure existed prior to the construction of the structure (including the premises of the inner and outer courtyards of such structure, commonly known as the Ram Janma Bhumi–Babri Masjid, in the area in which the structure stood in Village Kot Ramchandra in Ayodhya, in Pargana Haveli Avadh, in Tehsil Faizabad Sadar, in the district of Faizabad of the State of Uttar Pradesh;

2   And whereas the said area is located in Revenue Plot Nos. 159 and 160 in the said Village Kot Ramchandra;
3.   And whereas the said dispute has affected the maintenance of public order and harmony between different communities in the country;
4.   And whereas the aforesaid area vests in the Central Government by virtue of the Acquisition of Certain Area at Ayodhya Ordinance, 1993;
5.   **And whereas notwithstanding the vesting of the aforesaid area in the Central Government under the said Ordinance the Central Government proposes to settle the said dispute after obtaining the opinion of the Supreme Court of India and in terms of the said opinion;**

6. And whereas in view of what has been hereinbefore stated it appears to me that the question hereinafter set out has arisen and is of such a nature and of such public importance that it is expedient to obtain the opinion of the Supreme Court of India thereon;

7. Now, therefore, in exercise of the powers conferred upon me by clause (1) of Article 143 of the Constitution of India, I, Shanker Dayal Sharma, President of India, hereby refer the following question to the Supreme Court of India for consideration and opinion thereon, namely:

**Whether a Hindu temple or any Hindu religious structure existed prior to the construction of the Ram Janma Bhumi–Babri Masjid (including the premises of the inner and outer courtyards of such structure) in the area on which the structure stood?**

Sd/-
President of India

New Delhi;
Dated 7th January, 1993.'

[. . .]

47. As earlier stated, worship by Hindu devotees of the idols installed on the Ram Chabutra which stood on the disputed site within the courtyard of the disputed structure had been performed without any objection by the Muslims even prior to the shifting of those idols from the Ram Chabutra into the disputed structure in December 1949; in one of the suits filed in January 1950, the trial court passed interim orders whereby the idols remained at the place where they were installed in 1949 and worship of the idols there by the Hindu devotees continued; this interim order was confirmed by the High Court in April 1955; the District Judge ordered the opening of the

lock placed on a grill leading to the sanctum sanctorum of the shrine in the disputed structure on 1-2-1986 and permitted worship of the idols there to Hindu devotees; and this situation continued till demolition of the structure on 6-12-1992 when Ram Chabutra also was demolished. It was only as a result of the act of demolition on 6-12-1992 that the worship by the Hindu devotees in general of the idols at that place was interrupted. Since the time of demolition, worship of the idols by a pujari alone is continuing. This is how the right of worship of the idols practised by Hindu devotees for a long time from much prior to 1949 in the Ram Chabutra within the disputed site has been interrupted since the act of demolition on 6-12-1992 restricting the worship of the idols since then to only by one pujari. On the other hand, at least since December 1949, the Muslims have not been offering worship at any place in the disputed site though, it may turn out at the trial of the suits that they had a right to do so.

[. . .]

51. It may also be mentioned that even as Ayodhya is said to be of particular significance to the Hindus as a place of pilgrimage because of the ancient belief that Lord Rama was born there, the mosque was of significance for the Muslim community as an ancient mosque built by Mir Baqi in 1528 AD. **As a mosque, it was a religious place of worship by the Muslims. This indicates the comparative significance of the disputed site to the two communities and also that the impact of acquisition is equally on the right and interest of the Hindu community.** Mention of this aspect is made only in the context of the argument that the statute as a whole, not merely Section 7 thereof, is anti-secular being slanted in favour of the Hindus and against the Muslims.

[. . .]

53. Another effect of the freeze imposed by Section 7(2) of the Act is that it ensures that there can be no occasion for the Hindu community to seek to enlarge the scope of the practice of worship by them as on 7-1-1993 during the interregnum till the final adjudication on the basis that in fact a larger right of worship by them was in vogue up to 6-12-1992. It is difficult to visualise how Section 7(2) can be construed as a slant in favour of the Hindu community and, therefore, anti-secular. The provision does not curtail practice of right of worship of the Muslim community in the disputed area, there having been de facto no exercise of the practice or worship by them there at least since December 1949; and it maintains status quo by the freeze to the reduced right of worship by the Hindus as in existence on 7-1-1993. However, confining exercise of the right of worship of the Hindu community to its reduced form within the disputed area as on 7-1-1993, lesser than that exercised till the demolition on 6-12-1992, by the freeze enacted in Section 7(2) appears to be reasonable and just in view of the fact that the **miscreants who demolished the mosque are suspected to be persons professing to practise the Hindu religion. The Hindu community must, therefore, bear the cross on its chest, for the misdeed of the miscreants reasonably suspected to belong to their religious fold.**

[. . .]

### Conclusions

96. [. . .]

(1) (a) Since Sub-section (3) of Section 4 of the Act abates all pending suits and legal proceedings without providing for an alternative dispute resolution mechanism for resolution of the dispute between the parties thereto. This is an extinction of the judicial remedy for resolution of the despite amounting to

negation of the rule of law. Sub section (3) of Section 4 of the Act is, therefore, unconstitutional and invalid.

(b) The remaining provisions of the Act do not suffer from any invalidity on the construction made thereof by us. Sub-section (3) of Section 4 of the Act is severable from the remaining Act. Accordingly, the challenge to the constitutional validity of the remaining Act, expect for sub-section (3) of Section 4, is rejected.

**(2) Irrespective of the status of a mosque under the Muslim law applicable in the Islamic countries, the status of a mosque under the Mahomedan Law applicable in secular India is the same and equal to that of any other place of worship of any religion; and does not enjoy any greater immunity from acquisition in exercise of the sovereign or prerogative power of the State, than the places of worship of the other religions.**

(3) The pending suits and other proceedings relating to the disputed area within which the structure (including the premises of the inner and outer courtyards of such structure), commonly known as the Ram Janma Bhumi–Babri Masjid, stood, stand revived for adjudication.

(4) The vesting of the said disputed area in the Central Government by virtue of Section 3 of the Act is limited, as a statutory receiver, with the duty for its management and administration according to Section 7 requiring maintenance of status quo therein under sub-section (2) of Section 7 of the Act. The duty of the Central Government as the statutory receiver is to hand over the disputed area in accordance with Section 6 of the Act, in terms of the adjudication made in the suits for implementation of the final decision therein. This is the purpose for which the disputed area has been so acquired.

(5) The power of the courts in making further interim orders in the suits is limited to, and circumscribed by, the area outside the ambit of Section 7 of the Act.

(6) The vesting of the adjacent area, other than the disputed area, acquired by the Act in the Central Government by virtue of

Section 3 of the Act is absolute with the power of management
and administration thereof in accordance with sub-section (1)
of Section 7 of the Act, till its further vesting in any authority or
other body or trustees of any trust in accordance with Section 6
of the Act. The further vesting of the adjacent area, other than
the disputed area, in accordance with Sec. 6 of the Act has to
be made at the time and in the manner indicated, in view of the
purpose of its acquisition.

(7) The meaning of the word 'vest' in Section 3 and Section 6 of the
Act has to be so understood in the different contexts.

[. . .]

(9) The challenge to acquisition of any part of the adjacent area
unnecessary for achieving the professed objective of settling
the long-standing dispute cannot be examined at this stage.
However, the area found to be superfluous on the exact area
needed for the purpose being determined on adjudication of
the dispute, must be restored to the undisputed owners.

The minority on the bench—comprising justices A.M. Ahmadi
and S.P. Bharucha—dissented strongly, beginning by repeating
the narrative of the white paper:

100. [. . .]

On 6-12-1992, the disputed structure was demolished.

'The demolition . . . was a most reprehensible act. The
perpetrators of this deed struck not only against a place of
worship but also at the principles of secularism, democracy
and the rule of law . . .' (Para 1.35)

At 6.45 p.m. on that day the idols were replaced where the
disputed structure had stood and by 7.30 p.m. work had started on

the construction of a temporary structure for them. (Para 1.20) At about 9.10 p.m. the President of India issued a proclamation under the provisions of Article 356 assuming to himself all the functions of the Government of Uttar Pradesh and dissolving its Vidhan Sabha. (Para 1.21)

[. . .]

139.    Reference was made in the course of the proceedings to the provisions of the Places of Worship Special Provisions Act, 1991. It is a statute to prohibit the conversion of any place of worship and to provide for the maintenance of the religious character of any place of worship as it existed on 15-8-1947. It enjoins that no person shall convert any place of worship of any religious denomination or any section thereof into a place of worship of a different section of the same religious denomination or of a different religious denomination or any section thereof. It declares that the religious character of a place of worship existing on 15-8-1947, shall continue to be the same as it existed on that date. It is specified that nothing contained in the statute shall apply to the place of worship which was the disputed structure at Ayodhya and to any suit, appeal or other proceedings relating to it. Based upon The Places of Worship Act, it was submitted that what had happened at Ayodhya on 6-12-1992, could never happen again. The submission overlooks the fact that the Penal Code, 1860 contains provisions in respect of offences relating to religion. Section 295 thereof states that whoever destroys, damages or defiles any place of worship or any object held sacred by any class of persons with the object of thereby insulting the religion of any class of persons or with the knowledge that any class of persons is likely to consider such destruction, damage or defilement as an insult to their religion shall be punished. Section 295 provides for punishment of a person who with the deliberate and malicious intention of

outraging the religious feelings of any class of citizens of India, by words, either spoken or written, or by signs or by visible representation or otherwise insults or attempts to insult the religion or religious beliefs of that class. **Those who razed the disputed structure to the ground on 6-12-1992, were not deterred by these provisions. Others similarly minded are as little likely to be deterred by the provisions of the Places of Worship Act.**

140. The Preamble to the Constitution of India proclaims that India is a secular democratic republic. Article 15 in Part III of the Constitution, which provides for fundamental rights, debars the State from discriminating against any citizen on the ground of religion. Secularism is given pride of place in the Constitution. The object is to preserve and protect all religions, to place all religious communities on a par. **When, therefore, adherents of the religion of the majority of Indian citizens make a claim upon and assail the place of worship of another religion and, by dint of numbers, create conditions that are conducive to public disorder, it is the constitutional obligation of the State to protect that place of worship and to preserve public order, using for the purpose such means and forces of law and order as are required. It is impermissible under the provisions of the Constitution for the State to acquire that place of worship to preserve public order. To condone the acquisition of a place of worship in such circumstances is to efface the principle of secularism from the Constitution.**

141. We must add a caveat. If the title to the place of worship is in dispute in a court of law and public order is jeopardised, two courses are open to the Central Government. It may apply to the court concerned to be appointed Receiver of the place of worship, to hold it secure pending the final adjudication of its title, or it may enact legislation that makes it statutory Receiver of the place of worship pending the adjudication of

its title by the court concerned. In either event, the Central Government would bind itself to hand over the place of worship to the party in whose favour its title is found.

[. . .]

149. **The Act and the Reference, as stated hereinabove, favour one religious community and disfavour another; the purpose of the Reference is, therefore, opposed to secularism and is unconstitutional. Besides, the Reference does not serve a constitutional purpose.**

150. Secondly, the fifth recital to the Reference states that 'the Central Government proposes to settle the said dispute after obtaining the opinion of the Supreme Court of India and in terms of the said opinion'. (emphasis supplied) It is clear that the Central Government does not propose to settle the dispute in terms of the Court's opinion. It proposes to use the Court's opinion as a springboard for negotiations. Resolution of the dispute as a result of such negotiations cannot be said to be a resolution of the dispute 'in terms of the said opinion'. **Asked to obtain instructions and tell the Court that the mosque would be rebuilt if the question posed by the Reference was answered in the negative, the learned Solicitor General made the statement quoted above. It leaves us in no doubt that even in the circumstance that this Court opines that no Hindu temple or Hindu religious structure existed on the disputed site before the disputed structure was built thereon, there is no certainty that the mosque will be rebuilt.**

151. Thirdly, there is the aspect of evidence in relation to the question referred. It is not our suggestion that a court of law is not competent to decide such a question. It can be done if expert evidence of archaeologists and historians is led, and is tested in cross-examination. The principal protagonists

of the two stands are not appearing in the Reference; they will neither lead evidence nor cross-examine. The learned Solicitor General stated that the Central Government would lead no evidence, but it would place before the Court the material that it had collected from the two sides during the course of earlier negotiations. The Court being ill-equipped to examine and evaluate such material, it would have to appoint experts in the field to do so, and their evaluation would go unchallenged. Apart from the inherent inadvisability of rendering a judicial opinion on such evaluation, the opinion would be liable to the criticism of one or both sides that it was rendered without hearing them or their evidence. This would ordinarily be of no significance for they had chosen to stay away, but this opinion is intended to create a public climate for negotiations and the criticism would find the public ear, to say nothing of the fact that it would impair this Court's credibility.

152.   **Ayodhya is a storm that will pass. The dignity and honour of the Supreme Court cannot be compromised because of it.**

* * *

The storm may well have passed but it left a great deal of debris in its wake. Many people believe that the winds that blew did not spare the robust structure of the Supreme Court either. To be fair to the court, one might borrow from Charles Dickens and say, 'Those were the best of times, those were the worst of times.'

# Eleven

# Ayodhya to Allahabad

Much as the Ayodhya saga is repeatedly emphasized to be a title dispute, although with religious and political overtones, there is a clear religious spin given to it. And to understand it one needs to put in perspective how religious institutions were treated by the courts long before the Ayodhya judgment. The Constitution of India has a core of rights under the 'Fundamental Rights' chapter, dealing with Articles 14, 15, 16 (equality) 19, 21, 25–30 (fundamental rights). Central to the cluster of rights is the system of adjudication under Articles 32 (enforcement of fundamental rights by the Supreme Court), 136 (special appeals to the Supreme Court), 226–227 (judicial review by the high court) and 141–142 (Supreme Court laying down the law to do complete justice). As the country discovered in the ADM Jabalpur case,* rights become meaningless without adjudication and enforcement by courts of law.

---

* 'Additional District Magistrate, Jabalpur vs Shivakant Shukla', 1976, 2 SCC 521; AIR 1976 SC 1207. A landmark judgment pertaining to the right of habeas corpus, where it was decreed during the Emergency that a person's right to not be unlawfully detained could be suspended.

Naturally, the citizens (on both sides) had a major stake in the Ayodhya litigation and, therefore, a keen interest in how the high court and the Supreme Court would deal with the matter. The Allahabad High Court's full bench, comprising Justice Sudhir Agarwal, Justice D.V. Sharma and Justice S.U. Khan, decided five suits*, and all parties filed cross-appeals (essentially first appeals) before the Supreme Court. The suits, as noticed by the Supreme Court,† were as follows:

[. . .]

**Suit 1 - OOS No 1 of 1989 (Regular Suit 2 of 1950)**

**34. The suit was instituted on 13 January 1950 by Gopal Singh Visharad, a resident of Ayodhya in his capacity as a follower of Sanatan Dharm seeking:**

(i) A declaration of his entitlement to worship and seek the darshan of Lord Ram—according to religion and custom at the Janmabhumi temple without hindrance; and

(ii) A permanent and perpetual injunction restraining defendant nos 1 to 10 from removing the idols of the deity and other idols from the place where they were installed; from closing the way leading to the idols; or interfering in worship and darshan.

34.1 Defendant nos 1 to 5 are Muslim residents of Ayodhya; defendant no 6 is the State of Uttar Pradesh . . .

---

* Consolidated judgment in 'Gopal Singh Visharad vs Zahoor Ahmad and Others', Other Original Suit (OOS) No. 1/1989, and 'Nirmohi Akhara and Others vs Baboo Datt Ram and Others' (OOS) No. 3/1989, and 'The Sunni Central Board of Waqfs, UP and Others vs Gopal Singh Visharad and Others, (OOS) No. 4/1989, and 'Bhagwan Sri Ram Lala Virajman and Others vs Rajendra Singh and Others', (OOS) No. 5/1989; 2010 SCC OnLine All 1935.
† The Ram Janmabhoomi Temple case (supra).

34.2   The case of the plaintiff in Suit 1 is that, as a resident of
       Ayodhya, he was worshipping the idol of Lord Ram and Charan
       Paduka (foot impressions)—in that place of Janambhumi. The
       boundaries of the 'disputed place' as described in the plaint
       are as follows:

       Disputed place:
       East: Store and Chabutra of Ram Janam Bhumi
       West: Parti
       North: Sita Rasoi
       South: Parti

[. . .]

35.2      Defendant 10, the Sunni Central Waqf Board filed its written
       statement stating:

[. . .]

   (vi)   **The plaintiff was estopped from claiming the mosque as
          the Janmabhumi of Lord Ram as the claim in the Suit of
          1885 instituted by Mahant Raghubar Das** (described to be
          the plaintiff's predecessor) had been confined only to the
          Ramchabutra measuring seventeen by twenty-one feet
          outside the mosque; and

       [. . .]

   (viii) **There already existed a Ram Janmasthan Mandir, a
          short distance away from Babri Masjid. In the plaintiff's
          replication to the written statement of defendant nos
          1 to 5, it was averred that the disputed site has never
          been used as a mosque since 1934.** It was further stated
          that it was common knowledge that Hindus have been in

continuous possession by virtue of which the claim of the
defendants has ceased.

\* \* \*

During the course of proceedings O.S.S No. 2/1989 was withdrawn
as it sought similar relief to Suit No. 1.

\* \* \*

**Suit 3 - OOS no 3 of 1989 (Regular Suit no 26 of 1959)**

36.   The suit was instituted on 17 December 1959 by Nirmohi
      Akhara through Mahant Jagat Das seeking a decree for the
      removal of the receiver from the management and charge
      of the Janmabhumi temple and for delivering it to the
      plaintiff. Defendant no 1 in Suit 3 is the receiver; defendant
      no 2 is the State of Uttar Pradesh; defendant no 3 is the
      Deputy Commissioner, Faizabad; defendant no 4 is the City
      Magistrate, Faizabad; defendant no 5 is the Superintendent
      of Police, Faizabad; defendant nos 6 to 8 are Muslim residents
      of Ayodhya; defendant no 9 is the Sunni Central Waqf Board
      and defendant no 10 is Umesh Chandra Pandey.

36.1  The cause of action is stated to have arisen on 5 January
      1950 when the management and charge of the Janmabhumi
      temple was taken away by the City Magistrate and entrusted
      to the receiver. Nirmohi Akhara pleaded that:

[. . .]

      (iii) The Janmasthan is of ancient antiquity lying within the
            boundaries shown . . . in the sketch map appended to
            the plaint within which stands the 'temple building' . . .
            where the idols of Lord Ram with Lakshman, Hanuman and

Saligram have been installed. The temple building has been in the possession of Nirmohi Akhara and only Hindus have been allowed to enter the temple and make offerings . . .

[. . .]

(vi) No Mohammedan has been allowed to enter the temple building since 1934 . . .

37. In the written statement filed on behalf of defendant nos 6 to 8, Muslim residents of Ayodhya, it was stated that Babri Masjid was constructed by Emperor Babur in 1528 and has been constituted as a waqf, entitling Muslims to offer prayers. Moreover, it was submitted that:

(i) The Suit of 1885 by Raghubar Mahant Das was confined to Ramchabutra and has been dismissed by the Sub-Judge, Faizabad;

(ii) The property of the mosque was constituted as a waqf under the U.P. Muslim Waqf Act 1936;

(iii) **Muslims have been in continuous possession of the mosque since 1528 as a consequence of which all the rights of the plaintiffs have been extinguished;**

(iv) On the eastern and northern sides of the mosque, there are Muslim graves;

(v) Namaz was continuously offered in the property until 16 December 1949 and the character of the mosque will not stand altered if an idol has been installed surreptitiously; and

(vi) **There is another temple at Ayodhya which is known as the Janmasthan temple of Lord Ram which has been in existence for a long time.**

[. . .]

37.3  In the written statement filed by Defendant 10, Umesh
      Chandra Pandey, it was submitted:

[. . .]

   (v) **The place was virtually landlocked by a Hindu temple in
       which worship of the deity took place;**
   (vi) The Suit of the Nirmohi Akhara was barred by limitation
        having been instituted in 1959, though the cause of action
        arose on 5 January 1950; and
   (vii) Nirmohi Akhara did not join the proceedings under Section
         145 nor did they file a revision against the order passed by
         the Additional City Magistrate.

In the replication filed by Nirmohi Akhara to the written statement
of defendant no 10, there was a detailed account of the founding
of the denomination. Following the tradition of Shankaracharya
since the seventh century CE, the practice of setting up Maths was
followed by Ramanujacharya and later, by Ramanand. Ramanand
founded a sect of Vaishnavs known as 'Ramats', who worship Lord
Ram. The spiritual preceptors of the Ramanandi sect of Bairagis
established three 'annis' namely, the (i) Nirmohi; (ii) Digamber; and
(iii) Nirwani Akharas. These Akharas are Panchayati Maths. Nirmohi
Akhara owns the Ram Janmasthan temple which is associated with
the birth-place of Lord Ram. The outer enclosure was owned and
managed by Nirmohi Akhara until the proceedings under Section
145 were instituted.

**Suit 4 - OOS 4 of 1989 (Regular Suit no 12 of 1961)**

38. **Suit 4 was instituted on 18 December 1961 by the Sunni Central
    Waqf Board and nine Muslim residents of Ayodhya. It has been
    averred that the suit has been instituted on behalf of the entire
    Muslim community together with an application under Order I**

**Rule 8 of the CPC. As amended, the following reliefs have been sought in the plaint:**

(a) A declaration to the effect that the property indicated by letters A B C D in the sketch map attached to the plaint is public mosque commonly known as 'Babri Masjid' and that the land adjoining the mosque shown in the sketch map by letters E F G H is a public Muslim graveyard as specified in j para 2 of the plaint may be decreed.

(b) That in case in the opinion of the Court delivery of possession is deemed to be the proper remedy, a decree for delivery of possession of the mosque and graveyard in suit by removal of the idols and other articles which the Hindus may have placed in the mosque as objects of their worship be passed in plaintiff's favour, against the defendants.

(bb) That the statutory Receiver be commanded to hand over the property in dispute described in Schedule 'A' of the Plaint by removing the unauthorized structures erected thereon.

[Note: Prayer (bb) was inserted by an amendment to the plaint pursuant to the order of the High Court dated 25 May 1995].

38.1   Defendant no 1 in Suit 4 is Gopal Singh Visharad; defendant no 2 is Ram Chander Dass Param Hans; defendant no 3 is Nirmohi Akhara; defendant no 4 is Mahant Raghunath Das; defendant no 5 is the State of U.P. . . . .

38.2   The suit is based on the averment that in Ayodhya, there is an ancient historic mosque known commonly as Babri Masjid which was constructed by Babur more than 433 years ago following his conquest of India and the occupation of its territories. It has been averred that the mosque was built for the use of the Muslims in general as a place of worship and for the performance of religious ceremonies. The main construction of the mosque is depicted by the letters A B C D on the plan annexed to the plaint. Adjoining the land is a graveyard. According to the plaintiffs, both the mosque and the graveyard vest in the Almighty and since the construction of the mosque, it has been used by the Muslims for offering prayers while the graveyard has been used for burial. The plaint alleged that outside the main building of the mosque, Hindu worship was being conducted at a Chabutra admeasuring 17x21 feet on which there was a small wooden structure in the form of a tent.

[. . .]

**38.4  According to the plaintiffs, assuming without admitting that there existed a Hindu temple as alleged by the defendants on the site of which the mosque was built 433 years ago by Emperor Babur, the Muslims by virtue of their long exclusive and continuous possession commencing from the construction of the mosque and ensuing until its desecration perfected their title by adverse possession . . .**

[. . .]

**Suit 5 – OOS no 5 of 1989 (Regular Suit no 236 of 1989)**

40. The suit was instituted on 1 July 1989 claiming the following reliefs:

**(A) A declaration that the entire premises of Sri Rama Janma Bhumi at Ayodhya, as described and delineated in Annexure I, II and III belongs to the plaintiff Deities.**

(B) A perpetual injunction against the Defendants prohibiting them from interfering with, or raising any objection to, or placing any obstruction in the construction of the new

Temple building at Sri Rama Janma Bhumi, Ayodhya, after demolishing and removing the existing buildings and structures etc., situated thereat, in so far as it may be necessary or expedient to do so for the said purpose.

**40.1** **This suit has been instituted in the name of—'Bhagwan Sri Ram Virajman at Sri Ram Janmabhumi, Ayodhya also called Bhagwan Sri Ram Lalla Virajman'. The deity so described is the first plaintiff. The second plaintiff is described as—'Asthan Sri Rama Janambhumi, Ayodhya'.** Both the plaintiffs were represented by Sri Deoki Nandan Agrawala, a former judge of the Allahabad High Court as next friend. The next friend of the first and second plaintiffs is impleaded as the third plaintiff.

40.2    The defendants to the suit include:

(i)   Nirmohi Akhara which is the Plaintiff in Suit 3;
(ii)  Sunni Central Waqf Board, the Plaintiff in Suit 4;
(iii) Hindu and Muslim residents of Ayodhya; and
(iv) The State of Uttar Pradesh, the Collector and Senior Superintendent of Police.

Several other Hindu entities including the All India Hindu Mahasabha and a Trust described as the Sri Ram Janmabhumi Trust, are parties to the Suit as is the Shia Central Board of Waqfs.

40.3    The principal averments in Suit 5 are that:

(i)   The first and second plaintiffs are juridical persons: Lord Ram is the presiding deity of the place and the place is itself a symbol of worship;
(ii)  The identification of Ram Janmabhumi, for the purpose of the plaint is based on the site plans of the building, premises and adjacent area prepared by Sri Shiv Shankar

Lal, who was appointed as Commissioner by the Civil Judge at Faizabad in Suit 1 of 1950;

(iii)   The plaint contains a reference to the earlier suits instituted before the Civil Court and that the religious ceremonies for attending to the deities have been looked after by the receiver appointed in the proceedings under Section 145. Although seva and puja of the deity have been conducted, darshan for the devotees is allowed only from behind a barrier;

(iv)    Alleging that offerings to the deity have been misappropriated, it has been stated that the devotees desired to have a new temple constructed—after removing the old structure at Sri Ram Janmabhumi at Ayodhya. A Deed of Trust was constituted on 18 December 1985 for the purpose of managing the estate and affairs of the Janmabhumi;

(v)     **Though both the presiding deity of Lord Ram and Ram Janmabhumi are claimed to be juridical persons with a distinct personality, neither of them was impleaded as a party to the earlier suits. As a consequence, the decrees passed in those suits will not bind the deities;**

(vi)    Public records establish that Lord Ram was born and manifested himself in human form as an incarnation of Vishnu at the premises in dispute;

(vii)   **The place itself—Ram Janmasthan—is an object of worship since it personifies the divine spirit worshipped in the form of Lord Ram. Both the deity and the place of birth thus possess a juridical character. Hindus worship the spirit of the divine and not its material form in the shape of an idol. This spirit which is worshipped is indestructible. Representing this spirit, Ram Janmabhumi as a place is worshipped as a deity and is hence a juridical person;**

(viii)  The actual and continuous performance of puja of an immovable deity by its devotees is not essential for its existence since the deity represented by the land is indestructible;

(ix) **There was an ancient temple during the reign of Vikramadltya at Ram Janmabhumi. The temple was partly destroyed and an attempt was made to raise a mosque by Mir Baqi, a Commander of Emperor Babur. Most of the material utilised to construct the mosque was obtained from the temple including its Kasauti pillars with Hindu Gods and Goddesses carved on them;**

(x) The 1928 edition of the Faizabad Gazetteer records that during the course of his conquest in 1528, Babur destroyed the ancient temple and on its site a mosque was built. In 1855, there was a dispute between Hindus and Muslims. The gazetteer records that after the dispute, an outer enclosure was placed in front of the mosque as a consequence of which access to the inner courtyard was prohibited to the Hindus. As a result, they made their offerings on a platform in the outer courtyard;

(xi) The place belongs to the deities and no valid waqf was ever created or could have been created;

(xii) **The structure which was raised upon the destruction of the ancient temple, utilising the material of the temple does not constitute a mosque. Despite the construction of the mosque, Ram Janmabhumi did not cease to be in possession of the deity which has continued to be worshipped by devotees through various symbols;**

(xiii) The building of the mosque could be accessed only by passing through the adjoining places of Hindu worship. Hence, at Ram Janmabhumi, the worship of the deities has continued through the ages;

(xiv) **No prayers have been offered in the mosque after 1934. During the night intervening 22–23 December 1949, idols of Lord Ram were installed with due ceremony under the central dome.** At that stage, acting on an FIR, proceedings were initiated by the Additional City Magistrate under Section 145 of the CrPC and a preliminary order was passed on 29 December 1949. A receiver was appointed, in spite of which the possession of the plaintiff deities was not disturbed;

(xv) **The plaintiffs, were not a party to any prior litigation and are hence not bound by the outcome of the previous proceedings; and**

(xvi) **The Ram Janmabhumi at Ayodhya which contains, besides the presiding deity, other idols and deities along with its appertaining properties constitutes one integral complex with a single identity. The claim of the Muslims is confined to the area enclosed within the inner boundary wall, erected after the annexation of Oudh by the British.**

40.4. The plaint contains a description of the demolition of the structure of the mosque on 6 December 1992 and the developments which have taken place thereafter including the promulgation of an Ordinance and subsequently, a law enacted by the Parliament for acquisition of the land.

[. . .]

## N.5. Issues and findings of the High Court

421. The issues which were framed in the Suit and the findings of the three judges in the High Court are catalogued below:

421.1. **(1) Whether the first and second plaintiffs are juridical persons.**

- **S.U. Khan, J.** – *The idol is duly capable of holding property.*
- **Sudhir Agarwal, J.** – *Answered in the affirmative* – *both* Plaintiffs 1 and 2 are juridical persons.
- **D.V. Sharma, J.** – *Decided in favour of the plaintiffs.*

421.2. **(2) Whether the suit in the name of deities described in the plaint as the first and second plaintiffs is not maintainable through the third plaintiff as next friend.**
- **S.U. Khan, J.** – *Followed the decision of Sudhir Agarwal, J.*
- **Sudhir Agarwal, J.** – *Suit held to be maintainable.*
- **D.V. Sharma, J.** – *Suit held to be maintainable.*

421.3. **3(a) Whether the idol in question was installed under the central dome of the disputed building (since demolished) in the early hours of 23-12-1949 as alleged by the plaintiff in Para 27 of the plaint as clarified in their statement under Order 10 Rule 2 CPC.**
- **S.U. Khan, J.** – The idols were placed inside the mosque for the first time during the night of 22-12-1949/ 23-12-1949.
- **Sudhir Agarwal, J.** – *Answered in the affirmative.*
- **D.V. Sharma, J.** – *Answered in the affirmative.*

421.4. **3(b) Whether the same idol was reinstalled at the same place on a Chabutra under the canopy.**
- **S.U. Khan, J.** – *Adopted the findings of Sudhir Agarwal, J.*
- **Sudhir Agarwal, J.** – *Answered in the affirmative.*
- **D.V. Sharma, J.** – Answered in the affirmative.

421.5. **3(c) Whether the idols were placed at the disputed site on or after 6-12-1992 in violation of the court's order dated 14-12-1989 and 15-11-1991.**
- **S.U. Khan, J.** – Adopted the findings of Sudhir Agarwal, J.
- **Sudhir Agarwal, J.** – *Answered in the negative.*
- **D.V. Sharma, J.** – Decided in favour of the plaintiffs.

421.6. **3(d) If the aforesaid issue is answered in the affirmative, whether the idols so placed still acquire the status of a deity.**
- **S.U. Khan, J.** – Adopted the findings o Sudhir Agarwal, J.

- **Sudhir Agarwal, J.** – Answered in the affirmative.
- **D.V. Sharma, J.** – Answered in the affirmative.

421.7. **(4) Whether the idols in question had been in existence under the 'Shikhar' prior to 6-12-1992 from time immemorial as alleged in Para 44 of the additional written statement of Nirmohi Akhara (the third defendant).**

- **S.U. Khan, J.** – *The idols were placed inside the mosque for the first time on 22-12-1949/23-12-1949.*
- **Sudhir Agarwal, J.** – Answered in the negative; the idols under the central dome were in existence prior to 6-12-1992 but were placed during the night of 22-12- 1949/ 23-12-1949.
- **D.V. Sharma, J.** – *The idols were not under the central dome prior to 22-12-1949/23-12-1949.*

421.8. **(5) Is the property in question properly identified and described in the plaint.**

- **S.U. Khan, J.** – No temple was demolished for constructing the mosque. Until the mosque was constructed during the reign of Babur, the premises were neither treated nor believed to be the birth-place of Lord Ram.
- **Sudhir Agarwal, J.** – *There is no ambiguity in the identification or description of the property.*
- **D.V. Sharma, J.** – *Answered in favour of the plaintiffs.*

421.9. **(6) Is third plaintiff not entitled to represent Plaintiffs 1 and 2 as their next friend and is the suit not competent on this account.**

- **S.U. Khan, J.** – Adopted the findings of Sudhir Agarwal, J.
- **Sudhir Agarwal, J.** – *Answered in the negative, in favour of the plaintiffs.*
- **D.V. Sharma, J.** – *Decided in favour of the plaintiffs.*

421.10. **(7) Whether Nirmohi Akhara (the third defendant) alone is entitled to represent the first and second plaintiffs, and is the suit not competent on that account as alleged in Para 49 of the additional written statement of Nirmohi Akhara (the third defendant).**

- **S.U. Khan, J.** – Adopted the findings of Sudhir Agarwal, J.
- **Sudhir Agarwal, J.** – *Answered in the negative* against Nirmohi Akhara, in favour of the plaintiffs.
- **D.V. Sharma, J.** – *Answered against Nirmohi Akhara, in favour of the* plaintiffs.

421.11. **(8) Is the defendant Nirmohi Akhara the 'Shebait' of Bhagwan Sri Ram installed in the disputed structure.**

- **S.U. Khan, J.** – *Adopted the findings of* Sudhir Agarwal, J.
- **Sudhir Agarwal, J.** – *Answered against Nirmohi Akhara.*
- **D.V. Sharma, J.** – *Answered against Nirmohi Akhara, held that Nirmohi Akhara is incompetent to represent* the first and second plaintiffs.

421.12. **(9) Was the disputed structure a mosque known as Babri Masjid?**

- **S.U. Khan, J.** – *The mosque was constructed by or under the orders of Babur. Until 1934, Muslims offered regular prayers and* thereafter, until 22 December 1949 only Friday prayers were offered.
- **Sudhir Agarwal, J.** – *Answered against the plaintiffs.*
- **D.V. Sharma, J.** – *Answered against the Sunni* Central Waqf Board and in favour of the plaintiffs.

421.13. **(10) Whether the disputed structure could be treated to be a mosque on the allegations contained in Para 24 of the plaint.**

- **S.U. Khan, J.** – *The mosque was a valid mosque.*
- **Sudhir Agarwal, J.** – *Answered in the affirmative.*

- **D.V. Sharma, J.** – *The mosque was constructed upon demolition of the temple.*

421.14 **(11) Whether on the averments made in paragraph 25 of the plaint, no valid waqf was created in respect of the structure in dispute to constitute it as a mosque.**
- **S.U. Khan, J.** – *The mosque is a valid mosque.*
- **Sudhir Agarwal, J.** – *Answered in the affirmative.*
- **D.V. Sharma, J.** – *No valid waqf with respect to the disputed property.*

[. . .]

421.16. **(13) Whether the suit is barred by limitation.**
- **S.U. Khan, J.** – *The suit is not barred by limitation.*
- **Sudhir Agarwal, J.** – *The suit is not barred by limitation.*
- **D.V. Sharma, J.** – *The suit is not barred by limitation.*

421.17. **(14) Whether the disputed structure claimed to be Babri Masjid was erected after demolishing Janmasthan temple at its site.**
- **S.U. Khan, J.** – *No temple was demolished for the construction of the* mosque. Until the mosque was constructed during the reign of Babur, the premises were not believed to be the birth-place of Lord Ram.
- **Sudhir Agarwal, J.** – *Answered in the affirmative.*
- **D.V. Sharma, J.** – *Decided in favour of the plaintiffs, against the Sunni Central Waqf Board.*

421.18. **(15) Whether the disputed structure claimed to be Babri Masjid was always used only by the Muslims regularly for offering namaz ever since its alleged construction in 1528 AD to 22-12- 1949 as alleged by the Defendants 4 and 5.**

- **S.U. Khan, J.** – *Until 1934, Muslims were offering regular prayers in the mosque. Thereafter, until 22-12-1949, only Friday prayers were offered.*
- **Sudhir Agarwal, J.** – *At least from 1860, namaz was offered in the inner courtyard. The last namaz was on 16-12-1949.*
- **D.V. Sharma, J.** – *Connected with Issue 1-B(c), 2, 4, 12, 13, 14, 15, 19(a), 19(b), 19(c), 27 and 28 of Suit No. 4 which were decided against the Sunni Central Waqf Board.*

421.19  **(16). Whether the title of Plaintiffs 1 and 2, if any, was extinguished as alleged in Para 25 of the written statement of Defendant 4. If yes, have plaintiffs 1 and 2 reacquired title by adverse possession as alleged in Para 29 of the plaint.**

- **S.U. Khan, J.** – *Both parties were in joint possession before 1855 and hence, there was no need to decide the issue of adverse possession.*
- **Sudhir Agarwal, J.** – *The title of the first and second plaintiffs has never been extinguished.*
- **D.V. Sharma, J.** – Connected with Issue 1B-(c), 2, 4, 12, 13, 14, 15, 19(a), 19(b), 19(c), 27 and 28 of Suit No. 4 which were decided against the Sunni Central Waqf Board.

[. . .]

421.21  **(18) Whether the suit is barred by Section 34 of the Specific Relief Act as alleged in Para 42 of the additional written statement of Defendant 3 and also as alleged in Para 47 of the written statement of Defendant 4 and Para 62 of the written statement of Defendant 5.**

- **S.U. Khan, J.** – *Adopted the findings of* Sudhir Agarwal, J.

- **Sudhir Agarwal, J.** – *Answered in the negative against the third, fourth and fifth defendants.*
- **D.V. Sharma, J.** – *In favour of the plaintiffs, against the defendants.*

421.22. **(19) Whether the suit is bad for non-joinder of necessary parties, as pleaded in Para 43 of the additional written statement of Defendant 3.**
- **S.U. Khan, J.** – *Adopted the findings of Sudhir Agarwal, J.*
- **Sudhir Agarwal, J.** – *Answered in the negative.*
- **D.V. Sharma, J.** – *The suit held to* be maintainable.

421.23. **(20) Whether the alleged Trust creating the Nyas, Defendant 21, is void on the facts and grounds stated in Para 47 of the written statement of Defendant 3.**
- **S.U. Khan, J.** – *Not answered.*
- **Sudhir Agarwal, J.** – *Not answered.*
- **D.V. Sharma, J.** – *Answered in favour of the plaintiffs.*

421.24. **(21) Whether the idols in question cannot be treated as deities as alleged in Para 1, 11, 12, 21, 22, 27 and 41 of the written statement of Defendant 4 and in Para 1 of the written statement of Defendant 5.**
- **S.U. Khan** – Adopted the findings of Justice Sudhir Agarwal, J.
- **Sudhir Agarwal and D.V. Sharma, JJ.** – Answered against the Sunni Central Waqf Board and fifth defendant.

421.25 **(22) Whether the premises in question or any part thereof is by tradition, belief and faith the birth-place of Lord Ram as alleged in Para 19 and 20 of the plaint? If so, its effect.**
- **S.U. Khan, J.** – *Neither was any temple demolished for constructing the mosque nor until the construction of*

*the* mosque were the premises treated or believed to be birthplace of Lord Ram.

- **Sudhir Agarwal, J.** – *The place of birth of Lord Ram as believed and* worshipped by Hindus is covered under the central dome of the three-domed structure in the inner courtyard of the premises in dispute.
- **D.V. Sharma, J.** – *Connected with Issue 1, 1(a), 1(b), 1B-(b), 11, 19(d), 19(e) and 19(f) in Suit No. 4. Decided against the Sunni Central Waqf Board.*

421.26. **(23) Whether the judgment in Suit of 1885 filed by Mahant Raghubar Das in the Court of Special Judge, Faizabad is binding upon the plaintiffs by application of the principles of estoppel and res judicata as alleged by the Defendants 4 and 5.**

- **S.U. Khan, J.** – Section 11 CPC is not attracted as virtually nothing was decided in the Suit of 1885.
- **Sudhir Agarwal, J.** – *Answered in the negative.*
- **D.V. Sharma, J.** – *Answered in favour of the plaintiffs.*

421.27. **(24) Whether worship has been done of the alleged plaintiff deity on the premises in the suit since time immemorial as alleged in Para 25 of the plaint.**

- **S.U. Khan, J.** – Neither was any temple demolished for constructing the mosque nor were the premises treated or believed to be the birth-place of Lord Ram until the mosque was constructed.
- **Sudhir Agarwal, J.** – *Worship of the first and second plaintiffs has been since time immemorial: issue answered in the affirmative.*
- **D.V. Sharma, J.** – *Connected with Issue 1-B(c), 2, 4, 12, 13, 14, 15, 19(a), 19(b), 19(c), 27 & 28 of Suit No. 4. Answered against the Sunni Central Waqf Board.*

421.28. **(25) Whether the judgment and decree dated 30 March 1946 passed in Suit no 29 of 1945 is not binding upon the plaintiffs as alleged by the plaintiffs.**
- **S.U. Khan, J.** – Adopted the findings of Sudhir Agarwal, J.
- **Sudhir Agarwal, J.** – The plaintiffs were not a party to the suit and the judgment is therefore not binding on them.
- **D.V. Sharma, J.** – *Decided in favour of the plaintiffs.*

421.29. **(26) Whether the suit is bad for want of notice under Section 80 CPC as alleged by the defendants 4 and 5.**
- **S.U. Khan, J.** – Adopted the findings of Sudhir Agarwal, J.
- **Sudhir Agarwal, J.** – *Answered in favour of the plaintiffs.*
- **D.V. Sharma, J.** – Answered in favour of the plaintiffs.

421.30. **(27) Whether the plea of suit being bad for want of notice under Section 80 CPC can be raised by Defendants 4 and 5.**
- **S.U. Khan, J.** – Adopted the findings of Sudhir Agarwal, J.
- **Sudhir Agarwal, J.** – *Answered in favour of the plaintiffs.*
- **D.V. Sharma, J.** – Answered in favour of the plaintiffs.

421.31. **(28) Whether the suit is bad for want of notice under Section 65 of the U.P. Muslim Waqf Act 1960 as alleged by defendants 4 and 5. If so, its effect.**
- **S.U. Khan, J.** – Adopted the findings of Sudhir Agarwal, J.
- **Sudhir Agarwal, J.** – *The provision is not applicable.*
- **D.V. Sharma, J.** – *Decided in favour of the plaintiffs.*

421.32. **(29) Whether the plaintiffs are precluded from bringing the present suit on account of dismissal of Suit No. 57 of 1978 (Bhagwan Sri Ram Lalla v State) of the Court of Munsif Sadar, Faizabad.**
- **S.U. Khan, J.** – Adopted the findings of Sudhir Agarwal, J.

- **Sudhir Agarwal and D.V. Sharma, JJ.** – Answered in favour of the plaintiffs.

421.33. **(30) To what relief, if any, are plaintiffs or any of them entitled?**
   - **S.U. Khan, J.** – Adopted the findings of Sudhir Agarwal, J.
   - **Sudhir Agarwal, J.** – *The suit was partly decreed in accordance with the directions contained in para 4566.*
   - **D.V. Sharma, J.** – *The plaintiffs were held entitled to relief and the suit was decreed.*

422. Sudhir Agarwal, J. granted the following relief in the Suit: [. . .]

(i)    It is declared that the area covered by the central dome of the three-domed structure, i.e., the disputed structure being the deity of Bhagwan Ram Janamsthan and place of birth of Lord Rama as per faith and belief of the Hindus, belongs to plaintiffs (Suit No. 5) and shall not be obstructed or interfered in any manner by the defendants . . .

(ii)   The area within the inner courtyard . . . (excluding (i) above) belongs to members of both the communities, i.e., Hindus (here plaintiffs, Suit No. 5) and Muslims since it was being used by both since decades and centuries. It is, however, made clear that for the purpose of share of plaintiffs, Suit No. 5 under this direction the area which is covered by (i) above shall also be included.

(iii)  The area covered by the structures, namely, Ram Chabutra . . . Sita Rasoi . . . and Bhandar . . . in the outer courtyard is declared in the share of Nirmohi Akhara (Defendant 3) and they shall be entitled to possession thereof in the absence of any person with better title.

(iv)   The open area within the outer courtyard . . . (except that covered by (iii) above) shall be shared by Nirmohi Akhara (Defendant 3) and plaintiffs (Suit No. 5) since it has been generally used by the Hindu people for worship at both places.

(iv-a) It is however made clear that the share of Muslim parties shall not be less than one third (1/3) of the total area of the premises and if necessary it may be given some area of outer courtyard. It is also made clear that while making partition by metes and bounds, if some minor adjustments are to be made with respect to the share of different parties, the affected party may be compensated by allotting the requisite land from the area which is under acquisition of the Government of India.

(v) The land which is available with the Government of India acquired under Ayodhya Act 1993, for providing it to the parties who are successful in the suit for better enjoyment of the property shall be made available to the above concerned parties in such manner so that all the three parties may utilise the area to which they are entitled to, by having separate entry for egress and ingress of the people without disturbing each other's rights. For this purpose the concerned parties may approach the Government of India who shall act in accordance with the above directions and also as contained in the judgment of Apex Court in Dr. Ismail Faruqui.

(vi) A decree, partly preliminary and partly final, to the effect as said above (i) *to* (v) is passed. Suit No. 5 is decreed in part to the above extent. The parties are at liberty to file their suggestions for actual partition of the property in dispute in the manner as directed above by metes and bounds by submitting an application to this effect to the Officer on Special Duty, Ayodhya Bench at Lucknow or the Registrar, Lucknow Bench, Lucknow, as the case may be.

(vii) For a period of three months or unless directed otherwise, whichever is earlier, the parties shall maintain status quo as on today in respect of property in dispute.

423. S.U. Khan, J. issued the following directions: [. . .]

Accordingly, all the three sets of parties, i.e. Muslims, Hindus and Nirmohi Akhara are declared joint title holders of the property/ premises in dispute as described . . . in the map Plan-I prepared by Sri Shiv Shanker Lal, Pleader/Commissioner appointed by Court in Suit No.1 to the extent of one third share each for using and managing the same for worshipping. A preliminary decree to this effect is passed.

However, it is further declared that the portion below the central dome where at present the idol is kept in makeshift temple will be allotted to Hindus in final decree.

It is further directed that Nirmohi Akhara will be allotted share including that part which is shown by the words Ram Chabutra and Sita Rasoi in the said map.

It is further clarified that even though all the three parties are declared to have one third share each, however if while allotting exact portions some minor adjustment in the share is to be made then the same will be made and the adversely affected party may be compensated by allotting some portion of the adjoining land which has been acquired by the Central Government.

The parties are at liberty to file their suggestions for actual partition by metes and bounds within three months.

424.     Justice D.V. Sharma decreed the suit of the plaintiffs in the following terms: [. . .]

Plaintiffs' suit is decreed but with easy costs. It is hereby declared that the entire premises of Sri Ram Janm Bhumi at Ayodhya as described and delineated in annexure nos. 1 and 2 of the plaint belong to the plaintiff nos. 1 and 2, the deities. The defendants are permanently restrained from interfering with, or raising any objection to, or placing any obstruction in the construction of the temple at Ram Janm Bhumi Ayodhya at the site, referred to in the plaint.

# Twelve

# The Judgment: Final Word

On 9 November 2019, hours before Chief Justice Ranjan Gogoi retired, a constitution bench (five judges: Chief Justice Ranjan Gogoi and Justices Arvind Bobde, Ashok Bhushan, D.Y. Chandrachud and Abdul Naseer) heard the first appeal and pronounced its verdict of 929 (main judgment) plus 116 pages (addenda) in the almost-seventy-year-long Ram Janmabhoomi–Babri Masjid land dispute in Ayodhya. Before Chief Justice Gogoi's tenure, two successive chief justices, Jagdish Singh Khehar and Dipak Misra, had endeavoured to assemble benches to tackle the case but failed, as thousands of pages, in more than eighty-nine volumes, of pleadings, one volume of written submissions and dozens of books had to be translated and collated.

The bench that ultimately heard and decided the matter was interesting.

Chief Justice Gogoi was appointed to head the court on 3 October 2018 and completed his tenure on 17 November 2019, after a thirteen-month stint. He joined the Bar in 1978 and mainly practised in the Guwahati High Court. He was appointed as a permanent judge of the Guwahati High Court on 28 February 2001. Later, on 9 September 2010, he was transferred to the

Punjab and Haryana High Court. On 12 February 2011, he was appointed as chief justice of the Punjab and Haryana High Court. Chief Justice Gogoi was elevated as judge of the Supreme Court on 23 April 2012. He was part of the bench that thwarted the government's attempts to weaken the Lokpal Act, and pushed the Assam NRC (National Register of Citizens) to a logical conclusion. He issued contempt of court notice against former Supreme Court judge Markandey Katju. He also put in jail a sitting judge, Justice C.S. Karnan of Calcutta High Court, for contempt—the first time that a sitting judge of a high court had been so sentenced. Post his superannuation, Chief Justice Gogoi accepted a nomination to the Rajya Sabha.

Justice Sharad Arvind Bobde (as his lordship then was) was sworn in by President Ram Nath Kovind as the forty-seventh chief justice on 18 November 2019, after Chief Justice Gogoi recommended his name, as tradition has it. He held office till 23 April 2021. Born on 24 April 1956 in Nagpur, Chief Justice Bobde secured his BA and LLB degrees from Nagpur University. He was enrolled in the Bar Council of Maharashtra in 1978. Further, he practised at the Nagpur bench of the Bombay High Court, with appearances at Bombay before the Principal Seat and before the Supreme Court of India for over twenty-one years. He was elevated to the bench of the Bombay High Court on 29 March 2000 as additional judge. He was sworn in as chief justice of Madhya Pradesh High Court on 16 October 2012 and elevated as a judge of SC on 12 April 2013.

The son of former chief justice of India Y. V. Chandrachud, Justice Dr D.Y. Chandrachud obtained an LLM degree and a doctorate in juridical sciences from Harvard Law School, USA. Prior to this, he received a BA Hons (economics) from St Stephen's College, Delhi, and an LLB from Campus Law Centre, Delhi University. He was appointed as judge of the Supreme Court on 13 May 2016. Before this, he was appointed as the judge of Bombay High Court, from 29 March 2000 until his appointment as chief justice of the Allahabad High Court on 31 October 2013. He had served as additional solicitor general of India from 1998 until his appointment as a judge. He was part of the bench that decriminalized homosexuality and secured dignity to the LGBTQ community, pushed constitutional morality as the bedrock of our jurisprudence and has the distinction of overruling his father's judgment in 'ADM Jabalpur',* thus casting his lot with liberty.

Justice Ashok Bhushan was born on 5 July 1956 in the Jaunpur district of Uttar Pradesh. He graduated in arts in 1975 and obtained his law degree from the Allahabad University. Having served as a high court judge in Allahabad, he was sworn in as judge of the high court of Kerala on 10 July 2014 and took charge as acting chief justice on 1 August 2014. He was sworn in as chief justice on 26 March 2015 and elevated as judge of the Supreme Court of India on 13 May 2016.

Justice S. Abdul Nazeer was elevated as judge of the Supreme Court of India on 17 February 2017. He enrolled as an advocate in 1983 and practised in the high court of Karnataka. He was appointed as additional judge of the Karnataka High Court on 12 May 2003 and as a permanent judge on 24 September 2004. He was brought to the Supreme Court by Chief Justice Jagdish Singh Khehar, who had been his chief justice in Karnataka.

Justices Bhushan and Nazeer were members of the bench of three judges who had heard the applications for the Ayodhya matter to be placed before five judges. But that bench, by a majority of two to one, had turned down the request by confirming an earlier finding that a mosque is not an essential part of Islam. Of course, despite that finding by Chief Justice Dipak Misra and Justice Ashok Bhushan (with Justice Nazeer dissenting), the matter was heard, under Chief Justice Gogoi, by five judges. That was in itself somewhat unusual, because no constitutional issues were left to

---

* 'Additional District Magistrate, Jabalpur vs Shivakant Shukla', 1976, 2 SCC 521.

be decided in what was essentially a first appeal from a title suit decided by the Allahabad High Court.

While the papers, books and additional material were being prepared, the court took a chance to try mediation. Several past attempts had been stillborn, and Chief Justice Khehar's offer to be the mediator had not been accepted. However, this time, mediation did take place with some earnestness and was reported to have almost succeeded. The broad parameters were that the Muslim side would give up its claim to the site in Ayodhya, subject to an assurance that Mathura and Varanasi would be secured—i.e., if the Muslim side relinquished their claims on the birthplace of Ram, the Hindu side would desist from raising similar agitations against sites in Mathura and Varanasi, which could otherwise be sought to be wrestled back, as temples there had allegedly faced a similar fate at the hands of the 'Mughal invaders' in ages past.

The Ayodhya matter was heard for over forty-one days, with Dr Rajeev Dhawan in the lead for the Muslim side while the doyen K. Parasaran, former attorney general of the Congress government, presented the arguments for Ram Lalla. The proceedings were not without theatrics, such as Dr Rajiv Dhawan taking the chief justice on his word and tearing up a document that seemed not to persuade the court and was dismissed with the retort, 'You can tear it up.' Parasaran was offered by the court the indulgence to remain seated while arguing, but he politely declined.

The hon'ble court summed up the entire case before into several **'Points for determination'**, inter alia:

[. . .]

60.3. (iii)(a) Whether a Hindu temple existed at the disputed site?
    (b) Whether the temple was demolished by Babur or at his behest by his commander Mir Baqi in 1528 for the construction of the Babri Masjid?
    [. . .]

(d)  What, if any are the legal consequences arising out of the
      determination on (a)(b) and (c) above;

60.4 (iv) Whether the suit property is according to the faith and
      belief of the Hindus since time immemorial the birth-place of
      Lord Ram . . .

Unanimity among all judges of a constitution bench of the Supreme
Court is rare. Landmark cases like 'Keshavananda Bharti'* were
decided by a wafer-thin majority of seven to six. In the Ayodhya
case, the court had a month to write the judgment, given that
Chief Justice Gogoi was to retire on 18 November 2019. The
lucidly written judgment has indications as to its authorship, but
since the court chose not to specify, it is best left unstated. Of
course, the unusual and somewhat incomprehensible addenda,
which too is an unsigned judgment, does raise some questions.
Was it a judgment in agreement but with different reasons? Did
the chief justice prevail upon his colleagues to ensure unanimity?
Is it possible that this judgment would be used in the future to
revive the role of faith as a deciding factor in adjudication? All
these questions aside, clearly Chief Justice Gogoi's tenure will go
down in history as momentous in deciding a century-old, divisive
dispute between Hindus and Muslims.

* * *

The court essentially heard and decided five suits:

13. On 16-1-1950, a suit was instituted by a Hindu devotee, Gopal
    Singh Visharad, ('Suit No. 1') . . . alleging that he was being
    prevented by officials of the Government from entering the inner

---

* 'Keshavananda Bharti vs State of Kerela', 1973, 4 SCC 225; AIR 1973 SC
  1461.

courtyard of the disputed site to offer worship. A declaration
was sought to allow the plaintiff to offer prayers in accordance
with the rites and tenets of his religion ('Sanatan Dharm') at the
'main Janmabhumi', near the idols, within the inner courtyard,
without hindrance.

14. On 5-12-1950, another suit was instituted by Paramhans
Ramchandra Das ('Suit 2') . . . seeking reliefs similar to those in
Suit 1. Suit No. 2 was subsequently withdrawn on 18-9-1990.

[. . .]

16. On 17-12-1959, Nirmohi Akhara instituted a suit through its
Mahant ('Suit No. 3') . . . claiming that 'its absolute right' of
managing the affairs of the Janmasthan and the temple had
been impacted by the Magistrate's order of attachment and
by the appointment of a Receiver . . . A decree was sought to
hand over the management and charge of the temple to the
plaintiff . . .

17. On 18-12-1961, the Sunni Central Waqf Board and nine Muslim
residents of Ayodhya filed a suit ('Suit No. 4') . . . seeking a
declaration that the entire disputed site of the Babri Masjid
was a public mosque and for the delivery of possession upon
removal of the idols.

18. On 6-1-1964, the trial of Suits Nos. 1, 3 and 4 was consolidated
and Suit No. 4 was made the leading case.

19. On 25-1-1986, an application was filed by one Umesh Chandra
before the Trial Court for breaking open the locks placed on the
grill-brick wall and for allowing the public to perform darshan
within the inner courtyard. On 1-2-1986, the District Judge issued
directions to open the locks and to provide access to devotees
for darshan inside the structure. In a Writ Petition filed before
the High Court challenging the above order, an interim order
was passed on 3-2-1986 directing that until further orders, the
nature of the property as it existed shall not be altered.

20. On 1-7-1989, a Suit ('Suit No. 5') was . . . by the deity ('Bhagwan
    Shri Ram Virajman') and the birth-place('Asthan Shri Ram Janam
    Bhumi, Ayodhya'), through a next friend for a declaration of title
    to the disputed premises and to restrain the defendants from
    interfering with or raising any objection to the construction of a
    temple . . .

The court further noted that:

1028. The significant aspect of the case which has been pleaded in
Suit 4 is the construction of the mosque in 1528 A.D. and its use by
Muslims for the purpose of offering prayer thereafter. **But, a crucial
aspect of the evidentiary record is the absence of any evidence to
indicate that the mosque was, after its construction, used for offering
namaz until 1856–7.** Justice Sudhir Agarwal noticed this feature of the
case bearing on the lack of evidence of the use of the mosque for the
purpose of worship until the riots of 1856–1857. The learned Judge
also noted the submission of . . . the Sunni Central Waqf Board . . .

> '. . . even if for the purpose of the issues in question we assume
> that the building in dispute was so constructed in 1528 A.D.,
> there is no evidence whatsoever that after its construction,
> it was ever used as a mosque by Muslims at least till 1856–
> 1857 . . . [H]istorical or other evidence is not available to show
> the position of possession or offering of Namaz in the disputed
> building at least till 1855.'

1034.5. [. . .] [T]he High Court has noted that the documents would
show that financial assistance was provided by the British for the
purposes of maintenance of the mosque, but this would not amount to
proving that the structure was used for the purpose of offering namaz.

The court made it clear that the issue to be decided was a title suit
on the basis of evidence and not a matter of faith:

90. [. . .] **This Court, as a secular institution, set up under a constitutional regime must steer clear from choosing one among many possible interpretations of theological doctrine and must defer to the safer course of accepting the faith and belief of the worshipper.**

91. Above all, the practice of religion, Islam being no exception, varies according to the culture and social context. That indeed is the strength of our plural society. Cultural assimilation is a significant factor which shapes the manner in which religion is practiced . . . Our Court is founded on and owes its existence to a constitutional order. We must firmly reject any attempt to lead the court to interpret religious doctrine in an absolute and extreme form and question the faith of worshippers. Nothing would be as destructive of the values underlying Article 25 of the Constitution.

[. . .]

102. [. . .] **The law is hence a legislative instrument designed to protect the secular features of the Indian polity, which is one of the basic features of the Constitution. Non-retrogression is a foundational feature of the fundamental constitutional principles of which secularism is a core component. The Places of Worship Act is thus a legislative intervention which preserves non-retrogression as an essential feature of our secular values.**

## Juristic Personality of Deity

Among the issues that needed to be decided was the legal status of the deity, both for the claim on its behalf as well as the claim of the other side. A deity is a juristic person, but the court underscored the fact that the Hindu god is formless. The deity is a convenient object to focus obeisance and intent to do noble deeds for God.

Attempts were made to seek the status of juristic personality for the birthplace of Lord Ram itself, but the court negatived that claim. This finding is likely to have far-reaching implications for the future.

Juristic personality has the legal capacity to hold property and to sue as well as be sued. It is significantly different from a waqf, where the property is dedicated to Allah, to be used for the benefit of the sick, poor, indigent and orphans. The *mutawalli* is but a manager but does not hold title to the property, unlike an English trust, where the legal title rests in the trustee but the beneficial title rests in the beneficiaries. The hon'ble court dedicated substantial time to this discussion in the Ayodhya judgment, some of which is presented here:

128. At the outset, it is important to understand that the conferral of legal personality on a Hindu idol is not the conferral of legal personality on divinity itself, which in Hinduism is often understood as the 'Supreme Being'. The Supreme Being defies form and shape, yet its presence is universal. In the law of Hindu endowments and in the present proceedings, it has often been stated that legal personality is conferred on the 'purpose behind the idol'. The present judgment shall advert to the exact legal significance of this statement. **For the present, it is sufficient to note that legal personality is not conferred on the 'Supreme Being' itself. As observed by this Court in Ram Jankijee Deities v State of Bihar:**

'19. **God is omnipotent and omniscient and its presence is felt not by reason of a particular form or image but by reason of the presence of the omnipotent. It is formless, it is shapeless and it is for the benefit of the worshippers that there is a manifestation in the images of the supreme being. 'The supreme being has no attribute, which consists of pure spirit and which is without a second being i.e. God**

is the only being existing in reality, there is no other being
in real existence excepting Him.'

(emphasis supplied)

[. . .]

104. Hinduism understands the Supreme Being as existing in every
aspect of the universe. The Supreme Being is omnipresent. The
idea of a legal person is premised on the need to 'identify the
subjects' of the legal system. An omnipresent being is incapable
of being identified or delineated in any manner meaningful to
the law and no identifiable legal subject would emerge. This
understanding is reflected in the decisions of this Court as
well. In Yogendra Nath Naskar v Commissioner of Income Tax,
Calcutta, a three judge Bench of this Court . . . held:

'. . . Sankara, the great philosopher, refers to the one Reality, who,
owing to the diversity of intellects (Matibheda) is conventionally
spoken of (Parikalpya) in various ways as Brahma, Visnu and
Mahesvara. It is, however, possible that the founder of the
endowment or the worshipper may not conceive of this highest
spiritual plane but hold that the idol is the very embodiment of
a personal God, but that is not a matter with which the law is
concerned. Neither God nor any supernatural being could be a
person in law. But so far as the deity stands as the representative
and symbol of the particular purpose which is **indicated by the
donor, it can figure as a legal person. The true legal view is that
in that capacity alone the dedicated property vests in it** . . . Our
conclusion is that the Hindu idol is a juristic entity capable of
holding property and of being taxed through its Shebaits who are
entrusted with the possession and management of its property.'

(emphasis supplied)

131. Legal personality is not conferred on the Supreme Being. The Supreme Being has no physical presence for it is understood to be omnipresent—the very ground of being itself. The court does not confer legal personality on divinity. Divinity in Hindu philosophy is seamless, universal and infinite. Divinity pervades every aspect of the universe. The attributes of divinity defy description and furnish the fundamental basis for not defining it with reference to boundaries—physical or legal. For the reason that it is omnipresent it would be impossible to distinguish where one legal entity ends and the next begins. The narrow confines of the law are ill suited to engage in such an exercise and it is for this reason, that the law has steered clear from adopting this approach. In Hinduism, physical manifestations of the Supreme Being exist in the form of idols to allow worshippers to experience a shapeless being. The idol is a representation of the Supreme Being. The idol, by possessing a physical form is identifiable.

[. . .]

142. The conferral of juristic personality by courts is to overcome existing shortfalls in the law and ensure societally satisfactory and legally sound outcomes . . .

[. . .]

120. The recognition of juristic personality was hence devised by the courts to give legal effect to the Hindu practice of dedicating property for a religious or 'pious' purpose . . .

[. . .]

123. **The recognition of the Hindu idol as a legal or 'juristic' person is therefore based on two premises employed by courts.**

**The first is to recognise the pious purpose of the testator as a legal entity capable of holding property in an ideal sense absent the creation of a trust. The second is the merging of the pious purpose itself and the idol which embodies the pious purpose to ensure the fulfilment of the pious purpose. So conceived, the Hindu idol is a legal person. The property endowed to the pious purpose is owned by the idol as a legal person in an ideal sense . . .**

[. . .]

130. Mr K. Parasaran, learned Senior Counsel appearing on behalf of the plaintiffs in Suit 5 urged that the second plaintiff is a juristic person. He submitted that in Hindu Law the concept of a juridical person is not limited to idols . . . the relevant question is whether prayer is offered to the deity and not the form in which the deity appears. It was contended that 'Asthan Sri Ram Janam Bhoomi' is an object of worship and personifies the spirit of the divine . . .

[. . .]

178. The Privy Council in Madura[*] was concerned with the ownership of a barren hill in the Madura District of Madras. There was a mosque at the highest point of the hill. The Tirupparankundram Temple, represented by its manager, instituted a suit claiming the whole hill as temple property . . .

179. [. . .] The temple was held to have been in possession of the unoccupied portion of the hill from time immemorial which had been treated by the temple as temple property. The Privy

---

[*] 'Madura, Tirupparankundram vs Alikhan Sahib', 1931, SCC OnLine PC 47; (1931) 61 MLJ 285.

Council held that, save and except the mosque, there was 'no evidence of expropriation from the remainder' of the hill.

[. . .]

188. In Shiromani Gurdwara*, 56 persons moved a petition under Section 7(1) of the Sikh Gurdwaras Act 1925 for a declaration that certain disputed property was a Sikh Gurdwara . . .

[. . .]

190. Tracing the evolution of the concept of juristic person, Justice A.P. Misra noted that recognition in law of a juristic person is to sub-serve the needs of the law and society.

191. Misra, J. further noted [. . .]:

'[. . .]

    41. [. . .] [W]e do not find any strength in the reasoning of the High Court in recording a finding that the "Guru Granth Sahib" is not a "juristic person". The said finding is not sustainable both on fact and law.'

209. It cannot be said that the observations of the court in respect of the consecration or establishment of a valid deity apply with equal force to the conferral of juristic personality on property on the basis of the faith and belief of the devotees. The rationale underlying the approach adopted by this Court is clarified in the following observations: (Ram Jankijee Deities case[†])

---

* 'Shiromani Gurdwara Prabandhak Committee vs Som Nath Dass', 2000, 4 SCC 146.
† 'Ram Jankijee Deities vs State of Bihar', 1999, 5 SCC 50.

'17. One cardinal principle underlying idol worship ought to be borne in mind that whichever God the devotee might choose for purposes of worship and whatever image he might set up and consecrate with that object, the image represents the Supreme God and none else. There is no superiority or inferiority amongst the different Gods. Siva, Vishnu, Ganapati or Surya is extolled, each in its turn as the creator, preserver and supreme lord of the universe. The image simply gives a name and form to the formless God and the orthodox Hindu idea is that conception of form is only for the benefit of the worshipper and nothing else.'

[. . .]

210. The observations in Ram Jankijee Deities were made in the specific context of consecrating an image based on the faith and belief of devotees for the establishment of a deity to which valid dedications may be made. The observations in this case establish that the existence of a valid deity was not to be tested against Hindu Shastras but on the basis of the faith and belief of the devotees. Once the faith and belief of the devotees had been established, it was an express deed of dedication that resulted in the conferral of juridical personality on the idol. The observations in this case cannot be equated to the elevation of property itself as a juristic person.

[. . .]

216. In the present case, the recognition of 'Asthan Sri Ram Janam Bhumi' as a juristic person would result in the extinguishment of all competing proprietary claims to the land in question. This conferral of 'absolute title' (resulting from the conferral of legal personality on land) would in truth render the very concept of title meaningless. Moreover, the extinguishing of competing

claims would arise not by virtue of settled legal principles, but purely on the basis of the faith and belief of the devotees. This cannot be countenanced in law. The conferral of legal personality by courts is an innovation arising out of necessity and convenience. The conferral of legal personality on Hindu idols arose due to the fundamental question of who the property was dedicated to and in whom the dedicated land vested. The two clear interests that the law necessitated protection of were the interests of the devotees and the protection of the properties from mismanagement. In the present case, there exists no act of dedication and therefore the question of whom the property was dedicated to does not arise and consequently the need to recognise the pious purpose behind the dedication itself as a legal person also does not arise.

[. . .]

183. Mr Parasaran relied on the decision in Saraswathi Ammal v Rajagopal Ammal* to argue that the widespread belief and worship of the land styled as Ram Janmbhumi is sufficient to recognise it as a juristic person. The case concerned a settlement deed whereby a widow dedicated in perpetuity the revenue of certain immovable properties for the performance of daily puja and 'Gurupuja' of her former husband's tomb. It was urged by the appellants in the case that the dedication was for the performance of puja and an annual 'sradh' on a significant scale, and the dedication was thus for a religious and charitable purpose. In rejecting this contention [. . .] this Court observed:

'6. [. . .] To the extent, therefore, that any purpose is claimed to be a valid one for perpetual dedication on the ground of religious merit though lacking in public benefit, it must be shown to have a Shastric basis so far as Hindus are

---

* 'Saraswathi Ammal vs Rajagopal Ammal', 1954, SCR 277; AIR 1953 SC 491.

concerned. No doubt since then other religious practices and beliefs may have grown up and obtained recognition from certain classes, as constituting purposes conducive of religious merit. If such beliefs are to be accepted by courts as being sufficient for valid perpetual dedication of property therefor without the element of actual or presumed public benefit it must be at least shown that they have obtained wide recognition and constitute the religious practice of a substantial and large class of persons . . . [I]t cannot be maintained that the belief in this belief of one or more individuals is sufficient to enable them to make a valid settlement permanently tying up property. The heads of religious purposes determined by belief in acquisition of religious merit cannot be allowed to be widely enlarged consistently with public policy and needs of modern society.'

[. . .]

226. The above decision . . . deals with whether a substantial and widespread practice of a large number of Hindus would warrant its recognition as a religious or charitable practice. Further, the court expressly observes it was not necessary to answer this question as the ground of public policy is sufficient to discredit the practice of tomb-worship by a few stray individuals. It does not deal with the question when a court should confer juristic personality, either on an idol or on land. While a particular practice may or may not be recognised by a court as 'religious' or 'charitable' depending on the scale of adoption of the practice, a parallel cannot be drawn with the concept of juristic person which operates in an entirely different field of law. The decision does not support the contention that widespread belief in the religious nature of a site is sufficient to confer upon that site legal personality.

\* \* \*

As it is a matter of faith, it is difficult to be sceptical about the possibility of the deity making an appearance by itself instead of being installed. There are innumerable examples of such miracles being reported, often assisted by a willing imagination, such as when idols of Ganesha were reported to be drinking milk across the country. Having explained the law on a Hindu deity having juristic personality, the court proceeded to consider the argument whether the birthplace of Lord Ram, too, by itself had juristic personality and the idea of the Swayambhu deity:

229. This Court in Yogendra Nath Naskar[*] drew a distinction between the perception of the devotee that the idol is a manifestation of the Supreme Being and the position in law that legal personality is conferred on the pious purpose of the testator that is entitled to legal protection. Hinduism is an expansive religion that believes divinity in the form of the Supreme Being is present in every aspect of creation. **The worship of God in Hinduism is not limited to temples or idols but often extends to natural formations, animals and can even extend to everyday objects which have significance in a worshipper's life. As a matter of religion, every manifestation of the Supreme Being is divine and worthy of worship. However, as a matter of law, every manifestation of the Supreme Being is not a legal person. Legal personality is an innovation arising out of legal necessity and the need for adjudicative utility.** Each conferment of legal personality absent an express deed of dedication must be judged on the facts of the case and it is not a sound proposition in law to state that every manifestation of the Supreme Being results in the creation of a legal person.

230. In the present case, it was contended that the land forming the disputed site is itself the manifestation of Lord Ram. Significant reliance was placed on the existence of certain temples which

---

[*] 'Yogendra Nath Naskar vs CIT', 1969, 1 SCC 555.

do not possess idols, in particular the Chidambaram Temple in Tamil Nadu, to advance two legal propositions: First, that a Hindu deity possessing juristic personality could exist even absent an idol, and second that unadorned land, absent any distinguishing features, could constitute a Swayambhu deity and consequently a juristic person . . . [I]t is true than an idol is not a prerequisite for the existence of a juristic person. Where there exists an express deed of dedication, the legal personality vests in the pious purpose of the founder. The idol is the material embodiment of the pious purpose and is the site of jural relations. There are instances of the submergence or even destruction of the idol in spite of which it has been held that the legal personality continues to subsist. Even if a testator were to make a dedication to a religious purpose but the idol did not exist at the time the dedication was made or the manifestation of the divine was not in the form of the idol, but in the form of some other object of religious significance, the legal personality would continue to vest in the pious purpose of the dedication itself.

[. . .]

233. A Swayambhu deity is a manifestation of God that is 'self-revealed' or 'discovered as existing' as opposed to a traditional idol that is hand-crafted and consecrated by the prana pratishta ceremony. The word 'swayam' means 'self' or 'on its own', 'bhu' means 'to take birth'. A Swayambhu deity is one which has manifested itself in nature without human craftsmanship. Common examples of these deities are where a tree grows in the shape of a Hindu God or Goddess or where a natural formation such as ice or rock takes the form of a recognised Hindu deity.

[. . .]

235. A Swayambhu deity is the revelation of God in a material form which is subsequently worshipped by devotees. The recognition of a Swayambhu deity is based on the notion that God is omnipotent and may manifest in some physical form. This manifestation is worshipped as the embodiment of divinity. In all these cases, the very attribution of divinity is premised on the manifestation of the deity in a material form. Undoubtedly, a deity may exist without a physical manifestation, example of this being the worship offered to the Sun and the Wind. But a Swayambhu is premised on the physical manifestation of the Divine to which faith and belief attaches.

236. The difficulty that arises in the present case is that the Swayambhu deity seeking recognition before this Court is not in the form ordinarily associated with the pantheon of anthropomorphised Hindu Gods. The plaintiffs in Suit No. 5 have sought to locate the disputed land as a focal point by contending that the very land itself is the manifestation of the deity and that the devotees worship not only the idols of Lord Ram, but the very land itself. The land does not contain any material manifestation of the resident deity Lord Ram. Absent the faith and belief of the devotees, the land holds no distinguishing features that could be recognised by this court as evidence of a manifestation of God at the disputed site. It is true that in matters of faith and belief, the absence of evidence may not be evidence of absence. However, absent a manifestation, recognising the land as a self-manifested deity would open the floodgates for parties to contend that ordinary land which was witness to some event of religious significance associated with the human incarnation of a deity (e.g. the site of marriage, or the ascent to a heavenly abode) is in fact a Swayambhu deity manifested in the form of land. If the argument urged by Mr Parasaran that there is no requirement of a physical manifestation is accepted, it may well be claimed that any area of religious significance is a Swayambhu deity which deserves to be recognised as a juristic personality.

This problem is compounded by the fact that worship to a particular deity at a religious site and to the land underlying a religious site are for all intents and purposes, indistinguishable. Hence, in order to provide a sound jurisprudential basis for the recognition of a Swayambhu deity, manifestation is crucial. Absent that manifestation which distinguishes the land from other property, juristic personality cannot be conferred on the land.

237. It is conceivable that in certain instances the land itself would possess certain unique characteristics. For example, it may be claimed that certain patterns on a seashore or crop formations represent a manifestation of the divine. In these cases, the manifestation is inseparable from the land and is tied up to it. An independent question arises as to whether land can constitute the physical manifestation of the deity. Even if a court recognises land as a manifestation of a deity, because such land is also governed by the principles of immoveable property, the court will need to investigate the consequences which arise. In doing so the court must analyse the compatibility of the legal regime of juristic personality with the legal regime on immoveable property . . .

[. . .]

244. The conferral of juristic personality is a legal innovation applied by courts in situations where the existing law of the day has certain shortcomings or such conferral increases the convenience of adjudication. In the present case, the existing law is adequately equipped to protect the interests of the devotees and ensure against maladministration without recognising the land itself as a legal person. Where the law is capable of adequately protecting the interests of the devotees and ensuring the accountable management of religious sites without the conferral of legal personality, it is not necessary to

embark on the journey of creating legal fictions that may have unintended consequences in the future. There is therefore no merit in the argument that faith and belief, and the protection of faith and belief alone may necessitate the conferral of legal personality on the second plaintiff. On the contrary, there exists a substantial risk with adopting this argument. It may be contended by a section of a religion that a particular plot of land is the birth-place, place of marriage, or a place where the human incarnation of a deity departed for a heavenly abode; according to the faith and belief of the devotees. Corporeal property may be associated with myriad incidents associated with the human incarnation of a deity each of which holds a significant place in the faith and belief of the worshippers. Where does the court draw the line to assess the significance of the belief as the basis to confer juristic personality on property? In the absence of an objective criterion, the exercise will be fraught with subjectivity . . . This conferral would be to the detriment of bona fide litigants outside the faith—who may not share the same beliefs and yet find their title extinguished. Further, such conferral of legal personality on immovable property would be on the basis of the faith and belief of the devotees, which is fundamentally subjective and incapable of being questioned by this Court.

245. The purpose for which juristic personality is conferred cannot be 'evolved' into a trojan horse that permits, on the basis of religious faith and belief, the extinguishing of all competing proprietary claims over property as well stripping the property itself of the essential characteristic of immoveable property. If the contention urged [. . .] is accepted, it results in a position in law where claims to absolute title can be sustained merely on the basis of the faith and belief of the devotees. The conferral of legal personality on corporeal property would immunise property not merely from competing title claims, but also render vast swathes of the law that are essential for courts

to meaningfully adjudicate upon civil suits, such as limitation, ownership, possession and division, entirely otiose . . .

246. A final observation must be made on this aspect of the case which is of significant importance. The rejection of the contention [. . .] touches upon the heart of our constitutional commitment to secularism. The method of worship on the basis of which a proprietary claim may be sustained is relatable to a particular religion. The conferral of legal personality on idols stemming from religious endowments is a legal development applicable only to a practice of the Hindu community. The performance of the parikrama is a method of worship confined largely to Hinduism. Putting aside the fact that the argument . . . is a novel extension of the law applicable to Hindu religious endowments, this is a significant matter which requires our consideration.

247. Religious diversity undoubtedly requires the protection of diverse methods of offering worship and performing religious ceremonies. However, that a method of offering worship unique to one religion should result in the conferral of an absolute title to parties from one religion over parties from another religion in an adjudication over civil property claims cannot be sustained under our Constitution. This would render the law, which ought to be the ultimate impartial arbiter, conferring a benefit on a party with respect to her or his legal claims, not on the basis of the merits of a particular case, but on the basis of the structure or fabric of the religion to which they belong. If the contention . . . is accepted, the method of worship performed by one religion alone will be conferred with the power to extinguish all contesting proprietary claims over disputed property.

248. It is true that the connection between a person and what they consider divine is deeply internal. It lies in the realm of a personal sphere in which no other person must intrude. It is for this reason that the Constitution protects the freedom to

**profess, practise and propagate religion equally to all citizens. Often, the human condition finds solace in worship. But worship may not be confined into a straightjacket formula. It is on the basis of the deep entrenchment of religion into the social fabric of Indian society that the right to religious freedom was not made absolute. An attempt has been made in the jurisprudence of this court to demarcate the religious from the secular. The adjudication of civil claims over private property must remain within the domain of the secular if the commitment to constitutional values is to be upheld. Over four decades ago, the Constitution was amended and a specific reference to its secular fabric was incorporated in the Preamble. At its heart, this reiterated what the Constitution always respected and accepted: the equality of all faiths. Secularism cannot be a writ lost in the sands of time by being oblivious to the exercise of religious freedom by everyone.**

249. It is for all the reasons highlighted above that the law has till today yet to accept the conferral of legal personality on immoveable property. Religiosity has moved hearts and minds. The court cannot adopt a position that accords primacy to the faith and belief of a single religion as the basis to confer both judicial insulation as well as primacy over the legal system as a whole. **From Shahid Gunj to Ayodhya, in a country like ours where contesting claims over property by religious communities are inevitable, our courts cannot reduce questions of title, which fall firmly within the secular domain and outside the rubric of religion, to a question of which community's faith is stronger.**

## Archaeological Evidence and Conclusions

The archaeological evidence available to the court pointed to certain facts but was far from conclusive in establishing the claim that Lord Ram was born at the disputed site. The court gave considerable attention to archaeological evidence, although it might be argued that in a title suit it has very limited value. Yet, since the high court had granted permission to the ASI to excavate the disputed site and extensive material was available for its consideration, the court might have thought it best to leave no scope for speculation. Ultimately, the excavation findings did not provide a conclusive picture and certainly negatived the much-propagated narrative that a temple, particularly one dedicated to Lord Ram, was demolished to build the Babri Masjid.

730. [. . .] There is adequate basis in the material contained in the ASI report to lead to the following conclusions:

730.1. The Babri mosque was not constructed on vacant land;

730.2. The excavation indicates the presence of an underlying structure below the disputed structure;

730.3. The underlying structure was at least of equal, if not larger dimensions than the disputed structure;

730.4. The excavation of the walls of the underlying structure coupled with the presence of pillar bases supports the conclusion of the ASI of the presence of a structure underlying the disputed structure;

730.5. The underlying structure was not of Islamic origin;

730.6. The foundation of the disputed structure rests on the walls of the underlying structure; and

730.7. Artefacts, including architectural fragments which have been recovered during excavation have a distinct non-Islamic origin. Though individually, some of the artefacts could also have been utilised in a structure of Buddhist or Jain origins, there is no evidence of the underlying structure being of an Islamic religious nature. **The conclusion which has been drawn by the ASI that the nature of the underlying structure and the recoveries which have been made would on stylistic grounds suggest the existence of temple structure dating back to the twelfth century A.D. would on a balance of probabilities be a conclusion which is supported by evidence. The conclusion** cannot be rejected as unsupported by evidence or lying beyond the test of a preponderance of probabilities, which must govern a civil trial.

## Caveats

731.    Having said this, we must also read the ASI report with the following caveats:

731.1. Though the excavation has revealed the existence of a circular shrine, conceivably a Shiva shrine dating back to the seventh to ninth century A.D., the underlying structure belongs to twelfth century A.D. The circular shrine and the underlying structure with pillar bases belong to two different time periods between three to five centuries apart;

731.2. There is no specific finding that the underlying structure was a temple dedicated to Lord Ram; and

731.3. Significantly, the ASI has not specifically opined on whether a temple was demolished for the construction of the disputed structure though it has emerged from the report that the disputed structure was constructed on the site of and utilised the foundation and material of the underlying structure.

## The unanswered question of demolition

732.    The ASI report has been criticised on the ground that it fails to answer the question as to whether the disputed structure of a mosque was constructed on the demolition of a pre-existing temple at the site. The High Court dealt with this objection in the following observations of Sudhir Agarwal, J.:

'3990. ASI, in our view, has rightly refrained from recording a categorical finding whether there was any demolition or not for the reason when a building is constructed over another

and that too hundreds of years back, it may sometimes be
difficult to ascertain . . . in what circumstances building was
raised and whether the earlier building collapsed on its own
or due to natural forces or for the reason attributable to some
persons interested for its damage. Sufficient indication has
been given by ASI that the building in dispute did not have
its own foundation but it was raised on the existing walls. If
a building would not have been existing before construction of
the subsequent building, the builder might not have been able
to use foundation of the erstwhile building without knowing its
strength and capacity of bearing the load of new structure.

The floor of the disputed building was just over the floor of
earlier building. The existence of several pillar bases all show
another earlier existence of a sufficiently bigger structure, if
not bigger than the disputed structure then not lessor than that
also.'

[. . .]

733.    The High Court justified the inability of ASI to come to a
specific finding on whether an erstwhile structure of a
Hindu religious origin was demolished for the construction
of the mosque. The High Court noted that when a structure
has been constructed several hundred years ago, it is
difficult to conclude with any degree of certainty whether
the underlying structure on whose foundations it rests had
collapsed due to natural causes or whether the structure
was demolished to give way to the structure of a mosque.
This would indicate that the existence of the ruins of an
underlying structure is not reason in itself to infer that the
structure had been demolished for the construction of a new
structure which rests on its foundations. ASI, as an expert
body refrained from recording a specific finding on whether
the underlying structure was demolished for the purpose of

**the construction of a mosque.** Assuming that an inference in regard to demolition could have been made several hundred years later, ASI evidently did not find specific evidence to suggest that a structure had been demolished for the purpose of constructing a mosque. The report submitted by ASI is silent on this facet. The High Court, therefore, indicated that there could be one of two hypotheses: either that the underlying structure had collapsed due to natural forces or that its demolition was the work of human intervention as part of the process of building a mosque on its foundations. Though the ASI did not venture to enter a specific finding, the High Court seems to infer that since the foundation of the erstwhile structure was used for the construction of a mosque, the builder of the mosque would have been aware of the nature of the erstwhile structure and its foundation while constructing the mosque. This is an inference which the High Court has drawn though that is not a specific finding which the ASI has returned in the course of its report.

734.   Consequently, when the ASI report will be placed in balance in terms of its evidentiary value in the course of this judgment, it is crucial for the court to sift between what the report finds and what it leaves unanswered. The ASI report does find the existence of a pre-existing structure . . . The report concludes on the basis of the architectural fragments found at the site and the nature of the structure that it was of a Hindu religious origin. The report rejects the possibility . . . of the underlying structure being of Islamic origin. **But the ASI report has left unanswered a critical part of the remit which was made to it, namely, a determination of whether a Hindu temple had been demolished to pave way for the construction of the mosque. ASI's inability to render a specific finding on this facet is certainly a significant evidentiary circumstance which must be borne in mind when the cumulative impact of the entire evidence is considered in the final analysis.**

735. There is another aspect which needs to be flagged at this stage and which will be considered when the question of title is evaluated. That issue is whether a determination of title can rest on the basis of the ASI findings as they stand. Whether the construction of a mosque in 1528 A.D. (over 450 years ago) on the foundations of an erstwhile religious structure (dating back to the twelfth century A.D.) can result in a finding on the question of title is a distinct matter. At this stage, it will suffice to note that a determination of title was not obviously within the remit of ASI. This is a matter on which the court will need to draw a considered and objective conclusion when it deals with the issue of title later in this judgment.

[. . .]

772. From the testimony of the Hindu and Sunni Muslim witnesses, there appear three significant areas of dispute:

772.1. The first is about the presence of idols under the central dome of the three domed structure, which was a part of the Babri mosque to the Muslims and the 'Garbh Grih' to the Hindus. The oral accounts contain isolated references to the presence of a calendar bearing a photograph of the idol and of worship being offered to this pictorial representation. **The Hindu witnesses have however accepted that the idol of Lord Ram was shifted into the inner courtyard, below the central dome on the night between 22-12-1949/ 23-12-1949. The possibility of any idol under the central dome prior to 22-12-1949/23-12-1949. stands excluded on a preponderance of probabilities;**

772.2. Second, there are variations in regard to the statements of the Hindu witnesses on whether and, if so the nature of the prayers, that were offered inside the inner sanctum prior to **22-12-1949/23-12-1949**. While some witnesses have stated that they had entered the disputed structure for offering prayers below the central dome, other witnesses have stated that prayers were being offered only at the railing separating the inner and the outer courtyards. **The case that prayers were offered at the railing is inconsistent with the claim that prayers were being offered inside the three domed structure by the Hindus between 1934 and 1949. According to the Muslim witnesses, no prayers were being offered inside the three domed structure by the Hindus;**

772.3. Third, there is a variation between the statements of the Hindu and Muslim witnesses on whether namaz was offered inside the three domed structure of the mosque between 1934 and 1949. The Muslim witnesses consistently deposed that namaz was being offered and that the last Friday prayers were offered on **22-12-1949**. On the other hand, according to the Hindu witnesses, no Muslim offered prayers at the three domed structure and if anyone ventured near the premises, they were made to leave out of the fear of the sadhus and Bairagis in the neighbourhood.

[. . .]

795. Setting course through history, the cornerstone of the edifice for the Hindus is their faith and belief in the birthplace of Lord Ram as the incarnation of Vishnu. Their faith is founded principally on the significance attached to Ayodhya in the following:

795.1. Religious scriptures, principally the association of Ayodhya with the presiding deity of Lord Ram in Valmiki's Ramayan, Skand Puran and Shri Ramacharitmanas . . .

795.2. Travelogues, gazetteers and books.

796. In weaving through the wealth of documents produced before this Court, it is necessary to answer both the extent of judicial review of faith and belief and the evidentiary value of the reliance on travelogues, gazetteers and books.

The court went on to reiterate the extent of jurisdiction it assumed in matters of reversing the decisions of sovereign Mughal rulers:

[. . .]

997. **This Court cannot entertain claims that stem from the actions of the Mughal rulers against Hindu places of worship in a court of law today.** For any person who seeks solace or recourse against the actions of any number of ancient rulers, the law is not the answer. Our history is replete with actions that have been judged to be morally incorrect and even today are liable to trigger vociferous ideological debate. **However, the adoption of the Constitution marks a watershed moment where we, the people of India, departed from the determination of rights and liabilities on the basis of our ideology, our religion, the colour of our skin, or the century when our ancestors arrived at these lands, and submitted to the rule of law. Under our rule of law, this court can adjudicate upon private property claims that were expressly or impliedly recognised by the British sovereign and subsequently not interfered with upon Indian independence.** With respect to the disputed property, it is evident that the British Sovereign recognised and permitted the existence of both Hindu and Muslim communities at the disputed property upon the annexation of Oudh in 1856. This culminated with the construction of the railing in order to maintain law and order between the two communities. The acts of the parties subsequent to the annexation of Oudh in 1856 form the continued basis of the legal rights of the parties in the present suits and it is these acts that this Court must evaluate to decide the present dispute.

\* \* \*

One might summarize the main findings of the Supreme Court on the archaeological material thus: The mosque was built on the remains of a religious structure as per the ASI, but it could not be said that it was a temple or, more importantly, that a temple was demolished to build the mosque. For the historical dimension sought to be used by the Hindu side, despite contrary versions of respectable historians, this must be conclusive closure.

The case of Swayambhu was not accepted, nor the claim that in the absence of a deity the *janmasthan* might have juristic personality. This indicated some divergence between law and faith, with the former prevailing.

It was noted that it was conceded by the Muslim side that Hindus worshipped Lord Ram on the *chabutra* (platform) in the outer courtyard of the mosque and that Lord Ram was born in Ayodhya. That, too, may be a matter of faith, but the concession gave the court the opportunity of applying principles of law regarding undisturbed possession. The possession of the outer courtyard by the Hindu side was admitted by the Muslim side, but the latter's possession of the inner courtyard and the mosque was disputed and periodically challenged by the former.

However, the Muslims were, surprisingly, unable to show any evidence that they had continued to pray at the site from 1528 to 1856–57, the period under Mughal rule.

Given the enormity of the implications of the judgment, the court, having sensed that a decision on pure legal principles might not be appropriate, prepared the ground for making adjustments for the purpose of justice. The Supreme Court does that formally, under Article 142, but the underlining principle is that of justice, equity and good conscience. Ultimately, in balancing equities to compensate the Muslim side, that was exactly what the court did, setting a precedent for modern times, though disagreeing explicitly with the high court having done something similar by trifurcating the disputed plot where Babri Masjid stood before demolition. It could be argued that, in the absence of Article 142, a court of law has more restricted access to principles.

## O.5. Applicable legal regime and Justice, Equity and Good Conscience

[. . .]

**1022. The common underlying thread is that justice, good conscience and equity plays a supplementary role in enabling courts to mould the relief to suit the circumstances that present themselves before courts with the principal purpose of ensuring a just outcome. Where the existing statutory framework is inadequate for courts to adjudicate upon the dispute before them, or no settled judicial doctrine or custom can be availed of, courts may legitimately take recourse to the principles of justice, equity and good conscience to effectively and fairly dispose of the case.** A court cannot abdicate its responsibility to decide a dispute over legal rights merely because the facts of a case do not readily submit themselves to the application of the letter of the existing law. Courts in India have long availed of the principles of justice, good conscience and equity to supplement the incompleteness or inapplicability of the letter of the law with the ground realities of legal disputes to do justice between the parties. Equity, as an essential component of justice, formed the final step in the just adjudication of disputes. After taking recourse to legal principles from varied legal systems, scholarly written work on the subject, and the experience of the Bar and Bench, if no decisive or just outcome could be reached, a judge may apply the principles of equity between the parties to ensure that justice is done. This has often found form in the power of the court to craft reliefs that are both legally sustainable and just.

## The Doctrine of Lost Grant

The court explored all possible aspects of the Muslim claim, including waqf by user and lost-grant principles, lest it be thought that a preconceived opinion in favour of Hindus drove the final decision. The lost-grant doctrine applies in circumstances where there is no grant document or title papers, but the conduct of affairs since ancient times is indicative of an assumption that the grant was made. The doctrine is very similar to the setting up of a waqf by user, where the absence of a waqf deed is made up for by uninterrupted use of the property for a long period for purposes treated as charitable under Islamic law. In dealing with this concept, the court observed:

757. **Under the doctrine of lost grant, a long-continued use or possession can raise a legal presumption that the right exercised was previously conveyed to the user or possessor and that the instrument of conveyance has been lost . . .**

[. . .]

1173. From the analysis of the precedent on the subject, the following principles can be culled out:

1173.1. The doctrine of lost grant supplies **a rule of evidence**. The doctrine is applicable in the absence of evidence, due to a lapse of time, to prove the **existence of a valid grant issued in antiquity**. However, the court is not bound to raise the presumption where there is sufficient and convincing evidence to prove possession or a claim to a land in which case the doctrine of lost grant will have no applicability;

[. . .]

1173.4. **For the applicability of the doctrine of lost grant, there must be long, uninterrupted and peaceful enjoyment of an incorporeal right. Uninterrupted enjoyment includes continuous use or possession. The requisite period of use and possession is variable and to be determined from case to case.**

1173.5. A distinction has to be made between an assertion of rights due to a prolonged custom and usage and that by doctrine of lost grant.

[. . .]

1183. No documentary evidence has been brought on the record indicating the conferment of title in a form of the grant of the land underlying the mosque. The documentary evidence on which reliance has been placed essentially consists of grants which were made by the British Government for the upkeep and maintenance of the mosque. These grants are stated to be in continuation of those which have been made previously prior to the annexation of Oudh by the Colonial Government . . .

[. . .]

1200. The case of the plaintiffs in Suit No. 4 has to be evaluated on the basis of the entirety of the evidence on the record to deduce whether possession has been established on a preponderance of probabilities. The evidence reveals several significant features which must be noted:

1200.1. **Though, the case of the plaintiffs in Suit 4 is that the mosque was constructed in 1528 by or at the behest of Babur, there is no account by them of possession, use or offer of namaz in the mosque between the date of construction and 1856–7. For a period of over 325 years which elapsed since the date of the construction of the mosque until the setting up of a grill-brick wall by the British, the Muslims have not adduced evidence to establish the exercise of possessory control over the disputed site. Nor is there any account in the evidence of the offering of namaz in the mosque, over this period.**

[. . .]

1200.4. The communal riots that took place in 1856–7 resulted in the colonial administration setting up a grill-brick wall to bring about a measure of peace between the conflicting claims of the two communities. The immediate aftermath of the railing led to the dispute over the Ramchabutra, which was erected right outside the railing and from where the Hindus sought to offer worship to Lord Ram. The time of the setting up of the Chabutra, the place of its location and the offer of worship to Lord Ram on Chabutra are pointers in the direction of the Hindus continuing to offer worship immediately outside the railing when faced with a possible exclusion from the inner courtyard.

[. . .]

1200.11. **After 1934, evidence indicates that Muslim worship in the form of namaz had reduced as a result of the obstructions in their acces to the inner courtyard. By 16-12-1949 (the last Friday namaz) the mosque was being used for the purposes of Friday namaz.** The circumstances bearing upon the restoration of the damage which was done to the mosque in 1934, availing of the services of the Pesh Imam and the offering of namaz albeit to a reduced extent are circumstances which point to a reasonable inference that there was no total ouster of the Muslims from the inner structure prior to **22-12-1949/ 23-12-1949** though their access was intermittent and interrupted.

## Waqf by User

The doctrine of lost grant is obviously to fill the gap left by missing documents of property, employed when the title is presumed but not possible to prove through normal documentation. The doctrine applies in general to all situations and might not have been necessary in this particular case, given that the matter pertained to a waqf property, and a specific doctrine of waqf by user was available to be applied here.

Although no proof of dedication of waqf could be provided, the court noted that in Indian law there is scope for waqf by user.*

---

* A kind of waqf where the absence of a waqf deed is made up for by uninterrupted use of the property for a long period for purposes treated as charitable under Islamic law.

Thus, Babri Masjid was a waqf property. However, the possession of the Muslims was not found to be undisturbed. So, on the basis of the facts as found by the court, both lost-grant and waqf by user were found unsustainable. Curiously, the former might have been answered in the negative for the Hindu side as well, but somehow greater onus seems to have been placed on the Muslim side. Yet it is unclear why the court, having come to that conclusion, nevertheless expressed its concern that the Muslims had been repeatedly wronged and deserved some compensatory reparation.

1112. Before the High Court, it was not disputed by the litigating parties that the plot of land in which the disputed structure existed was recorded as Nazul land (i.e. land which is owned by the government) . . .

[. . .]

1119. [. . .] [I]t was urged that even in the absence of an express dedication, the long use of the disputed site for public worship as a mosque elevates the property in question to a 'waqf by user'.

[. . .]

**1121. This contention raises two points for determination: First, whether the notion of a waqf by user is accepted as a principle of law by our courts; and second, as a matter of fact, whether its application is attracted in the present case.**

[. . .]

1122. In the first paragraph of the plaint [in Suit No. 4], the plaintiffs set up the case that on its construction in 1528 AD by or at the behest of Babur, the mosque was dedicated as a site of religious worship for the Muslims to offer namaz:

'1. That in the town of Ajodhiya, pargana Haveli Oudh there
exists an ancient historic mosque, commonly known as
Babri Masjid, built by Emperor Babar more than 443 years
ago, after his conquest of India and his occupation of the
territories including the town of Ajodhiya, for the use of the
Muslims in general, as a place of worship and performance
of religious ceremonies.'

1123. There being no specific document to establish a dedication,
the plaintiffs, during the course of submissions, fall back upon the
pleading in regard to long use of the mosque as a site for religious
worship.

[. . .]

'2. That in the sketch map . . . the main construction of
the said mosque is shown . . . and the land adjoining the
mosque on the east, west, north and south, shown in the
sketch map . . . in the ancient graveyard of the Muslims,
covered by the graves of the Muslims, who lost the lives in
the battle between emperor Babur and the previous ruler
of Ajodhiya . . . The mosque and the graveyard is vested
in the Almighty. The said mosque has since the time of its
construction been used by the Muslims for offering prayers
and the graveyard is in Mohalla Kot Rama Chander also
known as Rama Kot Town, Ayodhya . . .'

1124. A waqf is a dedication of movable or immovable property for a
religious or charitable purpose recognised by Muslim law. Ordinarily,
a waqf is brought into existence by an express act of dedication in
the form of a declaration. Upon pronouncing the declaration from
the wakif as the person making the dedication and vests in the
Almighty, Allah. A waqf is a permanent and **irrevocable dedication
of property and once the waqf is created, the dedication cannot be**

**rescinded at a later date. The property of a validly created waqf is inalienable and cannot be sold or leased for private gain.**

[. . .]

1134. Our jurisprudence recognises the principle of waqf by user even absent an express deed of dedication or declaration. Whether or not properties are waqf property by long use is a matter of evidence. The test is whether the property has been used for public religious worship by those professing the Islamic faith. The evidentiary threshold is high, in most cases requiring evidence of public worship at the property in question since time immemorial . . .

[. . .]

1136. [. . .] [P]laintiffs in Suit No. 4, admitted that there is no evidence of possession, use or offering of worship in the mosque prior to 1856–1857. No evidence has been produced to establish worship at the mosque or possessory control over the disputed property . . . over the period of 325 years between the alleged date of construction in 1528 until the erection of railing by the colonial government in 1857 . . .

1137. The construction of the railing was not an attempt to settle proprietary rights. It was an expedient measure to ensure law and order. Disputes between 1858 and 1883 indicated that the attempt to exclude the Hindus from the inner courtyard by raising a railing was a matter of continuing dispute . . .

[. . .]

1140. **The evidence adduced does not demonstrate that the entire disputed property was utilised by the resident Muslim community for public religious worship. It is evident that the outer courtyard**

**was in fact used by and was in the possession of the devotees of Lord Ram. These portions of the property were admittedly not used for religious purposes by the members of the resident Muslim community and cannot be waqf property by long use . . .**

[. . .]

**1144. Though, [the plaint] dates the commencement of the possession of the Muslims from the date of the construction of the mosque, it has emerged that no records are available with respect to possession for the period between 1528 and 1860 . . .**

[. . .]

1156. The plaintiffs have failed to adopt a clear stand evidently because they are conscious of the fact that in pleading adverse possession, they must necessarily carry the burden of acknowledging the title of the person or the entity against whom the plea of adverse possession has not been adequately set up in the pleadings and as noted above, has not been put-forth with any certitude in the course of the submissions. Above all, it is impossible for the plaintiffs to set up a case of being in peaceful, open and continuous possession of the entire property.

\* \* \*

These paragraphs include curious findings of virtual admission by the Muslim side that they were unable to produce proof of user as a mosque from 1528 to 1856. This sounds strange as the entire period covered the Mughal Empire, and it makes little sense to believe that the mosque was built but prayers were not performed through the reigns of emperors Babur, Akbar, Jehangir, Shahjehan and Aurangzeb, the great Mughals. On the other hand, the court held that there was evidence of Hindus having prayed inside the mosque from time to time, including when in 1858 the Nihang intruded and placed idols on a low, makeshift platform. But there is a great difference between occupation, or possession, being disturbed periodically by a rival claimant, and adverse possession that defeats the title of the original owner.

So long as the origins of the mosque were established, or waqf by user was accepted, the only way of reversing that position would require uninterrupted possession by the Hindu party as a challenge to the Muslim claim. Interestingly, the court notes that the land concerned was recorded as 'Nazul', or land owned by the government, usually by escheat. However, in view of the government not seeking to press its claim, the issue became irrelevant for the purposes of the litigation. But we know that revenue records in this country are known to be manipulated, and given the importance of this case the facts certainly deserved further examination of the root of the revenue entries. It could not have been that for a hundred years several courts failed to notice this significant fact.

There is an interesting postscript to the analysis of the judgment by a brilliant young lawyer named Nizam Pasha, who was part of the team of lawyers who argued on behalf of the Muslim side in the Supreme Court. In a well-argued piece published in the Wire, he obviates the need to establish a waqf by user and insists that a proper reading and interpretation of the inscriptions inside (said to be destroyed in the damage caused in 1934) and outside (which were available till 1992)—and in both cases rubbings were available—would have been sufficient evidence of dedication for waqf. One might add that a waqf dedication can be oral, and all that is required is authentication by a witness. While Pasha's entire article merits reading, two major assertions might be highlighted here. Firstly, he makes a point that in the high court Justice Sudhir Agarwal not only lost sight of the correct translation of the concerned verses but also did not have the benefit of the facts about the predilections of the German Indologist Alois Anton

Führer, on whose translations and reports the court had relied but for which he had been dismissed from his post at the ASI:

> 'It might be of some relevance to note that A. Fuhrer was dismissed from the Archeological Survey of India in 1898, a few years after he made the transcripts of these inscriptions, on the proved charge of falsifying inscriptions, submitting false reports and adopting unmethodical and unbusinesslike practices. The ASI conducted an inquiry against him, based on which he was dishonourably dismissed from service. The inquiry report was published for the first time as part of an article in the Journal of the Royal Asiatic Society of London in January 2012. Since this was after the judgement of the high court, Justice Agarwal, to his credit, did not have the benefit of it."

Pasha tells us that this record was available to the Supreme Court, but during arguments Chief Justice Gogoi confessed that he was unfamiliar with Persian and Urdu, and requested therefore that the argument be presented in writing. However, there is no reference to the written arguments in the final judgment, making the author wonder if the correct metre of the verse might have changed the course of history.

The inscriptions that Pasha alluded to have been considered in section

**'G. The three inscriptions':**

61. The case of the . . . plaintiffs in Suit No. 4 is that in the town of Ayodhya 'there exists an ancient historic mosque commonly known as Babri Masjid built by Emperor Babur more than 433

* Nizam Pasha, 'Ayodhya Verdict: The Poems That Could Have Changed History', TheWire.in, 4 April 2020, https://thewire.in/law/the-ayodhya-verdict-the-poems-that-could-have-changed-history

years ago, after his conquest of India and his occupation of the territories including the town of Ayodhya'. The mosque, it has been pleaded, was for the use of Muslims in general as a place of worship and for the performance of religious ceremonies. The mosque and the adjoining graveyard are stated to vest 'in the Almighty' and the mosque since the time of its inscription is stated to have been used by Muslims for offering prayers. Thus, the plaintiffs have come forth with a positive case in regard to the:

(i) Existence of a mosque;
(ii) Construction of the mosque by Babur 433 years prior to the institution of the Suit in 1961;
(iii) Construction of the mosque as a place of worship and for religious ceremonies; and
(iv) Use of the mosque since its construction for the purpose of offering prayers.

62. Sudhir Aggrawal, J. recorded in his judgment that it is accepted [. . .] that the sole basis for determining the date of the construction of the mosque and correlating it to Babur consists of the inscriptions stated to have been installed on the mosque as referred to in the gazetteers and other documents. [T]he learned Judge observed:

'1435. Broadly, we find and in fact it is even admitted . . . that the sole basis for determining the period of construction of the disputed building and to co-relate it with Emperor Babur is/are the inscription(s) said to be installed in the disputed building referred to in certain Gazetteers, etc.'

Now both before the High Court and during the course of the present proceedings, there has been a debate on whether the texts of the alleged inscriptions on the mosque have been proved. Mr P.N. Mishra, learned counsel appearing on behalf of the Akhil

Bharatiya Shri Ram Janmabhumi Punrudhar Samiti has questioned the authenticity of the inscriptions. He sought to cast doubt on whether the mosque was constructed in 1528 AD by or at the behest of Babur.

63. The first document relied on is the text by Führer titled 'The Sharqi Architecture of Jaunpur with Notes on Zafarabad, Sahet-Mahet and Other Places in the North-Western Provinces and Oudh'* . . . In Chapter X, there is a reference to three inscriptions bearing Nos. XL, XLI, and XLII. It is from these three inscriptions that Führer formed an opinion that the Babri mosque was constructed at Ayodhya in 1523 AD or AH 930.

63.1. Inscription XL in Arabic is over the central mihrab and furnishes the Kalimah twice in the following words:

'There is no god but Allah, Muhammad is His Prophet.'

63.2. Inscription XLI was found on the mimbar and was written in Persian. The inscription as translated in English reads thus:

'1.   By order of Babar, the king of the world,
2.   This firmament-like, lofty,
3.   Strong building was erected.
4.   By the auspicious noble Mir Khan.
5.   May ever remain such a foundation,
6.   And such a king of the world.'

63.3. Inscription XLII was found above the entrance door. Also, in Persian, the inscription has been translated thus:

---

* Alois Anton Führer, Edmund W. Smith and James Burgess, *The Sharqi Architecture of Jaunpur: With Notes on Zafarabad, Sahet-Mahet and Other Places in the North-Western Provinces and Oudh*, 1994.

'1.  In the name of God, the merciful, the element.

2.  In the name of him who . . . may God perpetually keep him in the world.

3.  * * *

4.  Such a sovereign who is famous in the world, and in person of delight for the world.

5.  In his presence one of the grandees who is another king of Turkey and China.

6.  Laid this religious foundation in the auspicious Hijra 930.

7.  O God! May always remain the crown, throne and life with the king.

8.  May Babur always pour the flowers of happiness; may remain successful.

9.  His counsellor and minister who is the founder of this fort masjid.

10. This poetry, giving the date and eulogy, was written by the lazy writer and poor servant Fath-allah-Ghori, composer.'

63.4. After adverting to the inscriptions, Führer notes:

'The old temple of Ramachandra at Janamasthanam must have been a very fine one, for many of its columns have been used by the Mussalmans in the construction of Babar's masjid. These are of strong, close-grained, dark-coloured or black stone, called by the natives kasauti, "touch-stone slate," and carved with different devices. They are from seven to eight feet long, square at the base, centre and capital, and round or octagonal intermediately.'

64. The second piece of documentary evidence in which these inscriptions are purportedly translated is the 'Babur-Nama'. The translation by A.S. Beveridge was first published in 1921.* Apart

---

* William Erskine, John Leyden and Annette Susannah Beveridge, *The Babur-Nama in English (Memoirs of Babur)*, reprint edition, Low Price Publications, 2006.

from the book, extracts of some of its pages were exhibited by the parties to the proceedings. Appendix (U) refers to two inscriptions: one inside and another outside the mosque . . .

65. Beveridge obtained the text of the inscription through the Deputy Commissioner of Faizabad on a request made by her spouse. Beveridge notes that while reproducing the text she had made a few changes. The text of the inscription inside the mosque, as quoted by Beveridge is as follows:

'(1) By the command of the Emperor Babur whose justice is an edifice reaching up to the very height of the heavens.
(2) The good-hearted Mir Baqi built this alighting place of angels.
(3) It will remain an everlasting bounty, and (hence) the date of its erection became manifest from my words: It will remain an everlasting bounty.'

The text of the inscription outside the mosque is thus:

'1. In the name of One who is Great (and) Wise (and) who is Creator of the whole world and is free from the bondage of space.
2. After His praise, peace and blessings be on Prophet Muhammad, who is the head of all the Prophets in both the worlds.
3. In the world, it is widely talked about Qalandar Babur that he is a successful emperor.'

Beveridge stated that the second inscription outside the mosque was incomplete.

66. The third set of texts in support of the inscriptions is published in 'Epigraphia Indica-Arabic-Persian Supplement (In Continuation

of Epigraphia Indo-Moslemica) 1964 and 1965'* (reprinted in 1987). This has been published by the Director General, ASI and contains a reference to the inscriptions of Babur. The text is attributed to Maulvi M. Ashraf Husain and is edited by Z.A. Desai.

[. . .]

66.2. The text contains the following description in regard to the construction of Babri Masjid:

'The Baburi-Masjid, which commands a picturesque view from the riverside, was constructed according to A. Führer in AH 930 (1523–24 AD) but his chronology, based upon incorrect readings of inscriptions supplied to him, is erroneous. Babur defeated Ibrahim Lodi only in AH 933 (1526 AD), and moreover, the year of construction, recorded in two of the three inscriptions studied below, is clearly AH 935 (1528–29 AD). Again, it was not built by Mir Khan as stated by him. The order for building the mosque seems to have been issued during Babur's stay at Ajodhya in AH 934 (1527–28 AD), but no mention of its completion is made in the Babur Nama. However, it may be remembered that his diary for the year AH 934 (1527–28 AD) breaks off abruptly, and throws the reader into the dark in regard to the account of Oudh.'

66.3. The text also provides an account of the manner in which the author obtained an inked rubbing of one of the inscriptions from Sayyid Badru'l Hasan of Faizabad:

'The mosque contains a number of inscriptions. On the eastern facade is a chhajja, below which appears a Quranic

---

* Z.A. Desai (ed.), *Epigraphia Indica, Arabic and Persian Supplement (In Continuation of Epigraphia Indo-Moslemica)*, Archaeological Survey of India, 1987.

text and above, an inscription in Persian verse. On the central mihrab are carved religious texts such as the Kalima (First Creed), etc. On the southern face of the pulpit was previously fixed a stone slab bearing a Persian inscription in verse. There was also another inscription in Persian verse built up into the right hand side wall of the pulpit. Of these, the last-mentioned two epigraphs have disappeared. They were reportedly destroyed in the communal vandalism in 1934 AD, but luckily, I managed to secure an inked rubbing of one of them from Sayyid Badru'l Hasan of Fyzabad. The present inscription, restored by the Muslim community, is not only in inlaid Nasta'liq characters, but is also slightly different from the original, owing perhaps to the incompetence of the restorers in deciphering it properly.

The readings and translations of the historical epigraphs mentioned above, except in the case of one, were published by Führer and Mrs Beveridge, but their readings are so incomplete, inaccurate and different from the text that their inclusion in this article is not only desirable but also imperative.

The epigraph studied below was inscribed on a slab of stone measuring about 68 by 48 cm, which was built up into the southern side of the pulpit of the mosque, but is now lost, as stated above. It is edited here from the estampage obtained from Sayyid Badru'l Hasan of Fyzabad. Its three-line text consists of six verses in Persian, inscribed in ordinary Naskh characters within floral borders. It records the construction of the mosque by Mir Baqi under orders from Emperor Babur and gives the year AH 935 (1528–29 AD) in a chronogram.'

66.4. The author states that on the southern side of the pulpit of the mosque was an inscription fixed on a slab of stone measuring 68 cm × 48 cm but the original was lost. What is quoted is the version obtained from the inked rubbing noted above. The text of the first inscription was thus:

'(1) By the order of King Babur whose justice is an edifice, meeting the palace of the sky (i.e. as high as the sky).

(2) This descending place of the angels was built by the fortunate noble Mir Baqi.

(3) It will remain an everlasting bounty, and (hence) the date of its erection became manifest from my words: It will remain an everlasting bounty.'

66.5. As regards the second inscription, the judgment of Sudhir Aggrawal, J. notes: [. . .]

'1449. Führer's Inscription No. XLI which he mentions that the same was found inside the mosque on the mimbar (right hand side of the disputed building) has been termed as second inscription by Maulvi F. Ashraf Hussain. It consists of three couplets arranged in six lines. He (Hussain) clearly admits non-existence of the said inscription by observing "the epigraphical Tablet" which was built up into right hand side wall of the pulpit, does not exist now, and, therefore, the text of the inscription is quoted here from Führer's work, for the same reason, its illustration could not be given. Sri Husain/Desai however, did not agree to the reading of the inscription by Führer and observed that Führer's reading does not appear free from mistakes.'
(emphasis in original)

66.6. The text of the third inscription is as follows:

'(1) In the name of Allah, the Beneficent, the Merciful. And in Him is my trust.

(2) In the name of One who is Wise, Great (and) Creator of all the universe (and) is spaceless.
After His praise, blessings be upon the Chosen one (i.e. the Prophet), who is the head of prophets and best in the world. The Qalandar-like (i.e. truthful) Babur has become

celebrated (lit. a story) in the world, since (in his time) the world has achieved prosperity.

(3) (He is) such (an emperor) as has embraced (i.e. conquered) all the seven climes of the world in the manner of the sky.

In his court, there was a magnificent noble, named Mir Baqi the second Asaf, councillor of his Government and administrator of his kingdom, who is the founder of this mosque and fort-wall.

(4) O God, may he live for ever in this world, with fortune and life and crown and throne. The time of the building is this auspicious date, of which the indication is nine hundred (and) thirty-five (AH 935 = 1528–29 AD).

Completed was this praise of God, of Prophet and of king. May Allah illumine his proof. Written by the weak writer and humble creature, Eathu'llah Muhammad Ghori.'

66.7. As regards the inscriptions noted by Führer, certain significant aspects need to be noted. While the second inscription contains a reference to the order of Babur for the construction of the mosque, construction is attributed to Mir Khan (not Mir Baqi). The third inscription refers to the foundation of the construction of the mosque being laid in Hijri 930 which corresponds to 1523 AD. This is prior to the invasion by Babur and the Battle at Panipat which resulted in the defeat of Ibrahim Lodhi. As regards the work of Beveridge, it is evident that she had neither seen the original text nor had she translated the text of the inscriptions herself. Beveridge obtained a purported text of the inscriptions through her spouse from the Deputy Commissioner, Faizabad. Beveridge claimed that she received a copy of the text through correspondence initiated by her spouse who was an ICS officer in the Colonial Government. She had neither read the original nor is there anything to indicate that she was in a position to translate it. Beveridge states that she made 'a few slight changes in the term of expression'. What changes were made by Beveridge has not been explained. According to her, the text of the two inscriptions was incomplete and was not legible. The text provided by Führer shows that the construction of the mosque was not in 1528 AD. Inscription XLI mentions the name of Mir Khan while inscription XLII refers to the construction of the mosque as Hijri 930.

67. Sudhir Aggrawal, J. while adverting to the work of Ashraf Husain and Z.A. Desai took serious note of the 'fallacy and complete misrepresentation' of the author in publishing a text under the authority of the ASI without regard for its accuracy, correctness and genuineness: [. . .]

'1463. We are extremely perturbed by the manner in which Ashraf Husain/Desai have tried to give an impeccable authority to the texts of the alleged inscriptions which they claim to have existed on the disputed building though repeatedly said that the original text has disappeared. The fallacy and complete misrepresentation on the part of author in trying to give colour of truth to this text is writ large from a bare reading of the write-up. We are really at pains to find that such blatant fallacious kind of material has been allowed to be published in a book published under the authority of ASI, Government of India, without caring about its accuracy, correctness and genuineness of the subject . . . Both these inscriptions i.e. the one claimed to be on the southern face of the pulpit and the other on the right hand side wall of the pulpit are said to be non-available by observing "of these the last-mentioned two epigraphs have disappeared". The time of disappearance according to Maulvi Ashraf Husain was 1934 AD when a communal riot took place at Ayodhya. However, he claimed to have got an inked rubbing on one of the two inscriptions from Syed Badrul Hasan of Faizabad. The whereabouts of Syed Badrul Hasan, who he was, what was his status, in what way and manner he could get that ink rubbing of the said inscription and what is the authenticity to believe it to be correct when original text of the inscription are not known. There is nothing to co-relate the text he got as the correct text of the inscription found in the disputed building claimed to have lost in 1934.' [. . .]

67.1. The High Court observed that two inscriptions, those on the southern face of the pulpit and on the wall on the right of the pulpit were not available. According to Ashraf Husain, the epigraphs disappeared in 1934 at the time of the communal riot. However, reliance was sought to be placed on an alleged 'inked rubbing' without explaining the identity or whereabouts of the person from whom it was obtained. The criticism of the High Court is not without basis. The identity of the individual from whom the inked rubbings were obtained was not explained. Nor was there any explanation about the manner in which he had in turn obtained it. There was indeed nothing to co-relate the text which that individual had obtained with the translation in the text compiled by Ashraf Husain and Z.A. Desai. The High Court observed: [. . .]

'1464. [. . .] When the original was already lost and there was nothing to verify the text of restored inscription with the original, neither the restored one can be relied upon nor it is understandable as to how he could have any occasion to compare the restored one with the alleged . . . original . . .'

67.2. In this background, the High Court observed: [. . .]

'1466. [. . .] The text, description and whatever had been set up by Ashraf Husain in respect of the above inscription is unbelievable and lacks trustworthiness. We are constrained to observe at this stage that in the matter of historical events and that too, when it bears a religious importance and the matter has also seen serious disputes between two communities, the persons who are connected with history . . . must behave responsibly and before making any write-up, should check up, cross-check and verify very carefully what they are writing since the consequences of their write-up may be dangerous and irreparable.'

68. A fourth version of the inscriptions emerged pursuant to a direction of the Civil Judge dated 26-3-1946 in Shia Central Waqf Board v. Sunni Central Board of Waqf.[*] In pursuance of those directions, a person by the name of Sr. A. Akhtar Abbas is stated to have read an inscription and prepared his inspection note. The High Court, however, noted that the text as reproduced in the judgment dated 30-3-1946 states that in the first inscription, the words are 'by the order of Shah Babar, Amir Mir Baki built the resting place of angels in 923 AH i.e. 1516–17 AD'. In respect of the second inscription, there is a reference to 'Mir Baki of Isphahan in 935 AH i.e. 1528–29 AD'. The High Court observed that it was not apprised of whether in the entire Babur-Nama, there was a reference to any Mir Baki Isphahani though, there was a reference to Baki Tashkendi. Besides one of the two tablets was new and had been replaced for the original tablet which had been demolished during the communal riots of 1934. On the above state of the evidence, the High Court doubted the genuineness and authenticity of the transcripts of the inscriptions which were relied upon before it.

69. At this stage, it is necessary to make a reference to the 'Tuzuk-i-Babri'.[†] The Babur-Nama contains the daily diary of Babur commencing from 899 Hijri (1494 AD). Out of the lifespan of Babur, a description of eighteen years is available over different

---

[*] 'Shia Central Waqf Board vs Sunni Central Board of Waqf', regular suit no. 29 of 1945.

[†] Rashid Akhtar Nadvi, *Tuzk-e-Babri*, Sang-e-Mil, 1995.

periods. Babur came to India in 1526 AD. The description available until his death is for the following periods, (noted by Sudhir Aggrawal, J.): [. . .]

'1487. [. . .] 1. From 1 Safar 932 Hijri (17-11-1525 AD) till 12 Rajab 934 Hijri (2-4-1528 AD)
2.   From 3 Muharram 934 Hijri (18-9-1528 AD) till 3 Moharram 936 Hijri (7-9-1529 AD).'

The records for the period from 2-4-1528 till 17-9-1528 are missing. Out of this period, the period from 2-4-1528 to 15-9-1528 was of 934 Hijri while the period from 15-9-1528 to 17-9-1528 was of 935 Hijri. Sudhir Aggrawal, J. noted in the High Court that the crucial year was 935 Hijri and the missing record was only of three days. Babur defeated Ibrahim Lodhi at Panipat on 20-4-1526. On 28-3-1528, Babur reached the junction of the Rivers Ghaghara and Saryu. After a reference to the date 2-4-1528, there is a break until 15-9-1528.

70. Beveridge's translation of Babur-Nama refers to the employment of artisans in the construction of buildings at several places including at Agra and Gwalior:

'1533. [. . .] 'Another good thing in Hindustan is that it has unnumbered and endless workmen of every kind. There is a fixed caste (jam'i) for every sort of work and for every thing, which has done that work or that thing from father to son till now. Mulla Sharaf, writing in the Zafar-nama about the building of Timur Beg's Stone Mosque, lays stress on the fact that on it 200 stonecutters worked, from Azarbaijan, Fars, Hindustan and other countries. But 680 men worked daily on my buildings in Agra and of Agra stonecutters only; while 1491 stonecutters worked daily on my buildings in Agra, Sikri, Biana, Dulpur, Gualiar and Kuil. In the same way there are numberless artisans and workmen of every sort in Hindustan.'

70.1. In this context, Aggrawal, J. observed: [. . .]

'1534. There is mention of buildings in Babur-Nama at different places including temple of Gwalior, mosque at Delhi, Agra, Gwalior and other several places but it is true that neither there is mention of demolition of any religious place by Babur in Awadh area nor is there anything to show that he either entered Ayodhya or had occasion to issue any direction for construction of a building and in particular a mosque at Ayodhya.'

70.2. The High Court recorded the submission made before it by . . . the Sunni Central Waqf Board, in para 1577 of the judgment that since Babur did not enter Ayodhya himself, there was no question of a demolition of a temple by him and a construction of a mosque. The absence in Babur-Nama of a reference to the construction of a mosque has been relied upon as a factor to discredit the inscriptions which have been analysed earlier. This line of enquiry must be read with the caution which must be exercised while drawing negative inferences from a historical text.

71. [. . .] Counsel adverted to the work of Niccolao Manucci titled 'Indian Texts Series—Storia Do Mogor or Mogul India 1653-1708',* translated in English by William Irvine. Manucci identifies 'the chief temples destroyed' by Aurangzeb, among them being:

(i)   Maisa (Mayapur);
(ii)  Matura (Mathura);
(iii) Caxis (Kashi); and
(iv)  Hajudia (Ajudhya).

---

* Niccolò Manucci and William Irvine, *Storia do Mogor, or, Mogul India, 1653–1708*, J. Murray, 1907.

Manucci was a traveller who had visited India during the reign of Aurangzeb. Besides, the work of Manucci, there is the 'Ain-e-Akbari'* written by Abul Fazal Allami. Ain-e-Akbari deals with the province of Oudh and refers to Ayodhya and its association with Lord Ram. The text refers to 'two considerable tombs of six and seven yards in length' near the city. The text identified several sacred places of pilgrimage. It specifically speaks of Ayodhya where during the month of Chaitra, a religious festival is held. Mr Mishra urged that there is no reference in the Ain-e-Akbari to the construction of a mosque at Ayodhya. The text refers to certain cities as being dedicated to the divinities, among them being Kashi and Ayodhya. By its order dated 18-3-2010, the High Court permitted the above text to be relied on under the provisions of Section 57(13) of the Evidence Act, 1872.

[. . .]

73. Having set out the material which was presented before the High Court in support of the plea that the mosque was constructed in 1528 by Mir Baki, on the instructions of Emperor Babur following the conquest of the subcontinent, it becomes necessary to analyse the conclusions which have been arrived at by the three Judges of the High Court.

(i) **Justice S.U. Khan**

73.1 S.U. Khan, J. held: [. . .]

'Muslims have not been able to prove that the land belonged to Babur under whose orders the mosque was constructed.'

Moreover, the learned Judge held that the inscriptions on the mosque as translated by Führer, Beveridge and Z.A. Desai were

---

* Abu al-Fazl ibn Mubārak and H. Blochmann, *The Ain-i-Akbari*, reprint of 1989, Low Price Publications.

not authentic and hence, on the basis of these inscriptions alone, it could not be held either that the disputed building was constructed by or under the orders of Babur or that it was constructed in 1528. S.U. Khan, J. specifically observed that:

> '. . . In this regard detailed reasons have been given by my learned Brother S. Aggrawal, J. with which I fully agree.'

73.2. However, in the course of his conclusions titled as 'Gist of the Findings' Khan, J. held: [. . .]

> '1.   The disputed structure was constructed as mosque by or under orders of Babur.
> 2.   It is not proved by direct evidence that premises in dispute including constructed portion belonged to Babur or the person who constructed the mosque or under whose orders it was constructed.'

73.3. The conclusion in Point 1 in the above extract of the conclusions is contrary to the earlier finding that it could not be held either that the mosque was constructed by or under the orders of Babur or that it was constructed in 1528. The finding on Point 1 is also contrary to the specific observation that S.U. Khan, J. was in agreement with the decision of Sudhir Aggrawal, J. in regard to the lack of authenticity of the inscriptions.

**(ii)  Justice Sudhir Aggrawal**

73.4. Sudhir Aggrawal, J. held: [. . .]

> '1679. [. . .] it is difficult to record a finding that the building in dispute was constructed in 1528 AD by or at the command of Babur since no reliable material is available for coming to the said conclusion. On the contrary the preponderance of

probability shows that the building in dispute was constructed at some later point of time and the inscriptions thereon were fixed further later but exact period of the two is difficult to ascertain.

* * *

1681. In the absence of any concrete material to show the exact period and the reign of the Mughal emperor concerned or anyone else during which the above construction took place, we are refraining from recording any positive finding on this aspect except that the building in dispute, to our mind, may have been constructed much later than the reign of Emperor Babur and the inscriptions were fixed further thereafter and that is why there have occurred certain discrepancies about the name of the person concerned as also the period. The possibility of change, alteration or manipulation in the inscriptions cannot be ruled out.'

73.5. While answering the issues framed in the suits, Aggrawal, J. held: [. . .]

'1682. [. . .] The defendants have failed to prove that the property in dispute was constructed by . . . Emperor Babur in 1528 AD. Accordingly, the question as to whether Babur constructed the property in dispute as a "mosque" does not arise and needs no answer.

(B) [. . .] The plaintiffs have failed to prove that the building in dispute was built by Babar. Similarly Defendant 13 has also failed to prove that the same was built by Mir Baqi. The further question as to when it was built and by whom cannot be replied with certainty since neither there is any pleading nor any evidence has been led nor any material has been placed before us to arrive at a concrete finding on this aspect. However, applying the principle of informed guess, we are of the view that the building in dispute may have been constructed, probably, between 1659 to 1707 AD i.e. during the regime of Aurangzeb.'

73.6. In the last part of the above findings, the Judge has recorded that it was not possible to enter a finding of fact with any certainty as to when the structure was constructed in the absence of pleading or evidence. The 'informed guess' at the end of the above observation that the structure was probably constructed by Aurangzeb between 1659–1707 cannot be placed on the pedestal of a finding of fact.

### (iii) Justice D.V. Sharma

73.7. D.V. Sharma, J. in the course of his decision arrived at the finding that: [. . .]

'17. [. . .] Thus, on the basis of the opinion of the experts, evidence on record, circumstantial evidence and historical accounts . . . it transpires that the temple was demolished and the mosque was constructed at the site of the old Hindu temple by Mir Baqi at the command of Babur . . .'

74. The High Court entered into the controversy surrounding the authenticity of the inscriptions on the basis of the hypothesis that the inscriptions were the sole basis for asserting that the mosque had been constructed by Babur. Aggrawal, J. came to the conclusion that the inscriptions were not authentic and hence a finding that the mosque was constructed by or at the behest of Babur in 1528 AD could not be arrived at. S.U. Khan, J.'s reasoning in the text of the judgment was in accord with the view of Aggrawal, J. but then, as we have noted, his ultimate conclusion that the disputed structure was constructed as a mosque by or under the orders of Babur is not consistent with the earlier part of the reasons. Sharma, J. held that the mosque was constructed by Mir Baqi at the command of Babur.

75. The basic issue, however, is whether it was necessary for the High Court to enter into this thicket on the basis of the pleadings of the parties. In the suit instituted by the Sunni Central Waqf Board (Suit No. 4), the case is that the mosque was constructed by Babur after his conquest and occupation of the territories, including the town of Ayodhya. Significantly, Suit No. 5 which has been instituted on behalf of Lord Ram and Ram Janmabhumi through a next friend also proceeds on the basis that the mosque was constructed by Mir Baqi who was the commander of Babur's forces.

75.1. The pleading in the plaint in Suit No. 5 reads thus: [. . .]

'23. That the books of history and public records of unimpeachable authenticity, establish indisputably that there was an ancient Temple of Maharaja Vikramaditya's time at Shri Rama Janma Bhumi, Ayodhya. That Temple was destroyed partly and an attempt was made to raise a mosque thereat, by the force of arms, by Mir Baqi, a commander of Babar's hordes. The material used was almost all of it taken from the Temple including its pillars which were wrought out of kasauti or touch-stone, with figures of Hindu gods and goddesses carved on them. There was great resistance by the Hindus and many battles were fought from time to time by them to prevent the completion of the mosque. To this day it has no minarets, and no place for storage of water for vazoo. Many lives were lost in these battles. The last such battle occurred in 1855. Shri Rama Janma Bhumi, including the building raised during Babar's time by Mir Baqi, was in the possession and control of Hindus at that time.' [. . .]

75.2. Immediately following the text of the pleading in the above extract, is a reference to the 1928 Edn. of the Faizabad Gazetteer. The text of the gazetteer is incorporated in the plaint and reads thus: [. . .]

'23. [. . .] In 1528 Babur came to Ayodhya and halted here for a week. He destroyed the ancient temple and on its site built a mosque, still known as Babar's mosque. The materials of the old structure were largely employed, and many of the columns are in good preservation, they are of close-grained black stone, called by the natives kasauti and carved with various devices.'

76. The pleading in Suit No. 5 demonstrates that even according to the plaintiffs, the mosque was built by Mir Baqi, a commander of Babur's forces, during the time of Babur. Hence, both in the pleading in Suit No. 4 and in Suit No. 5, there was essentially no dispute about the fact that the mosque was raised in 1528 AD by or at the behest of Babur. The case in Suit No. 5 is that the Hindus retained possession and control over the mosque. This is a separate matter altogether which has to be adjudicated upon. But, from the pleadings both in Suit No. 4 and in Suit No. 5, there appears to be no dispute about the origin or the date of construction of the mosque. Nirmohi Akhara in Suit No. 3 did not accept that the structure is a mosque at all for, according to it, the structure has always been a Hindu temple which has been managed by the Nirmohis at all material times. The Nirmohis disputed the very existence of a mosque, claiming it to be a temple. The case of the Nirmohis will be considered separately while assessing the pleadings, evidence and issues which arise in Suit No. 3. But, on the basis of the pleadings in Suit No. 4 and Suit No. 5, the controversy in regard to the authenticity of the inscriptions will not have any practical relevance.

77. There is another reason for adopting this line of approach. In the ultimate analysis, whether the mosque was built in 1528 (as both sets of plaintiffs in Suit No. 4 and Suit No. 5 have pleaded) or thereafter would essentially make no difference to the submissions of the rival sides. The plaintiffs in Suit No. 4 have stated before this Court that the records on which they place

reliance in regard to their claim of worship, use and possession
commence around 1860. This being the position, the precise
date of the construction of the mosque is a matter which has
no practical relevance to the outcome of the controversy having
regard to the pleadings in Suits Nos. 4 and 5 and the positions
adopted by the contesting Hindu and Muslim parties before this
Court.

* * *

The acts of 1934 (damage to the mosque), 1949 (the desecration,
when idols were placed) and 1992 (the demolition), against
assurance to the Supreme Court, were all unlawful. These findings
cut both ways for the critics of the judgment. Having found the
acts to be unlawful, the court, as the critics believe, rewarded the
wrongdoers by giving the site to them to build a temple. The critics
of the judgment test the court's thesis by asking if the decision
would have been the same if the mosque was still intact and 6
December 1992 had been averted.

## Secularism

One wonders why the court found it necessary to fortify its position
by underscoring the seminal significance of secularism. Was it
a concern that whatever decision the judges arrived at would be
questioned for being partisan in favouring either of the communities?
Be that as it may, the court held that the secular commitment of
India was reflected in the Places of Worship Act 1991 and that the
high court was wrong to qualify it and cut down its ambit.

103. In a nine judge Bench decision of this Court in S.R. Bommai v
     Union of India*, Justice B.P. Jeevan Reddy held:

---

* 'S.R. Bommai vs Union of India', 1994, 3 SCC 1.

'304. [. . .] How are the constitutional promises of social justice, liberty of belief, faith or worship and equality of status and of opportunity to be attained unless the State eschews the religion, faith or belief of a person from its consideration altogether while dealing with him, his rights, his duties and his entitlements? Secularism is thus more than a passive attitude of religious tolerance. It is a positive concept of equal treatment of all religions. This attitude is described by some as one of neutrality towards religion or as one of benevolent neutrality. This may be a concept evolved by western liberal thought or it may be, as some say, an abiding faith with the Indian people at all points of time. That is not material. What is material is that it is a constitutional goal and a basic feature of the Constitution as affirmed in Kesavananda Bharati[*] and Indira N. Gandhi v. Raj Narain[†]. Any step inconsistent with this constitutional policy is, in plain words, unconstitutional . . .

The Places of Worship Act is intrinsically related to the obligations of a secular state. It reflects the commitment of India to the equality of all religions. Above all, the Places of Worship Act is an affirmation of the solemn duty which was cast upon the State to preserve and protect the equality of all faiths as an essential constitutional value, a norm which has the status of being a basic feature of the Constitution. There is a purpose underlying the enactment of the Places of Worship Act. The law speaks to our history and to the future of the nation. Cognizant as we are of our history and of the need for the nation to confront it, Independence was a watershed moment to heal the wounds of the past. Historical wrongs cannot be remedied by the people taking the law in their own hands. In preserving the character of places of public worship, Parliament has mandated in no uncertain terms that history and its wrongs shall not be used as instruments to oppress the present and the future.'

---

[*] 'Kesavananda Bharati vs State of Kerala', 1973, 4 SCC 225; 1973 Supp SCR 1.
[†] 1975 Supp SCC 1 : (1976) 2 SCR 347.

104. The observations made on the Places of Worship Act by Justice
     D.V. Sharma are contrary to the scheme of the law as they are
     to the framework of constitutional values.

Curiously, despite that clear message, the result condones the act
of people taking the law into their hands. Of course, we know
that the Places of Worship Act exempted Ayodhya from its strict
ambit—perhaps one more example of compromising on a noble
principle in order to preserve it from outright rejection.

## Places of Worship (Special Provisions) Act, 1991

It would be recalled that in an attempt to ringfence the Ayodhya
dispute and ensure that there is no replication of the conflict
elsewhere in India, the then government had passed a legislation
that preserved the status quo of religious sites, with the reference
date of Independence Day 1947. Significantly, an exception was
made for Ayodhya in view of the pending litigation. However, the
high court sought to underscore the wide exceptions, emphasizing
the departure of the position of law in dealing with the site of
Ayodhya as noted in the present judgment:

92. Parliament enacted the Places of Worship (Special Provisions) Act
    1991. Sections 3, 6 and 8 of the legislation came into force at once
    on the date of enactment (18-9-1991) while the other provisions
    are deemed to have come into force on 11 July 1991. The long
    title evinces the intent of Parliament in enacting the law, for it is:

    'An Act to prohibit conversion of any place of worship and to
    provide for the maintenance of the religious character of any
    place of worship as it existed on the 15th day of August, 1947,
    and for matters connected therewith or incidental thereto.'

[. . .]

93. The expression 'place of worship' is defined in Section 2(c) thus:

'2. (c) "**place of worship**" means a temple, mosque, gurdwara, church, monastery or any other place of public religious worship of any religious denomination or any section thereof, by whatever name called.'

[. . .]

93.2. Section 3 enacts a bar on the conversion of a place of worship of any religious denomination or a section of it into a place of worship of a different religious denomination or of a different segment of the same religious denomination:

'3. **Bar of conversion of places of worship.**—No person shall convert any place of worship of any religious denomination or any section thereof into a place of worship of a different section of the same religious denomination or of a different religious denomination or any section thereof.'

93.3. Section 4 preserves the religious character of a place of worship as it existed on 15-8-1947:

'4. **Declaration as to the religious character of certain places of worship and bar of jurisdiction of courts, etc.**—(1) It is hereby declared that the religious character of a place of worship existing on the 15th day of August, 1947 shall continue to be the same as it existed on that day.

(2) If, on the commencement of this Act, any suit, appeal or other proceeding with respect to the conversion of the religious character of any place of worship, existing on the 15th day of August, 1947, is pending before any court, tribunal or other authority, the same shall abate, and no suit, appeal or other proceeding with respect to any such

matter shall lie on or after such commencement in any court, tribunal or other authority:

Provided that if any suit, appeal or other proceeding, instituted or filed on the ground that conversion has taken place in the religious character of any such place after the 15th day of August, 1947, is pending on the commencement of this Act, such suit, appeal or other proceeding shall not so abate and every such suit, appeal or other proceeding shall be disposed of in accordance with the provisions of sub-section (1).

(3) Nothing contained in sub-section (1) and sub-section (2) shall apply to—

(a) any place of worship referred to in the said sub-sections which is an ancient and historical monument or an archaeological site or remains covered by the Ancient Monuments and Archaeological Sites and Remains Act, 1958 (24 of 1958) or any other law for the time being in force;

(b) any suit, appeal or other proceeding, with respect to any matter referred to in sub-section (2), finally decided, settled or disposed of by a court, tribunal or other authority before the commencement of this Act;

(c) any dispute with respect to any such matter settled by the parties amongst themselves before such commencement;

(d) any conversion of any such place effected before such commencement by acquiescence;

(e) any conversion of any such place effected before such commencement which is not liable to be challenged in any court, tribunal or other authority being barred by limitation under any law for the time being in force.'

[. . .]

94. **The Places of Worship Act however contains an exemption from the application of its provisions to the place of worship**

'**commonly known as Ram Janam Bhumi-Babri Masjid'** and to any suit, appeal or proceeding relating to it. Section 5 stipulates:

'5. **Act not to apply to Ram Janma Bhumi-Babri Masjid.**— Nothing contained in this Act shall apply to the place or place of worship commonly known as Ram Janma Bhumi–Babri Masjid situated in Ayodhya in the State of Uttar Pradesh and to any suit, appeal or other proceeding relating to the said place or place of worship.'

[. . .]

96. Section 7 confers upon the Places of Worship Act overriding force and effect:

'7. **Act to override other enactments.**—The provisions of this Act shall have effect notwithstanding anything inconsistent therewith contained in any other law for the time being in force or any instrument having effect by virtue of any law other than this Act.'

97. The law imposes two unwavering and mandatory norms:

97.1. A bar is imposed by Section 3 on the conversion of a place of worship of any religious denomination or a section of a denomination into a place of worship either of a different section of the same religious denomination or of a distinct religious denomination. The expression 'place of worship' is defined in the broadest possible terms to cover places of public religious worship of all religions and denominations.

97.2. **The law preserves the religious character of every place of worship as it existed on 15-8-1947.** Towards achieving this purpose, it provides for the abatement of suits and legal proceedings with respect to the conversion of the religious character of any place of worship existing on 15-8-1947.

Coupled with this, the Places of Worship Act imposes a bar on the institution of fresh suits or legal proceedings. The only exception is in the case of suits, appeals or proceedings pending at the commencement of the law on the ground that conversion of a place of worship had taken place after 15-8-1947. The proviso to sub-section (2) of Section 4 saves those suits, appeals and legal proceedings which are pending on the date of the commencement of the Act if they pertain to the conversion of the religious character of a place of worship after the cut-off date. Sub-section (3) of Section 4 however stipulates that the previous two sub-sections will not apply to:

(a)  Ancient and historical monuments or archaeological sites or remains governed by Act 24 of 1958 or any other law;
(b)  A suit or legal proceeding which has been finally decided settled or disposed of;
(c)  Any dispute which has been settled by the parties before the commencement of the Act;
(d)  A conversion of a place of worship effected before the commencement of the Act by acquiescence; and
(e)  Any conversion of a place of worship before the commencement of the Act in respect of which the cause of action would be barred by limitation.

98. **Section 5 stipulates that the Act shall not apply to Ram Janmabhumi–Babri Masjid** and to any suit, appeal or any proceeding relating to it. Consequently, there is a specific exception which has been carved out by the provisions of the Places of Worship Act in respect of the present dispute.

[. . .]

99. The purpose of enacting the law was explained by the Union Minister of Home Affairs on the floor of the Lok Sabha on 10-9-1991 . . .

'We see this Bill as a measure to provide and develop our glorious traditions of love, peace and harmony. These traditions are part of a cultural heritage of which every Indian is justifiably proud. Tolerance for all faiths has characterised our great civilisation since time immemorial.

These traditions of amity, harmony and mutual respect came under severe strain during the pre-Independence period when the colonial power sought to actively create and encourage communal divide in the country. After Independence we have set about healing the wounds of the past and endeavoured to restore our traditions of communal amity and goodwill to their past glory. By and large we have succeeded, although there have been, it must be admitted, some unfortunate setbacks. Rather than being discouraged by such setbacks, it is our duty and commitment to take lesson from them for the future.'

[. . .]

100. The Union Minister of Home Affairs indicated that the law which sought to prohibit the forcible conversion of places of worship was not 'to create new disputes and to rake up old controversies which had long been forgotten by the people . . . but facilitate the object sought to be achieved' . . . Speaking in support of the cut-off date of 15-8-1947, one of the Members (Shrimati Malini Bhattacharya) explained [. . .]:

'But I think this 15-8-1947 is crucial because on that date we are supposed to have emerged as a modern, democratic and sovereign State thrusting back such barbarity into the past once and for all. From that date, we also distinguished ourselves . . . as State which has no official religion and which gives equal rights to all the different religious denominations. So, whatever may have happened before that, we all expected that from that date *there should be no such* retrogression into the past.'

[. . .]

101. **The Places of Worship Act which was enacted in 1991 by Parliament protects and secures the fundamental values of the Constitution. The Preamble underlines the need to protect the liberty of thought, expression, belief, faith and worship. It emphasises human dignity and fraternity. Tolerance, respect for and acceptance of the equality of all religious faiths is a fundamental precept of fraternity.** This was specifically adverted to by the Union Minister of Home Affairs in the course of his address before the Rajya Sabha [. . .] on 12-9-1991 by stating:

'I believe that India is known for its civilisation and the greatest contribution of India to the world civilisation is the kind of tolerance, understanding, the kind of assimilative spirit and the cosmopolitan outlook that it shows . . .

The Advaita philosophy . . . clearly says that there is no difference between God and ourselves. We have to realise that God is not in the mosque or in the temple only, but God is in the heart of a person . . .

Let everybody understand that he owes his allegiance to the Constitution, allegiance to the unity of the country: the rest of the things are immaterial.'

102. **In providing a guarantee for the preservation of the religious character of places of public worship as they existed on 15-8-1947 and against the conversion of places of public worship, Parliament determined that independence from Colonial Rule furnishes a constitutional basis for healing the injustices of the past by providing the confidence to every religious community that their places of worship will be preserved and that their character will not be altered.** The law addresses itself to the State as much as to every citizen of the nation. Its norms bind those who govern the affairs of the nation at every level. Those norms implement the Fundamental Duties under Article

51-A and are hence positive mandates to every citizen as well. The State, has by enacting the law, enforced a constitutional commitment and operationalised its constitutional obligations to uphold the equality of all religions and secularism which is a part of the basic features of the Constitution. The Places of Worship Act imposes a non-derogable obligation towards enforcing our commitment to secularism under the Indian Constitution. The law is hence a legislative instrument designed to protect the secular features of the Indian polity, which is one of the basic features of the Constitution. Non-retrogression is a foundational feature of the fundamental constitutional principles of which secularism is a core component. The Places of Worship Act is thus a legislative intervention which preserves non-retrogression as an essential feature of our secular values.

[. . .]

103. In a nine-Judge Bench decision of this Court in S.R. Bommai v. Union of India, B.P. Jeevan Reddy, J. held: [. . .]

'304. . . . **How are the constitutional promises of social justice, liberty of belief, faith or worship and equality of status and of opportunity to be attained unless the State eschews the religion, faith or belief of a person from its consideration altogether while dealing with him, his rights, his duties and his entitlements? Secularism is thus more than a passive attitude of religious tolerance. It is a positive concept of equal treatment of all religions. This attitude is described by some as one of neutrality towards religion or as one of benevolent neutrality. This may be a concept evolved by western liberal thought or it may be, as some say, an abiding faith with the Indian people at all points of time. That is not material. What is material is that it is a constitutional goal and a basic feature of the Constitution as affirmed in Kesavananda Bharati and**

**Indira Nehru Gandhi v. Raj Narain. Any step inconsistent with this constitutional policy is, in plain words, unconstitutional.'**
[. . .]

**The Places of Worship Act is intrinsically related to the obligations of a secular State. It reflects the commitment of India to the equality of all religions. Above all, the Places of Worship Act is an affirmation of the solemn duty which was cast upon the State to preserve and protect the equality of all faiths as an essential constitutional value, a norm which has the status of being a basic feature of the Constitution. There is a purpose underlying the enactment of the Places of Worship Act. The law speaks to our history and to the future of the nation. Cognizant as we are of our history and of the need for the nation to confront it, Independence was a watershed moment to heal the wounds of the past. Historical wrongs cannot be remedied by the people taking the law in their own hands. In preserving the character of places of public worship, Parliament has mandated in no uncertain terms that history and its wrongs shall not be used as instruments to oppress the present and the future.**

104. **The observations made on the Places of Worship Act by D.V. Sharma, J. are contrary to the scheme of the law as they are to the framework of constitutional values.** D.V. Sharma, J. observed as follows: [. . .]

'89. [. . .] In absence of any ecclesiastical courts any religious dispute is cognizable, except in very rare cases where the declaration sought may be what constitutes religious rite. Places of Worship (Special Provisions) Act, 1991 does not debar those cases where declaration is sought for a period prior to the Act came into force or for enforcement of right which was recognised before coming into force of the Act.'

The above conclusion of D.V. Sharma, J. is directly contrary to the provisions of Section 4(2).

D.V. Sharma, J. postulates in the above observations that the Places of Worship Act will not debar cases of the following nature being entertained, namely:

(i)   Where a declaration is sought for a period prior to the enforcement of the Places of Worship Act; or

(ii)  Where enforcement is sought of a right which was recognised before the enforcement of the Places of Worship Act.

105. Section 4(1) clearly stipulates that the religious character of a place of worship as it existed on 15-8-1947 shall be maintained as it existed on that day. Section 4(2) specifically contemplates that all suits, appeals and legal proceedings existing on the day of the commencement of the Places of Worship Act, with respect to the conversion of the religious character of a place of worship, existing on 15-8-1947, pending before any court, tribunal or authority shall abate, and no suit, appeal or proceeding with respect to such matter shall lie after the commencement of the Act. The only exception in the proviso to sub-section (2) is where a suit, appeal or proceeding is instituted on the ground that the conversion of the religious character of a place of worship had taken place after 15-8-1947 and such an action was pending at the commencement of the Places of Worship Act. **Clearly, in the face of the statutory mandate, the exception which has been carved out by D.V. Sharma, J. runs contrary to the terms of the legislation and is therefore erroneous.**

* * *

The court, in upholding the unqualified validity of the Places of Worship Act, 1991, virtually closed the door on any ambition of the Hindu side to attempt a repeat performance of Ayodhya in Mathura and Varanasi—not a small achievement from the point of view of secularism.

Having settled the law on several issues, the court then proceeded to deal with the central point of contest on which the outcome of the case depended: the title to the disputed property.

1203.      A stage has now been reached to marshal together the evidence on the claim of title in Suit 4 and Suit 5 to pave the way for the ultimate determination of the relief to be granted.

1204. I.    The report of the ASI indicates the following position:

1204.1.    Archaeological finds in the area of excavation reveal significant traces of successive civilisations, commencing with the age of the North Black Polished Ware traceable to the second century B.C.

1204.2.    The excavation by the ASI has revealed the existence of a preexisting underlying structure dating back to the twelfth century. The structure has large dimensions, evident from the fact that there were 85 pillar bases comprised in 17 rows each of five pillar bases.

1204.3.    On a preponderance of probabilities, the archaeological findings on the nature of the underlying structure indicate it to be of Hindu religious origin, dating to twelfth century A.D.

1204.4.    The mosque in dispute was constructed upon the foundation of the pre-existing structure. The construction of the mosque has taken place in such a manner as to obviate an independent foundation by utilising the walls of the pre-existing structure.

1204.5.    The layered excavation at the site of excavation has also revealed the existence of a circular shrine together with a makara pranala indicative of Hindu worship dating back to the eighth to tenth century.

1205.        A reasonable inference can be drawn on the basis of the standard of proof which governs civil trials that:

1205.1.     The foundation of the mosque is based on the walls of a large pre-existing structure;

1205.2.     The pre-existing structure dates back to the twelfth century.

1205.3.     The underlying structure which provided the foundations of the mosque together with its architectural features and recoveries are suggestive of a Hindu religious origin comparable to temple excavations in the region and pertaining to the era.

1206. II.    **The conclusion in the ASI report about the remains of an underlying structure of a Hindu religious origin symbolic of temple architecture of the twelfth century A.D. must however be read contextually with the following caveats:**

1206.1.     **While the ASI report has found the existence of ruins of a preexisting structure, the report does not provide:**

1206.1.1.   **The reason for the destruction of the pre-existing structure.**

1206.1.2.   **Whether the earlier structure was demolished for the purpose of the construction of the mosque.**

1206.2.     **Since the ASI report dates the underlying structure to the twelfth century, there is a time gap of about four centuries between the date of the underlying structure and the construction of the mosque. No evidence is available to explain what transpired in the course of the intervening period of nearly four centuries.**

1206.3.     **The ASI report does not conclude that the remnants of the preexisting structure were used for the purpose of constructing the mosque (apart, that is, from the construction of the mosque on the foundation of the erstwhile structure).**

1206.4.     The pillars that were used in the construction of the mosque were black Kasauti stone pillars. ASI has found no evidence to show that these Kasauti pillars are relatable to the underlying pillar bases found during the course of excavation in the structure below the mosque.

1207. III. **A finding of title cannot be based in law on the archaeological findings which have been arrived at by ASI. Between the twelfth century to which the underlying structure is dated and the construction of the mosque in the sixteenth century, there is an intervening period of four centuries. No evidence has been placed on the record in relation to the course of human history between the twelfth and sixteen centuries. No evidence is available in a case of this antiquity on (i) the cause of destruction of the underlying structure; and (ii) whether the pre-existing structure was demolished for the construction of the mosque. Title to the land must be decided on settled legal principles and applying evidentiary standards which govern a civil trial.**

1208. IV. Historical records of travellers (chiefly Tieffenthaler and the account of Montgomery Martin in the eighteenth century) indicate:

1208.1. **The existence of the faith and belief of the Hindus that the disputed site was the birth-place of Lord Ram;**

1208.2. **Identifiable places of offering worship by the Hindus including Sita Rasoi, Swargdwar and the Bedi (cradle) symbolising the birth of Lord Ram in and around the disputed site;**

1208.3. Prevalence of the practice of worship by pilgrims at the disputed site including by parikrama (circumambulation) and the presence of large congregations of devotees on the occasion of religious festivals; and

1208.4. The historical presence of worshippers and the existence of worship at the disputed site even prior to the annexation of Oudh by the British and the construction of a brick-grill wall in 1857.

1209.   Beyond the above observations, the accounts of the travellers must be read with circumspection. Their personal observations must carefully be sifted from hearsay—matters of legend and lore. Consulting their accounts on matters of public history is distinct from evidence on a matter of title. An adjudication of title has to be deduced on the basis of evidence sustainable in a court of law, which has withstood the searching scrutiny of cross-examination. Similarly, the contents of gazetteers can at best provide corroborative material to evidence which emerges from the record. The court must be circumspect in drawing negative inferences from what a traveller may not have seen or observed. Title cannot be established on the basis of faith and belief above. **Faith and belief are indicators towards patterns of worship at the site on the basis of which claims of possession are asserted. The court has evaluated the rival claims to possessory title in a situation in which the state has expressly stated in its written statement that it claims no interest in the land.**

1210.V.   The evidence indicates that despite the existence of a mosque at the site, Hindu worship at the place believed to be the birth-place of Lord Ram was not restricted. The existence of an Islamic structure at a place considered sacrosanct by the Hindus did not stop them from continuing their worship at the disputed site and within the precincts of the structure prior to the incidents of 1856–7. The physical structure of an Islamic mosque did not shake the faith and belief of Hindus that Lord Ram was born at the disputed site. On the other hand, learned counsel fairly stated that the evidence relied on by the Sunni Central Waqf Board to establish the offering of namaz by the Muslim residents commences from around 1856–7.

1211.VI. The setting up of a railing in 1857 by the British around the disputed structure of the mosque took place in the backdrop of a contestation and disputes over the claim of the Hindus to worship inside the precincts of the mosque. This furnished the context for the riots which took place between Hindus and Muslims in 1856–7. The construction of a grill-brick wall by the colonial administration was intended to ensure peace between the two communities with respect to a contested place of worship. **The grill-brick wall did not constitute either a subdivision of the disputed site which was one composite property, nor did it amount to a determination of title by the colonial administration.**

1211.VII. **Proximate in time after the setting up of the railing, the Ramchabutra was set up in or about 1857. Ramchabutra was set up in close physical proximity to the railing. Essentially, the setting up of Ramchabutra within a hundred feet or thereabouts of the inner dome must be seen in the historical context as an expression or assertion of the Hindu right to worship at the birth-place of Lord Ram. Even after the construction of the dividing wall by the British, the Hindus continued to assert their right to pray below the central dome.** This emerges from the evidentiary record indicating acts of individuals in trying to set up idols and perform puja both within and outside the precincts of the inner courtyard. Even after the setting up of the Ramchabutra, pilgrims used to pay obeisance and make offerings to what they believed to be the 'Garbh Grih' located inside the three domed structure while standing at the iron railing which divided the inner and outer courtyards. There is no evidence to the contrary by the Muslims to indicate that their possession of the disputed structure of the mosque was exclusive and that the offering of namaz was exclusionary of the Hindus;

1213.VIII. **Hindu worship at Ramchabutra, Sita Rasoi and at other religious places including the setting up of a Bhandar clearly indicated their open, exclusive and unimpeded possession of the outer courtyard. The Muslims have not been in possession of the outer courtyard**. Despite the construction of the wall in 1858 by the British and the setting up of the Ram chabutra in close proximity of the inner dome, Hindus continued to assert their right to pray inside the three-domed structure;

1214.IX. In or about 1877, at the behest of the Hindus, another door to the outer courtyard was allowed to be opened by the administration on the northern side (Sing Dwar), in addition to the existing door on the east (Hanumat Dwar). The Deputy Commissioner declined to entertain a complaint against the opening made in the wall. The Commissioner while dismissing the appeal held that the opening up of the door was in public interest. The opening of an additional door with the permission of the British administration indicates recognition of the presence of a large congregation of Hindu devotees necessitating additional access to the site in the interest of public peace and safety;

1215.X. **Testimonies of both Hindu and Muslim witnesses indicate that on religious occasions and festivals such as Ram Navami, Sawan Jhoola, Kartik Poornima, Parikrama Mela and Ram Vivah, large congregations of Hindu devotees visited the disputed premises for darshan. The oral testimony of the Hindu devotees establishes the pattern of worship and prayer at Sita Rasoi, Ramchabutra and towards the 'Garb Grih', while standing at the railing of the structure of the brick wall.**

1216.XI. Hindu witnesses have indicated that Hindus used to offer prayer to the Kasauti stone pillars placed inside the mosque. Muslim witnesses have acknowledged the presence of symbols of Hindu religious significance both inside and outside the mosque. Among them, is the depiction of Varah, Jai-Vijay and Garud outside the three domed structure. They are suggestive not merely of the existence of the faith and belief but of actual worship down the centuries.

1217.XII. **There can no denying the existence of the structure of the mosque since its construction in the sixteenth century with the inscription of 'Allah' on the structure. The genesis of the communal incident of 1856–1857 lies in the contestation between the two communities over worship. The setting up of the railing in 1856–1857 was an attempt by the administration to provide a measure of bifurcation to observe religious worship—namaz by the Muslims inside the railing within the domed structure of the mosque and worship by the Hindus outside the railing. Attempts by the Sikhs or faqirs to enter into the mosque and set up religious symbols for puja were resisted by the Muslims, resulting in the administration evicting the occupier.**

1218.XIII. After the construction of the grill-brick wall in 1857, there is evidence on record to show the exclusive and unimpeded possession of the Hindus and the offering of worship in the outer courtyard. Entry into the three-domed structure was possible only by seeking access through either of the two doors on the eastern and northern sides of the outer courtyard which were under the control of the Hindu devotees;

1219.XIV. **On a preponderance of probabilities, there is no evidence to establish that the Muslims abandoned the mosque or ceased to perform namaz in spite of the contestation over their possession of the inner courtyard after 1858. Oral evidence indicates the continuation of namaz.**

1220.XV. The contestation over the possession of the inner courtyard became the centre of the communal conflict of 1934 during the course of which the domes of the mosque sustained damage as did the structure. The repair and renovation of the mosque following the riots of 1934 at the expense of the British administration through the agency of a Muslim contractor is indicative of the fact that despite the disputes between the two communities, the structure of the mosque continued to exist as did the assertion of the Muslims of their right to pray. Namaz appears to have been offered within the mosque after 1934 though, by the time of incident of 22/23 December 1949, only Friday namaz was being offered. **The reports of the Waqf Inspector of December 1949 indicate that the Sadhus and Bairagis who worshipped and resided in the outer courtyard obstructed Muslims from passing through the courtyard, which was under their control, for namaz within the mosque. Hence the Waqf Inspector noted that worship within the mosque was possible on Fridays with the assistance of the police.**

1221.XVI. The events preceding 22-12-1949/23-12-1949 indicate the build-up of a large presence of Bairagis in the outer courtyard and the expression of his apprehension by the Superintendent of Police that the Hindus would seek forcible entry into the precincts of the mosque to install idols. In spite of written intimations to him, the Deputy Commissioner and District Magistrate (K.K. Nayyar) paid no heed and rejected the apprehension of the Superintendent of Police to the safety of the mosque as baseless. The apprehension was borne out by the incident which took place on the night **between** 22-12-**1949/23-12-1949, when a group of fifty to sixty persons installed idols on the pulpit of the mosque below the central dome. This led to the desecration of the mosque and the ouster of the Muslims otherwise than by the due process of law. The inner courtyard was thereafter attached in proceedings under Section 145 CrPC 1898 on 29 December 1949 and the receiver took possession;**

1222.XVII. **On 6 December 1992, the structure of the mosque was brought down and the mosque was destroyed. The destruction of the mosque took place in breach of the order of status quo and an assurance given to this Court. The destruction of the mosque and the obliteration of the Islamic structure was an egregious violation of the rule of law;**

1223.XVIII. The net result, as it emerges from the evidentiary record is thus:

1223.1. **The disputed site is one composite whole. The railing set up in 1856–7 did not either bring about a sub-division of the land or any determination of title.**

1223.2. **The Sunni Central Waqf Board has not established its case of a dedication by user.**

1223.3. The alternate plea of adverse possession has not been established by the Sunni Central Waqf Board as it failed to meet the requirements of adverse possession.

1223.4. **The Hindus have been in exclusive and unimpeded possession of the outer courtyard where they have continued worship.**

1223.5. **The inner courtyard has been a contested site with conflicting claims of the Hindus and Muslims.**

1223.6. **The existence of the structure of the mosque until 6 December 1992 does not admit any contestation.** The submission that the mosque did not accord with Islamic tenets stands rejected. **The evidence indicates that there was no abandonment of the mosque by Muslims. Namaz was observed on Fridays towards December 1949, the last namaz being on 16 December 1949;**

1223.7. **The damage to the mosque in 1934, its desecration in 1949 leading to the ouster of the Muslims and the eventual destruction on 6 December 1992 constituted a serious violation of the rule of law; and**

1223.8.   Consistent with the principles of justice, equity and good
          conscience, both Suits 4 and 5 will have to be decreed
          and the relief moulded in a manner which preserves
          the constitutional values of justice, fraternity, human
          dignity and the equality of religious belief.

1224.XIX.  **The Hindus have established a clear case of a possessory
          title to the outside courtyard by virtue of long,
          continued and unimpeded worship at the Ramchabutra
          and other objects of religious significance. The Hindus
          and the Muslims have contested claims to the offering
          worship within the three domed structure in the
          inner courtyard.** The assertion by the Hindus of their
          entitlement to offer worship inside has been contested
          by the Muslims.

* * *

The court, however, disagreed with the path adopted by the high
court:

1229. The High Court has adopted a path which was not open to
      it . . . It granted reliefs which were not the subject-matter of
      the prayers in the suits [before it].

      [. . .]

1232. There is another serious flaw in the entire approach of the
      High Court in granting relief of a three-way bifurcation of
      the disputed site. Having come to the conclusion that Suit
      No. 3 (filed by Nirmohi Akhara) and Suit No. 4 (filed by Sunni
      Central Waqf Board) were barred by limitation, the High
      Court proceeded to grant relief in Suit No. 5 to the plaintiffs in
      Suits Nos. 3 and 4. This defies logic and is contrary to settled
      principles of law. Moreover, the claim by the Nirmohi Akhara

was as a shebait who claimed a decree for management and charge. On its own case, Nirmohi Akhara could not have been granted an independent share of the land. By this judgment, the finding of the High Court that the suit of Nirmohi Akhara was barred by limitation has been upheld but the finding in regard to the bar of limitation being attracted to Suit No. 4 has been reversed. This aspect will be dealt with while analysing the final relief which will be granted.

[...]

1233. **The facts, evidence and oral arguments of the present case have traversed the realms of history, archaeology, religion and the law. The law must stand apart from political contestations over history, ideology and religion. For a case replete with references to archaeological foundations, we must remember that it is the law which provides the edifice upon which our multicultural society rests. The law forms the ground upon which, multiple strands of history, ideology and religion can compete. By determining their limits, this Court as the final arbiter must preserve the sense of balance that the beliefs of one citizen do not interfere with or dominate the freedoms and beliefs of another. On 15 August, 1947, India as a nation realised the vision of self-determination. On 26, January 1950 we gave ourselves the Constitution of India, as an unwavering commitment to the values which define our society. At the heart of the Constitution is a commitment to equality upheld and enforced by the rule of law. Under our Constitution, citizens of all faiths, beliefs and creeds seeking divine provenance are both subject to the law and equal before the law.** Every Judge of this Court is not merely tasked with but sworn to uphold the Constitution and its values. The Constitution does not make a distinction between the faith and belief of one religion and another. All forms of belief, worship and prayer are equal. Those whose duty it is to interpret the Constitution, enforce it and engage with it can ignore this only to the peril of our society and nation. The Constitution speaks to the judges who interpret it, to those who govern who must enforce it, but above all, to the citizens who engage with it as an inseparable feature of their lives.

1234. **In the present case, this Court is tasked with an adjudicatory task of unique dimension. The dispute is over immovable property. The court does not decide title on the basis of faith or belief but on the basis of evidence.** The law provides us with parameters as clear but as profound as ownership and possession. In deciding title to the disputed property, the court applies settled principles of evidence to adjudicate upon which party has established a claim to the immovable property.

1235. **On the balance of probabilities, there is clear evidence to indicate that the worship by the Hindus in the outer courtyard continued unimpeded in spite of the setting up of a grill-brick wall in 1857. Their possession of the outer courtyard stands established together with the incidents attaching to their control over it.**

1236. As regards the inner courtyard, there is evidence on a preponderance of probabilities to establish worship by the Hindus prior to the annexation of Oudh by the British in 1857. **The Muslims have offered no evidence to indicate that they were in exclusive possession of the inner structure prior to 1857 since the date of the construction in the sixteenth century. After the setting up of the grill-brick wall, the structure of the mosque continued to exist and there is evidence to indicate that namaz was offered within its precincts. The report of the Waqf Inspector of December**

**1949 indicates that Muslims were being obstructed in free and unimpeded access to mosque for the purposes of offering namaz.** However, there is evidence to show that namaz was offered in the structure of the mosque and the last Friday namaz was on 16 December 1949. **The exclusion of the Muslims from worship and possession took place on the intervening night between 22/23 December 1949 when the mosque was desecrated by the installation of Hindu idols. The ouster of the Muslims on that occasion was not through any lawful authority but through an act which was calculated to deprive them of their place of worship.** After the proceedings under Section 145 of CrPC 1898 were initiated and a receiver was appointed following the attachment of the inner courtyard, worship of the Hindu idols was permitted. **During the pendency of the suits, the entire structure of the mosque was brought down in a calculated act of destroying a place of public worship. The Muslims have been wrongly deprived of a mosque which had been constructed well over 450 years ago.**

1237. **We have already concluded that the three-way bifurcation by the High Court was legally unsustainable. Even as a matter of maintaining public peace and tranquillity, the solution which commended itself to the High Court is not feasible.** The disputed site admeasures all of 1500 square yards. Dividing the land will not subserve the interest of either of the parties or secure a lasting sense of peace and tranquillity.

1238. Suit 5 has been held to be maintainable at the behest of the first plaintiff (the deity of Lord Ram) who is a juristic person. The third plaintiff (next friend) has been held to be entitled to represent the first plaintiff. We are of the view that on the one hand a decree must ensue in Suit 5, Suit 4 must also be partly decreed by directing the allotment of alternate land to the Muslims for the construction of a mosque and associated activities. The allotment of land to the Muslims is necessary because though on a balance of probabilities, the evidence in respect of the possessory claim of the Hindus to the composite whole of the disputed property stands on a better footing than the evidence adduced by the Muslims, the **Muslims were dispossessed upon the desecration of the mosque on 22-12-1949/23-12-1949 which was ultimately destroyed on 6-12-1992. There was no abandonment of the mosque by the Muslims. This Court in the exercise of its powers under Article 142 of the Constitution must ensure that a wrong committed must be remedied. Justice would not prevail if the Court were to overlook the entitlement of the Muslims who have been deprived of the structure of the mosque through means which should not have been employed in a secular nation committed to the rule of law. The Constitution postulates the equality of all faiths. Tolerance and mutual co-existence nourish the secular commitment of our nation and its people.**

1239. **The area of the composite site admeasures about 1500 square yards. While determining the area of land to be allotted, it is necessary to provide restitution to the Muslim community for the unlawful destruction of their place of worship. Having weighed the nature of the relief which should be granted to the Muslims, we direct that land admeasuring 5 acres be allotted to the Sunni Central Waqf Board either by the Central Government out of the acquired land or by the Government of Uttar Pradesh within the city of Ayodhya.** This exercise, and the consequent handing over of the land to the Sunni Central Waqf Board, shall be conducted simultaneously with the handing over of the disputed site comprising of the inner and outer courtyards as a consequence of the decree in Suit 5. Suit 4 shall stand decreed in the above terms.

* * *

Jumping back in the judgment for a moment, let us look at how the court dealt with our commitment to the values enshrined in the Constitution:

## Commitment to constitutional values

246. A final observation must be made on this aspect of the case which is of significant importance. The rejection of the contention urged on behalf of the plaintiffs in Suit No. 5 touches upon the heart of our constitutional commitment to secularism. The method of worship on the basis of which a proprietary claim may be sustained is relatable to a particular religion. The conferral of legal personality on idols stemming from religious endowments is a legal development applicable only to a practice of the Hindu community. The performance of the parikrama is a method of worship confined largely to Hinduism. Putting aside the fact that the argument raised by the plaintiffs in Suit No. 5 is a novel extension of the law applicable to Hindu religious endowments, this is a significant matter which requires our consideration.

247. **Religious diversity undoubtedly requires the protection of diverse methods of offering worship and performing religious ceremonies. However, that a method of offering worship unique to one religion should result in the conferral of an absolute title to parties from one religion over parties from another religion in an adjudication over civil property claims cannot be sustained under our Constitution. This would render the law, which ought to be the ultimate impartial arbiter, conferring a benefit on a party with respect to her or his legal claims, not on the basis of the merits of a particular case, but on the basis of the structure or fabric of the religion to which they belong.** If the contention urged on behalf of the plaintiffs in Suit No. 5 is accepted, the method of worship performed by one religion alone will be conferred with the power to extinguish all contesting proprietary claims over disputed property.

248. It is true that the connection between a person and what they consider divine is deeply internal. It lies in the realm of a personal sphere in which no other person must intrude. It is for this reason that the Constitution protects the freedom to profess, practise and propagate religion equally to all citizens. Often, the human condition finds solace in worship. But worship may not be confined into a straitjacket formula. It is on the basis of the deep entrenchment of religion into the social fabric of Indian society that the right to religious freedom was not made absolute. An attempt has been made in the jurisprudence of this Court to demarcate the religious from the secular. The adjudication of civil claims over private property must remain within the domain of the secular if the commitment to constitutional values is to be upheld. Over four decades ago, the Constitution was amended and a specific reference to its secular fabric was incorporated in the Preamble. At its heart, this reiterated what the Constitution always respected and accepted: the equality of all faiths. Secularism cannot be a writ lost in the sands of time by being oblivious to the exercise of religious freedom by everyone.

249. It is for all the reasons highlighted above that the law has till today yet to accept the conferral of legal personality on immovable property. Religiosity has moved hearts and minds. The Court cannot adopt a position that accords primacy to the faith and belief of a single religion as the basis to confer both judicial insulation as well as primacy over the legal system as a whole. **From Shahid Gunj to Ayodhya, in a country like ours where contesting claims over property by religious communities are inevitable, our courts cannot reduce questions of title, which fall firmly within the secular domain and outside the rubric of religion, to a question of which community's faith is stronger.**

\* \* \*

And now, at last, we will look at the final directions of the hon'ble court at the end of this lengthy and significant judgment:

## Q. Reliefs and directions

1243.  We accordingly order and direct as follows:

1    (i) Suit 3 instituted by Nirmohi Akhara is held to be barred by limitation and shall accordingly stand dismissed;

(ii)  Suit 4 instituted by the Sunni Central Waqf Board and other plaintiffs is held to be within limitation. The judgment of the High Court holding Suit 4 to be barred by limitation is reversed; and

(iii)  Suit 5 is held to be within limitation.

2.   Suit 5 is held to be maintainable at the behest of the first plaintiff who is represented by the third plaintiff. There shall be a decree in terms of prayer clauses (A) and (B) of the suit, subject to the following directions:

(i)   The Central Government shall, within a period of three months from the date of this judgment, formulate a scheme pursuant to the powers vested in it under Sections 6 and 7 of the Acquisition of Certain Area at Ayodhya Act 1993. The scheme shall envisage the setting up of a trust with a Board of Trustees or any other appropriate body under Section 6. The scheme to be framed by the Central Government shall make necessary provisions in regard to the functioning of the trust or body including on matters relating to the management of the trust, the powers of the trustees including the construction of a temple and all necessary, incidental and supplemental matters;

(ii)  Possession of the inner and outer courtyards shall be handed over to the Board of Trustees of the Trust or to the body so constituted. The Central Government will be at liberty to make suitable provisions in respect of the rest of the acquired land by handing it over to the Trust or body for management and development in terms of the scheme framed in accordance with the above directions; and

(iii) Possession of the disputed property shall continue to vest in the statutory receiver under the Central Government, until in exercise of its jurisdiction under Section 6 of the Ayodhya Act of 1993, a notification is issued vesting the property in the trust or other body.

3 (i) Simultaneously, with the handing over of the disputed property to the Trust or body under clause 2 above, a suitable plot of land admeasuring 5 acres shall be handed over to the Sunni Central Waqf Board, the plaintiff in Suit 4.

(ii) The land shall be allotted either by:

(a) The Central Government out of the land acquired under the Ayodhya Act 1993; or

(b) The State Government at a suitable prominent place in Ayodhya; The Central Government and the State Government shall act in consultation with each other to effectuate the above allotment in the period stipulated.

(iii) The Sunni Central Waqf Board would be at liberty, on the allotment of the land to take all necessary steps for the construction of a mosque on the land so allotted together with other associated facilities;

(iv) Suit 4 shall stand decreed to this extent in terms of the above directions; and

(v) The directions for the allotment of land to the Sunni Central Waqf Board in Suit 4 are issued in pursuance of the powers vested in this Court under Article 142 of the Constitution.

4. In exercise of the powers vested in this Court under Article 142 of the Constitution, we direct that in the scheme to be framed by the Central Government, appropriate representation may

be given in the Trust or body, to the Nirmohi Akhara in such manner as the Central Government deems fit.

5.  The right of the plaintiff in Suit 1 to worship at the disputed property is affirmed subject to any restrictions imposed by the relevant authorities with respect to the maintenance of peace and order and the performance of orderly worship.

\* \* \*

The addenda is difficult to place in perspective on principles of judicial precedents. Yet it provides valuable insights and is thus noteworthy. After detailing history, along the lines of the unanimous judgment, in two crucial paragraphs, it comes to a conclusion, the basis of which was specifically ruled out by the judgment itself.

1416. **The sequence of the events as noticed above clearly indicate that faith and belief of Hindus was that birthplace of Lord Ram was in the three-dome structure Mosque which was constructed at the Janamasthan.** It was only during the British period that grilled wall was constructed dividing the walled premises of the Mosque into inner courtyard and outer courtyard. Grilled iron wall was constructed to keep Hindus outside the grilled iron wall in the outer courtyard. In view of the construction of the iron wall, the worship and puja started in Ram Chabutra in the outer courtyard. Suit of 1885 was filed seeking permission to construct temple on the said Chabutra where worship was permitted by the British Authority. **Faith and belief of the Hindus as depicted by the evidence on record clearly establish that the Hindus' belief that at the birthplace of Lord Ram, the Mosque was constructed and three-dome structure is the birthplace of Lord Ram.** The fact that Hindus were by constructing iron wall, dividing Mosque premises, kept outside the three-dome structure cannot be said to alter their faith and belief regarding the birthplace of Lord Ram. **The worship on the Ram Chabutra in the outer courtyard was symbolic worship of Lord Ram who was believed to be born in the premises.**

170.   **It is thus concluded on the conclusion that faith and belief of Hindus since prior to construction of Mosque and subsequent thereto has always been that Janmaasthan of Lord Ram is the place where Babri Mosque has been constructed which faith and belief is proved by documentary and oral evidence discussed above.**

* * *

As mentioned earlier, the addenda to the judgment is not only somewhat sui generis, in not explaining or amplifying any part of the main judgment, but indeed quite contrary to its main premise. Furthermore, written like a judgment, it does not indicate the author. In the circumstances, one can only conclude that it is a dissenting or contrary judgment and was relegated to being addenda owing to the court's endeavour to give a unanimous judgment. Nevertheless, the addenda poses fundamental questions about plural societies. Respect for other religions and beliefs is imperative among people. Fortunately, there are many significant differences among the several religions that are followed in India but none that cause fundamental philosophical or theological differences in terms of irreconcilable beliefs. Such a case might have arisen if the court had attempted to answer the Ayodhya conundrum on the basis of faith and indeed believed that both faiths had an essential feature associated with the disputed site at Ayodhya.

In crafting the final relief, given that Hindus were found to have better possessory title to the inner courtyard as well as admitted title to the outer courtyard, it was appropriate to hand over the entire disputed plot of 2.77 acres to the Hindus, but the

Muslims were also to be given 5 acres from the acquired 67 acres or elsewhere in the city of Ayodhya, to compensate them for their loss. The three-way partition done by the high court was held neither legal nor appropriate for preventing further disputes. It is far from clear whether the court, having rejected adverse possession and having concluded that the outer as well as the inner courtyards were one composite whole, with the grill only a temporary measure to prevent clashes, finally found aggregate possession of the Hindus to be the deciding factor in their favour; or whether in the totality of circumstances, the court opted to do complete justice by giving Muslims a larger plot of land elsewhere, instead of the 170 x 80 they would have received as the inner courtyard.

There are generally always winners and losers in a judgment, depending on how the two parties perceive their claims and the result of the case. But for the lawyer, all that matters is the legal reasoning and the impact the judgment makes as a precedent for future cases. From that perspective, one might summarize the case as follows.

As already noted earlier, the case was decided on settled principles of title in property law. To begin with the first thing one looks at in such cases are the documents of title, which in this case were neither available with the mosque party nor with the temple party. In the absence of documents or any revenue record—except that the land was recorded as 'Nazul' or escheat, but the State laid no claim or in effect gave up its claim—what remained was to take stock of user (that, in the case of a waqf, was enough proof of title) and in conjunction with that the doctrine of lost grant in favour of the Muslims.

Inexplicably, the Muslim side also pleaded adverse possession, but for that they had to admit the initial title of the Hindu side. The Hindu side laid claim to the property on the grounds that this had been a site of a twelfth-century temple, as established by the ASI excavation, and that the land itself was a deity and thus in was their possession from times immemorial. All those pleas having been rejected by the court, all that was left for it was to take recourse to the principle of Section 110 of the Evidence Act, 1872, which relies upon possession to grant relief. The court was able to hold that the Hindu side had established that Hindus had been worshipping at the site and had its possession for at least 100 years prior to 1857 (presumably on accounts of travellers, etc.), and that they had exclusive possession of the outer courtyard since then. The former seems doubtful, while the latter was admitted by the Muslim side. On the other hand, the Muslim side could show exclusive possession of the inner courtyard only since 1857. In the absence of claim to partition the two courtyards, the court found itself compelled to decide the fate of the entire property and, on a balance of probability, held that the Hindus had established possessory title.

Yet there seems no mention in the entire discussion by the court of the fact that Babri Masjid was registered as a waqf property and, by virtue of the gazette notification, that becomes final and binding on the whole world, unless challenged within one year. It is surprising that Zafaryab Jilani, who argued on behalf of the Personal Law Board, did not rely upon this fact, given the noise he had made about the issue when the Waqf Amendment Act was passed in 2013 under my stewardship of the Ministry of Minority Affairs.

We were cleaning up the Act and clarifying the jurisdiction of the revamped Waqf Tribunals. Since there was an existing provision for the registration of all waqfs, we provided for tribunals to hear matters pertaining to registered waqfs, with unregistered waqfs being in the purview of the civil courts. Jilani publicly decried that to be an attempt by the UPA government to derail the Babri Masjid case. No effort to explain the logic worked on him or the Personal Law Board. In fact, a little research disclosed that the Babri Masjid was indeed registered many decades ago, in 1944. under the UP Waqf Act, 1936, but the Faizabad Civil Court had rejected the registration in 1966, due to inadequate details of the

mutawallis. Subsequently, it was once again registered and given
the same registration number: no. 26.

That registration should have been used to bolster the case
of the masjid. However, although in the written submissions it
was argued that the 1944 registration being held void would not
affect the validity of the waqf, there is no mention that there was
a fresh registration—one that has not been questioned or held
void. Perhaps when the case is examined dispassionately, history
will judge how diligently and effectively the case of the masjid
was presented by those who made a lifetime career of political
advocacy. Who is there to blame now, unlike in the past when
they made a point to campaign in my constituency, Farrukhabad,
and against Sonia Gandhi in Amethi?

After the Ayodhya verdict, there was no impromptu
celebration or protest across the length and breadth of India. All
political parties had repeatedly announced their resolve to abide by
the decision of the Supreme Court, and that was what they did,
with the exception of individual leaders repeatedly voicing their
support for a 'bhavya mandir' without any mention of the masjid.
Meanwhile, despite reiterating their position to accept the court's
decision, the Muslim parties went into a huddle to ponder over the
possibility of filing a review and generally rejecting the offer of 5
acres of 'charity'.

Gradually, Ayodhya began to look like a contest between
Hindu groups (Nirmohi Akhara versus the Temple Trust to be
established) on the one hand and Muslim groups on the other
(Muslim Personal Law Board and Babri Masjid Committee versus
the Sunni Waqf Board). The differences among the latter surfaced
in the ungainly 'sacking' of Rajeev Dhawan, the senior counsel who
did an admirable job for the Muslim cause. His tireless advocacy
before the constitution bench had several dramatic moments,
including when he tore a site plan presented by another counsel
on behalf of the temple. The chief justice had probably meant to
be ironic in suggesting that the document could be torn up, but it

took the inimitable Dr Dhawan to show such candour and actually do it.

An important point must be made about the monopoly sought by certain groups among Hindus and Muslims to represent the respective cause of the two communities. What should have been a matter for widespread consultation with opinion-makers and community leaders was kept close to the chest of a few lawyers and their self-professed clients. During the early stages of the hearing, with the court giving instructions for the tidying up of the voluminous record, some groups that had laboriously collected material, which would have been immensely helpful, attempted to be impleaded or at least be allowed to intervene. But vigorous opposition by the counsel for the Waqf Board left the court helpless in the matter. Surprisingly, even the offer to merely file all the material was resisted.

Unelected representatives chose to decide the future of entire communities, obstinately obstructing any fresh inputs or participation. Sadly, the price will be paid by those who were never told why something was done—why some members of the community decided they must be the only voice of the community, and speak for all, for better or worse. Thus far we have not seen signs of people celebrating their victory or defeat, but many are convinced that the building of the temple will not be without considerable political fanfare and careful calibration of schedules to match election dates. But as they say, a closed fist fascinates only till it is opened and the truth becomes apparent. Indian politics, held captive in one way or the other by Ayodhya, may now well seek its emancipation from this issue, and the pursuit of welfare.

The unanimity among the five justices, both unusual and perhaps consciously accomplished, served a purpose: of underscoring our social need for unity. But scholars and professionals remain perplexed about the addenda attached to the judgment. If it was a draft judgment, it certainly points to a wide difference of opinion about the nature of the task assumed by the court. While the judgment firmly rejects appeals to faith (except to the limited extent of evidence of conduct) and avowedly sticks to the principles of evidence relevant to the title suit, the addenda squarely reposes trust in faith, as it were, and goes on to find that Hindus' faith in the Ram Janmabhoomi or the Ram Janmasthan must trump other considerations of possession and title.

Is the present judgment, then, a compromise between faith and law that therefore looks a little askew because of the court's reluctance to acknowledge that? This is not the first time that reluctance to acknowledge the role of faith has forced the court to tread into slippery territory. In the entire series of cases concerning the banning of cow slaughter,* the court's reluctance to read the cow slaughter-related directive principles as being concerned with the Hindu faith forced it to take positions that were neither constitutionally consistent nor sustainable over a period on the grounds of technological changes and best practices in animal husbandry.

## A Summary of the Findings

The mosque was built on the remains of a religious structure, possibly a Hindu one, from the twelfth century, as per the ASI. But it can't be said that it was a temple or, more importantly, that a temple was demolished to build the mosque. That virtually rejected the case made by the RSS and VHP, and justified their demand for reparation for the destruction of their temple.

There was no case of the Swayambhu deity established, neither on grounds of theology nor on the facts as proved. The essential element—of the manifestation of divine character—was missing. In the absence of a consecrated deity, it could not be said that the janmasthan, too, was a juristic person.

---

* 'Mohd. Hanif Quareshi and Others vs State of Bihar', 1959, SCR 629; 'State of Gujarat vs Mirzapur Moti Kureshi Kassab Jamat and Others', 2005, 8 SCC 534.

It was conceded by the Muslim side that Hindus worshipped Lord Ram on the chabutra in the outer courtyard of the mosque and that Lord Ram was born in Ayodhya. However, the idea that the concession about one clearly demarcated part of the property should have impact on the status of the other part is surprising.

The Muslim side was unable to show evidence that Muslims had continued to pray in the mosque from 1528 to 1856–57. But throughout, the court had accepted that it was a mosque and was never abandoned, and even when obstructions were created for people to visit the mosque, Friday prayers continued to be performed there till the idols were placed.

Since there was no proof of dedication, and uninterrupted use was not established, it could not be said that there was a waqf. This was held despite the court finding that from 1934 to 1949 the keys of the mosque remained with the Muslims, but since they had to traverse past the Hindu places of worship, like the chabutra and Sita Rasoi, they were able to perform namaz only on Fridays.

The last word, for the present, on the judgment: Despite the careful steps to find a balance between stated legal principles and acceptability by the masses, but with a concern to keep the secular fabric of our society intact, it will be said that ultimately the case was decided on the basis of the myopic pleadings of the Muslim side not seeking the portion that was admittedly the mosque. Besides that, there was the backdrop of the rejection of their claim of adverse possession, inexplicably sought against the non-owner. Finally, of course, the somewhat obscure concept of possessory title of the mosque being held to be doubtful because the other side made periodic attempts to intrude and occupy.

All this gives sadly the impression that the wrongdoer generally benefits. As does the candid admission by the court that Article 142 would be used to do complete justice by holding that the inner courtyard was established to be a mosque yet it would remain a contentious issue, since it would be surrounded and virtually landlocked by the mandir property.

# Thirteen

# The New Dawn

*'Ye dagh dagh ujala, ye shabguzida sehar,*
*Jis sehar ka intazar tha ye wo sehar to nahi.'*

'This shadowy, patchy light, the night-like morning,
This morning is not the much-awaited morning.'

Senior Advocate Rajiv Dhawan, who worked tirelessly to seek justice on behalf of the mosque, remains unconvinced by the judgment. In a recent interview he reflected on the gradual march of the reasoning that made the judgment possible:[*]

The first judgment on this, in my view, was a judgment in 1966 called Yagnapur Das Ji, where Justice . . . Gajendragadkar indicated that everybody is a Hindu . . . For temple entry, they may be all Hindus, which were the facts of the case, but he said we must take an

---

[*] Betwa Sharma, 'Ram Mandir: Supreme Court Judgements Have Contributed to "Hindu-isation" of India, Says Advocate Rajeev Dhavan', Huffpost.com, 30 July 2020, https://www.huffpost.com/archive/in/entry/ram-mandir-supreme-court-babri-masjid-rajeev-dhavan_in_5f228940c5b656e9b097a249

expansive view of Hindu to cover everybody. It covered everybody (Jains, Buddhists) except Christians and Muslims. This to my mind was the first judgment of expansive Hindu-isation.

The second judgment came in 1995–1996 . . . when the Supreme Court said that 'Hindutva' is a way of life. A three judge bench decided that you can appeal to your own religion, but not slander their religion. This in practical terms means a Hindu can go on and on about the greatness of Hinduism as long as he does not tell the Christians and the Muslims that their religion is bad . . . in campaigns what happens is that the Hindu juggernaut is much stronger.

The 1996 judgment on election appeal—Dr Ramesh Yeshwant Prabhoo versus Shri Prabhkar Kashinath Kunte—was reversed by the Supreme Court in Abhiram Singh versus CD Commachen in 2017.

While the majority (4–3) seized this opportunity to clarify that no appeals to religion is permissible in an election, a minority wrote a dissent which properly interpreted meant that you can always appeal to your own religion.

[. . .]

Babri. The Muslims proved their possession from 1858 because there were land grants by the British. Against the entire evidence it was decided that Hindus were in possession throughout from 1858 even though a judgment of 1886 clearly says Muslims have title and Hindus have a prescriptive right to pray. The Hindu side did not have to prove possession at all . . . The [Ayodhya verdict] judgment is the oddest in the history of the Supreme Court.

There is a flow. The court has always expanded its Hinduism to the extent that it has always wanted to. The first judgment is for a mahayana Hinduism. The second one appeals to religion in elections. When you look at the Gujarat riot cases, Supreme Court showed sympathy, but didn't exactly support the Muslims except on narrow points of law. When judgments co-opt a movement, you find the judiciary responding to, running away from or running on to muscular nationalism.

That is how a transformation in the country has taken place. Mild at first and then it becomes stronger because of the rath yatra and Babri Masjid and stronger and stronger and stronger until we reach the CAA (Citizenship Amendment Act). So the Hindu fundamentalism was always there but its muscularity has suddenly made it offensive.

Former Chief Justice (Ramesh Chandra) Lahoti (2004–2005), just before he retired, was very concerned about cows not being killed. So he wanted to reverse the five judge bench of 1958. The retiring Chief Justice suddenly put cows on the anvil and decided the cow was indeed sacred and we should not kill it. (In 1958, a five-judge bench in Mohd. Hanif Quareshi & Others vs The State Of Bihar, ruled against a complete ban on cow slaughter, confining it to 'useless' cows. In 2005, a seven-judge bench in State Of Gujarat vs Mirzapur Moti Kureshi Kassab ruled in favour of a complete ban, famously stating that the 'the value of dung is much more than even the famous Kohinoor diamond'.)

What was going on in the country was not just Ayodhya. What was going on was that the cow movement, the conversion movement, muscular nationalism was playing out against the minorities at various levels.

Another senior advocate, Rakesh Dwivedi, made the following comment:*

> Strikingly, the judgment rolls over in favour of Hindus on a slender basis. While it is found that Hindus have been worshipping in the inner courtyard and had exclusive possession of outer courtyard, the fact that mosque existed on the spot since the 16th century, and that Muslims were illegally ousted from

---

* Rakesh Dwivedi, 'Ayodhya Verdict: Balancing While Condemning the 1992 Demolition', *Economic Times*, https://economictimes.indiatimes.com/news/politics-and-nation/ayodhya-verdict-balancing-while-condemning-the-1992-demolition/articleshow/72007260.cms

worship in 1949 is also found to be established. Illegal ouster
of Muslims would be of no consequence. Thus inner courtyard
was in joint possession of Hindus and Muslims.

Actually, the judgement denies restitution to Muslims
which should ordinarily follow the finding of illegal demolition
and desecration of mosque. The court takes the compensation
route rather than restitution by invoking Article 142. It is better
evidence of possessory title which seems to have titled in favour
of Hindus. Landwise Muslims have got twice the land which was
under the mosque, and it is to be at a prominent place in Ayodhya.
In the circumstances Hindus and Muslims need to move forward.

The Ayodhya saga was undoubtedly related to certain organized
groups among Hindus and Muslims trying to secure leadership
of their respective communities by tilting the scales in favour
of a mandir and a mosque, respectively. The politics shaped by
the mandir–masjid contest drove the Congress to an existential
crisis in Uttar Pradesh and, after temporary empowerment of the
Samajwadi Party and Bahujan Samajwadi Party, gave the BJP
a springboard for dominance in the state and in Centre. Many
arguments that cut ice with the common folk in the build-up to
the current state of affairs have lost their grip after the judgment.
The food and shelter issues of daily existence cannot be obfuscated
by ideological indoctrination indefinitely. This is increasingly
becoming apparent. Liberty, too, does not remain in prolonged
retreat, as the world has repeatedly seen. Although religion
remains the opiate of the masses (as Karl Marx said), it has its
uses, and it is still relevant to Indian society. There may well be
a rediscovery of religion in this society and then the rebirth of a
faithful and constitutional morality.

Constitutional morality is another term for Ram Rajya.
Mahatma Gandhi often used the term Rama Rajya to explain
his idea of the world we must build and aspire to. It was a noble
vision and, for Gandhi, touched by the best humanist dimension

of Hinduism: 'By Ramarajya I do not mean Hindu Raj. I mean by Ramrajya Divine Raj, the Kingdom of God. For me Ram and Rahim are one deity. I acknowledge no other God but the one God of truth and righteousness . . . Whether Ram of my imagination lived or not on this earth, the ancient ideal of Ramarajya is undoubtedly One of true democracy in which the meanest citizen could be sure of swift justice without an elaborate and costly procedure.'[*]

Interestingly, in Islam the concept of Nizam-e-Mustafa has similar humanist attributes. Thus it might not be incorrect to assert that Ram Rajya and Nizam-e-Mustafa are indeed the same idea in different cultures and languages.

As the sun rises for Hindus and Muslims alike, it would be less than honest if the shadows of doubt are not recognized. These are not discordant voices but words of caution and concern.

Justice A.K. Ganguly, a former Supreme Court judge, said he was shocked 'beyond measure' by the Ayodhya verdict, as 'the conclusions of the judgment are not matched by its reasons'. Speaking at a discussion on 'The Consequences of the Ayodhya Judgment of the Supreme Court',[†] Justice Ganguly said: 'I've never heard in my humble career as a judge for 18 years that there can be addendum to a judgment . . . After reading the judgment, my first reaction in one sentence is "the conclusions of the judgment are not matched by its reasons, rather they are mutually destructive".'

The former judge said: 'In 1934, there were communal disturbances. Damage was made to the mosque . . . it was restored by the British government, and Hindus were fined. I find that our colonial masters, they protected the rights of minorities better than this constitutionally formed government under the Constitution where secularism is a basic feature.'

---

[*] M.K. Gandhi, *Ramrajya*, MKgandhi.org, available at https://www.mkgandhi. org/momgandhi/chap67.htm

[†] Pheroze L. Vincent, 'Ayodhya Conclusions Not Matched by Reasons: Justice Ganguly', *Telegraph*, 2 December 2019, https://www.telegraphindia.com/india/ ayodhya-conclusions-not-matched-by-reasons-justice-ganguly/cid/1723810

Pointing out that 'Hindu idols were surreptitiously placed in the mosque' just a month after the Constitution was adopted, Justice Ganguly quoted the judgment: 'The allotment of land to the Muslims is necessary because though on a balance of probabilities, the evidence in respect of the possessory claim of the Hindus to the composite whole of the disputed property stands on a better footing than the evidence adduced by the Muslims, the Muslims were dispossessed upon the desecration of the mosque on 22/23 December 1949, which was ultimately destroyed on 6 December 1992. There was no abandonment of the mosque by the Muslims . . . How does it become a better footing, on what better footing? Hindus have always encroached upon it illegally . . . Does demolition of the mosque constitute a better possessory title of the Hindus?'

Recalling that in 2017 the Supreme Court had ordered a fast-track trial against former Uttar Pradesh chief minister Kalyan Singh and other BJP leaders for criminal conspiracy to demolish the mosque, Justice Ganguly said: 'The court was so shocked by the enormity of the crime that it gives an extraordinary direction. And that is considered act of possession? . . . And now the central government is directed to frame a scheme on the same plot of land where stood a mosque, on the demolition of which the Supreme Court directed a trial with such seriousness.'

He finally added: 'All that was being asked is that "not only we (Muslims) have a right to that land, we also have a right to This Land (India). We are here in shared citizenship with everybody else. We can kindly adjust, but it has to come from us." Today all that is being told is that there is a responsibility to keep quiet. It doesn't affect only the Muslims but all of us who believe in our holy book, the Constitution . . .'

Another former judge of the Supreme Court, Justice Markandey Katju had equally caustic remarks to make about the judgment[*]:

---

[*] Markandey Katju, 'The Ayodhya Verdict is Based on a Strange Feat of Logic', TheWire.in, 11 November 2019, https://thewire.in/law/the-ayodhya-verdict-is-based-on-a-strange-feat-of-logic

The recent Ayodhya verdict of the Supreme Court will go down in the annals of Indian legal history in the same category as its 1975 decision in *ADM Jabalpur vs Shivakant Shukla*—except that unlike the latter, in this one there is not a single courageous dissent. In substance, the court has said that might is right, and has laid down a dangerous precedent sanctifying aggression.

[. . .] [T]he court has observed that the Muslim side adduced no evidence to show that from 1528, when the mosque was constructed, to 1857, it was in possession of Muslims who offered *namaz* there. But what evidence could possibly be adduced? There cannot be any eyewitnesses alive belonging to that period, and it is well known that in the 1857 war of independence, almost all records in Avadh were destroyed. In any case, it is common sense that when a house of worship, whether a temple, mosque, church or gurdwara is built, it is built for use, and not just for decoration.

[. . .] [I]t is stated [that], 'The exclusion of Muslims from worship and possession took place on the intervening night between 22/23.12.1949 when the mosque was desecrated by installation of Hindu idols. Ouster of Muslims was not through lawful authority, and Muslims have been wrongly deprived of a mosque that had been constructed well over 450 years ago'. Despite this clear finding, the court has handed over the site to Hindus by a strange feat of logic!

We know that appellate judges, like others, often disagree. But the nature and content of the disagreement, or dissent as it is called, matters far more when it comes to judgments. In this case, not only was there no 'courageous' dissent, as Justice Katju observed, but there is also no chance of the judgment ever being overruled. Yet the public criticism of the judgment by former judges raises important questions. There is obviously some scope of honest disagreement amongst judges on a bench, but it might well be that the choice of particular judges can swing the decision one way or another. This problem in Indian courts does not seem to get resolved, despite judges of the highest court expressing their discomfort in this regard periodically.

Immediately after the judgment was pronounced, some civil servants came together to voice their feelings in the following petition:

**Pledge Not to Allow the Constitution 'To Be Emptied of Its Soul'**

We, a collective of retired civil servants deeply committed to the values and guarantees of the Indian constitution, share with our fellow Indians our extreme grief and deep concern about where India stands today, 27 years after the demolition of the Babri Masjid in Ayodhya on 6 December, 1992.

2.    We recall that 6 December is also the anniversary of the day on which the man who led the creation of one of the finest constitutions in the world, Dr Bhimrao Ambedkar, left this world. The battle for the land on which the medieval mosque in Ayodhya stood was at its core a battle for the defence of the highest values of this constitution.

3.    This was not simply a title dispute over a tiny piece of land in a dusty small town. It was not even a contest between a medieval mosque, now razed, with a grand temple, still imagined. It was a dispute about what kind of country this is and will be in the future, to who does it belong, and on what terms must people of different identities and beliefs live together in this vast and teeming land.

4.    We feel intense anguish because 27 years after the mosque was demolished, those who were responsible for this crime which

* Concerned Citizens, 'Former Civil Servants Express "Anguish" Over the "Injustice" of Ayodhya', TheCitizen.in, 4 December 2019, https://www.thecitizen.in/index.php/en/NewsDetail/index/9/17957/Former-Civil-Servants-Express-Anguish-Over-the-Injustice-of-Ayodhya

tore India apart and led to the highest levels of communal bloodletting after the Partition riots, have still not been punished, even though the Supreme Court directed that this criminal case be heard on a day-to-day basis. Instead, many of those who led and participated in this assault not just on a mosque but on India's constitutional morality, have held some of the highest offices in this country.

5.  We worry also that the recent judgment of the Supreme Court of India in effect rewards this grave crime. It also creates a false and illusory notion that a verdict favouring those who claim to speak for the majority community can result in peace and reconciliation and everyone should move on, injustice notwithstanding.

6.  In this deeply troubling moment in the journey of this country which we love, we contest resolutely the message that it seems to convey to India's religious minorities that their claim to this country and its democratic institutions is subordinate to anyone. We would like to recall the famous dictum 'Freedom is the outcome of the tranquillity of peace and peace emanates from justice.' Freedom and justice are the soul of our constitution.

7.  This is a time when every Indian should recall Mahatma Gandhi's last fast, two weeks before he was assassinated. One of his three demands was that the mosques and dargahs in Delhi in which Hindu idols had been inserted should be returned respectfully to the Muslims. Hinduism, he said, would be emptied for him of meaning if a single place of worship of another faith was desecrated in the name of the Hindu faith.

8.  We who sign this letter to the Indian people include a Jain, Hindus, Muslims, Christians, Sikhs, atheists and agnostics. We are together convinced that true religion never teaches violence and hate of another. Therefore, on 6 December, we first express our collective agony and atonement that a place of worship was pulled down with such hate. We also pledge that we will not allow our great Constitution to be emptied of its soul.

The letter was signed by forty-six concerned retired IAS, IFS, IC&CES, IPS, IPoS and IRS officers, who had served in high positions in the government in various ministries and states.

There are similar voices emanating from different quarters: senior journalists, social activists, academics, et al. They will probably fade away gradually as people move on to other issues, but it is important that we don't allow Ayodhya to become a deep-seated scar that manifests itself when least expected. Inevitably, the debate on nationalism (as assumed by the emergent ideology) and secularism (held dear for long by the establishment but maligned and deliberately distorted by the Right) will continue unabated. It is to be seen if the pressure of false perceptions will undermine the commitment of true secular India. Nothing will be worse than secularists abandoning their creed because of transitory defeats. Furthermore, all sides of the political spectrum swear by the Constitution and its values, like secularism and equality. Yet there are serious disagreements about what these ideas mean. Of late, there is even disagreement on the meaning of democracy, not so much in terms of its deficits as its outcomes.

These are alarming developments for a democracy. Kashmir has become a living (perhaps more correct to say, dying) example of this deterioration. Just as the man on the horseback speaks of temporary suspension of rights for the greater good, we have talk of guided democracy and even painstaking efforts to explain shocking incidents of mob lynching and, even worse, shameless police encounters to eliminate inconvenient accused.

The Constitution belongs to us all. So does this land: India, Bharat, Hindustan. But can we impose interpretations on all those to make them appear quite different from what we have believed for millennia and even more so since Independence? Disappointment and pain are inevitable where there is togetherness. But this doesn't mean one can't expect the wrongs to be righted. If Muslims are made to feel more wanted as Indians by other Indians, the sacrifice of Ayodhya would be worth everything, or else it would be darkness at noon.

The test of Indian democracy, increasingly, is to make citizens understand that this irreplaceable system is not merely about numbers. Even highly educated persons often make the mistake of believing that this is all there is to a democracy. Numbers are important but within the limits of constitutional morality. Furthermore, although faith has prominence in articulation of certain rights, it cannot be a trump card against other people's rights and their separate faith. It is meaningless to close all discussion by citing faith in the Constitution without deciphering the contours of each constitutional value. To swear allegiance to the Constitution and, in the same breath, label the implementation of minority rights as 'appeasement for votes' is hypocritical in the extreme. People who celebrate the death of liberalism or the fundamental right to dissent are playing with the life of democracy.

# Postscript

Several review petitions filed against the judgment indicate resistance to the conclusions reached by the court, despite public reiteration by parties to the suits of acceptance and intent to honour the judgment. On the other hand, the judgment came in a climate of anxiety about the socio-political ambience being created in the country: vigilante squads of *gau rakshaks* lynching people on the streets; threats of introducing NRC in the entire country; the Citizenship Amendment Act.

The dismissal of the review petitions was a foregone conclusion—these were dispatched promptly, with the place on the bench vacated by Chief Justice Gogoi filled by Justice Sanjeev Khanna. But that news was rapidly overtaken by the spontaneous protests that erupted against the Citizenship Amendment Bill, which has now been converted into an Act by Parliament. The protests, which displayed surprising intensity and passion, were responded to by the police with predictable barbarity. Once again, blood and gore became the content of contemporary history. The movement shows all signs of bypassing the Hindu–Muslim binary, particularly because of the role of the North-east. The exceptions made in the Act to placate the troubled region, where scars of the All Assam Students Union (AASU) movement have been scratched again, will highlight the inherent contradictions in the stand of the BJP. This may turn out to be the Achilles' heel for the ruling party but not without massive damage to our governance.

Protests in our democracy have a way of settling down with the passage of time and some accommodation by adversaries. However, we are now being forced into resisting permanent and unwholesome changes in our lives. It is unlikely that a detente can be reached.

In the context of the Ayodhya verdict, despite a few discordant voices, there has largely been a conspicuous silence on all sides: no visible or audible celebration by Hindus, and no expression of dismay or protest by Muslims or their institutions. But the latter do sometimes discreetly express that they have not received justice. Yet there is unanimity of opinion that the judgment has removed all cause of division among communities along religious lines.

It is suggested in some quarters that the CAA–NRC–NPR controversy was consciously stoked by the ruling dispensation in order to keep alive divisive tendencies in society. However, the spontaneous reactions across the country, in which young and old, cutting across religious communities, rose in opposition to the government's plans, were in stark contrast to other issues that went unchallenged, like Article 370, Triple Talaq, etc. Although the former is still to be tested in the Supreme Court, the latter has been laid to rest by a constitutional bench majority judgment that held Triple Talaq had no place in Islam (Justice Kurien Joseph) and that it was *non est* in the eyes of the law (Justices Rohinton Nariman and Uday U. Lalit). Yet the government brought legislation to invalidate Triple Talaq and made its pronouncement a criminal offence.* Neither before nor after this judgment was any data produced to show a troubling incidence or the efficacy of the legislation.

---

* Muslim Women (Protection of Rights on Marriage) Act, 2019.

This time around the Constitution itself became the rallying point for the widespread protests. Ostensibly directed against a departure from Article 14 equality provisions, the movement was clearly against the intent to destroy the inclusive spirit of the Constitution and its replacement by exclusionary systems. The basic question is whether the range of options available in routine democratic choice today are the same as those available at the time of the drafting and adoption of the Constitution. We seem to have a difficult choice between the evolution of a constitutional model and a revolution that aims to throw it overboard and replace it with another, dramatically different one.

In the course of visiting the dogged protests at Jamia and Shaheen Bagh in Delhi, trying to discover the exact sentiment leading people to put up 24/7 demonstrations, I engaged with a young teacher of Jamia Millia Islamia university. Our conversation drifted to Babri Masjid, and I asked why we were refusing to accept the offer by the court to build a mosque at the alternative site. 'Because that will foreclose our right to claim the Babri Masjid in the future, when fortunes turn,' was his reply. Similarly, the five men who stood in front of the university gate, with candles in their hands, gently said, 'They have taken our mosque, now they want to take away our citizenship.'

The Supreme Court has perhaps not encountered a seminal moment as the present one since the Emergency of 1975 or 'ADM Jabalpur'.* While on one plane it has to simply look at the jurisprudence of Articles 14 and 21, it also has to take stock of what is happening around the country. Despite the hyperbole employed to decry the Emergency, including calling it a dark period of Indian democracy, an undeclared form of emergency in recent times poses greater threats to the rule of law. A direct challenge to civil liberties draws the battle lines clearly, but this steady and

_____
* 'ADM Jabalpur' (supra).

insidious attrition of rights, without any public pronouncement, may prove more dangerous.

There is clearly a growing divide in the country between those who have preferred ways of life and those who attempt to perceive matters in terms of majority and minority. When majorities seek to impose majoritarian ethos, it is for established institutions, particularly the courts, to preserve and protect the constitutional ethos.

The CAA protests have given occasion to certain elements in our national life to push the false narrative of 'anti-national sentiment' being the core of the protest, with the popular protest slogan of 'azadi' or freedom portrayed as the defining expression of unpatriotic intent. But in truth, the protests are virtually the last stand for the idea of liberty as enshrined in the Preamble of the Constitution. Interestingly, the movement has also opened a new chapter in the history of India's Muslim minority, whose apprehension at being forced into invisibility on the political landscape has been reversed in a spontaneous assertion of rights.

The cumulative impact of virulent, divisive electoral campaigns by the BJP in 2014 and 2019—their spectacular success, aggressive pursuing of a majoritarian agenda, with Triple Talaq being criminalized, abrogation of Article 370, reduction of J&K state to the status of a union territory and, indeed, Ayodhya—has been aggravated by speculation about the integrity and independence of the judicial edifice. Former Chief Justice Ranjan Gogoi accepting his nomination to the Rajya Sabha within weeks of superannuation, having delivered controversial judgments that gave critical relief to the government, has added to the widespread disquiet, not least among his own community, of former judges of the Supreme Court and high courts.[*]

---

[*] 'Ranjan Gogoi Takes Oath as Member of Rajya Sabha Amid "Shame" Slogans', *Indian Express*, 19 March 2019, https://indianexpress.com/article/india/ranjan-gogoi-takes-oath-rajya-sabha-6321599/; PTI, 'Gogoi's Nomination to Rajya

Suddenly, it has become difficult to explain to people that the Ayodhya judgment may have had no role in the government's decision to nominate Chief Justice Gogoi to the Rajya Sabha. 'Would he have been nominated even if the judgment had gone the other way?' is, sadly, a question one finds difficult to answer. This is in the same league as the following question: What might the decision have been if the structure of the mosque was still standing or had, as was promised immediately after the demolition, been restored? Whatever explanation Chief Justice Gogoi might have for his decision to accept the offer of the government, it will be difficult to separate it from an ideological tilt. As far as the Ayodhya judgment is concerned, this development does add to the overall air of scepticism. Chief Justice Gogoi is, of course, correct in saying that he was not alone in pronouncing the judgment—it was a unanimous judgment of five judges. But the role of the chief in steering the bench, having had the right to pick the judges as the master of the roster, may well have been significant.

Before the Supreme Court hearings began in right earnest and preliminary matters were being sorted out before the bench headed by the then chief justice Dipak Misra, my colleague Kapil Sibal, appearing for the Muslim side, had created a flutter by suggesting that the court ought not to hear the matter before the next general elections. Opinion at the Bar was divided on the propriety of that suggestion. But clearly, it was a cry to keep the judiciary protected against real or perceived political influence. Chief Justice Gogoi's decision puts that plea in a different light and vindicates the concern felt by some people back then.

There has been a steady flow of criticism and indignation since the news of Ranjan Gogoi's nomination for a seat in the Rajya Sabha was made public. Many former Supreme Court judges,

Sabha Draws Criticism from Former Judges', *New Indian Express*, 17 March 2020, https://www.newindianexpress.com/nation/2020/mar/17/gogois-nomination-to-rajya-sabha-draws-criticism-from-former-judges-2117976.html including some who were known to be reasonably close to him, spoke out in public with unprecedented candour. Several persons at the top of the lawyer fraternity also expressed their dismay. Some of these critics will encounter the former chief justice in his new avatar as a member of Parliament, and he in turn will discover what it feels like to be judged by others. Of course, the former chief justice has briefly presented his point of view and spoken of joining hands with the legislature to participate in the exercise of nation-building. In an interview, he seems to have hinted at a lobby of Lutyens's lawyers being anathema to judicial independence and at some outspoken former judges who have much to explain.* It was thought that perhaps we would become privy to more details as he settled in after taking the oath of office. However, despite the furore at his nomination, his tenure as Rajya Sabha member has been otherwise uneventful.

When I was asked by news agencies to comment on this development, my reply was that the court was too dear and irreplaceable in my estimate and that we can't allow it to suffer any further unintended damage, beyond what some people say has already befallen it. For each issue that followers of the court find disturbing, there are several admirable dimensions of its performance as the temple of justice. For each judge whose demeanour or judicial conscience makes us uneasy, there are innumerable judges who surpass all expectations of compassion, intellectual integrity, unimpeachable personal morality and sheer brilliance of mind. Like all institutions, it is larger than the men and women who occupy it. I therefore consciously declined to make any further comment. But the barrage of comments that

---

* 'FULL INTERVIEW: Ex-CJI Ranjan Gogoi Speaks to Arnab Goswami on His Rajya Sabha Nomination', Republic World's YouTube Channel, 20 March 2020, https://www.youtube.com/watch?v=3sRgQhtVZbg; 'Ranjan Gogoi Says "Lobby" Is Holding Judiciary to Ransom, Rejects Quid Pro Quo Allegations', TheWire.in, 20 March 2020, https://thewire.in/government/former-cji-ranjan-gogoi-rajya-sabha-nomination

have been made by responsible and respectable persons persuaded me to break my silence as a citizen, a senior advocate and a former minister for law and justice, and record my response.

I politely sought permission to pose a question about the institution that we hold in great esteem: Is there something wrong with our judicial system? There can be no gainsaying that there is. But why should one pose this question in regard to the courts alone? Our entire society is under stress and seemingly adrift. Yet it is the courts that can be the ballast to keep the ship of state steady. In recent months, our polity has been faced with a lack of consensus on issues concerning collective national life. We know that these differences cannot always be settled by counting heads democratically. Indeed, that may well be a part of the problem rather than the solution. Constitutional government has its moorings in the will of the majority. But if we truly understand our Constitution and recall the guidance of the Supreme Court, governance cannot be limited to just that. If we understand that, we would understand how integral constitutional courts are to the great democratic enterprise. We swear by the Constitution and hold the national flag as the symbol of our national esteem. But each of these landmarks of our patriotism will be rendered meaningless without the assurance and comfort that we receive from our connect with, and our faith in, the judiciary.

There are perfectionist activists among lawyers who advocate zero tolerance when it comes to aberration in judicial conduct and performance. Yet their repeated attempts to impose accountability have seen little success. It can be said here that none of us is perfect and nor is the judiciary, which reflects the make-up of our society. The higher standards that we apply to the judiciary as the beacon of rectitude are indeed agreed-upon, consensual principles. But it might be wise not to publicly highlight every perceived shortcoming or failing, as long as the internal corrective system responds to keep the ship steady.

Of late, there have been questions raised about several matters, but we need to be clear and honest with ourselves as to how much can be addressed without hurting the system and which problems hurt our institutions to the extent of calling for public redressal. It was with that in mind that I chose to disassociate myself from the steps some colleagues advocated for the impeachment of the incumbent chief justice in the aftermath of the press conference of four senior judges to which Justice Gogoi (as he then was) was party. Distressed as we might be about recent developments, it is difficult to say with confidence that the critical inflection point has come, or if public debate is enough to solve our problems. It is a difficult choice between letting people assume that we are impervious to change or be prepared for conduct unbecoming and disloyal to the institution we cherish. Finally, it seems clear that prevailing public perception, as indeed the perception among the judicial community, nudges us towards a response.

It was thus with a heavy heart and in view of such concerns that I urged the incumbent chief justice, as the head of the judicial family and a critical balancing point in constitutional governance, to take cognizance of the outcry and agony, and address concerns about independence of the judiciary—all the real and imagined perceptions on that score.

Meanwhile, in civil society, an important choice will have to be made by the majority and minority alike. Are we to be an inclusive, plural society that embraces diversity, or must we accept cultural and social uniformity? Both the process and the result will require intervention and adjudication by courts. Therefore, more than anything else, we need to preserve and protect the courts that, in turn, will protect us.

Judicial history has been written. Now, it will be etched in stone, by way of the grand temple, the design of which seems to grow by the day. In August 2020, Prime Minister Narendra Modi and Uttar Pradesh's chief minister Yogi Adityanath participated in the bhoomi poojan along with a few select invitees.

People recalled how Jawaharlal Nehru had stayed away from the inaugural ceremony of the refurbished Somnath temple in 1951. But those were times when India aspired to move from being a traditional society towards a modern one, inspired and guided by the Constitution. Contemporary aspirations, blessed by official government policy, aim for a return to tradition as part of the restoration of faith in society. Undoubtedly, the PM will await a grand inaugural of a completed Ram Mandir. As politicians across the political spectrum seek to capitalize on the prevailing public sentiment, whether real or presumed, it is forgotten that the Supreme Court has directed that land be given for a mosque as well. The temple is for everyone, but as yet it seems that the mosque belongs to the UP Sunni Waqf Board alone. Are we dealing with a government that seeks to divide not just Hindus from other communities but a section of Muslims from other Muslims as well? If only the PM had expressed the wish to see a mosque come up and be invited to its inauguration, we might have felt reassured that we live in a modern, secular, constitutional India, free of injustices past and present.

The new dawn in Ayodhya has been described in contrasting terms, with some calling it a true tryst with destiny, the foundation of the Hindu Rashtra, while others regarding it with unease and suspicion—the repudiation of constitutional values, the appropriation of Maryada Purshottam by a political movement. There are some hushed voices reminding us that Mathura and Varanasi are next on the BJP's agenda. The main Opposition party, the Indian National Congress, has stretched itself between 'disappointment at shift of emphasis on core values' and welcoming the construction of the temple but with the reservation that the 'mahurat' was inauspicious. Thus, the debate remains inconclusive.

Lord Ram will have his temple, but will Vishnu, the preserver, heal the scars that stretch across the landscape? When the din of temple bells and holy chants grow quiet, India will speak in a voice that combines obeisance to the deity and commitment to the Constitution. Satyamev Jayate.

Curiously, the term 'Ram Rajya' is accepted as a description of ideal governance. It might be said that the Hindutva version fundamentally challenges that universal concept, which, as I have mentioned earlier in the book, also fits easily with the Islamic idea of Nizam-e-Mustafa. Mahatma Gandhi's bhajan contemplates that unity:

रघुपति राघव राजाराम,
पतित पावन सीताराम

सीताराम सीताराम,
भज प्यारे तू सीताराम

ईश्वर अल्लाह तेरो नाम,
सब को सन्मति दे भगवान

राम रहीम करीम समान
हम सब है उनकी संतान

सब मिला मांगे यह वरदान
हमारा रहे मानव का ज्ञान


*Raghupati raghava raja Ram,*
*Patita paavana Sita Ram,*
*Bhaj pyaare tu Sita Ram*
*Ishwar Allah tero naam,*
*Sabko sanmati de Bhagwan.*


(O Lord Ram, descendant of Raghu, uplifter of the fallen,
You and your beloved consort, Sita, are to be worshipped.
All names of God refer to the same Supreme Being,
including Ishvara and Allah.
O Lord, please give peace and brotherhood to everyone,
as we are all your children.
We all request that this eternal wisdom of humankind prevail.)

# Acknowledgements

I must acknowledge my debt to Imtiaz Ahmed, advocate; he closely monitored the Ayodhya litigation, from the Allahabad High Court to the Supreme Court, and kept me abreast. We sadly lost him to COVID before he could get his hands on the manuscript.

Thanks to Zafar Khurshid and Aadya Mishra, both very bright, young lawyers, for diligently assisting me with the research and preparation of the manuscript.